ONCE IN A HOUSE ON FIRE

Andrea Ashworth

METROPOLITAN BOOKS

Henry Holt and Company / New York

Metropolitan Books
Henry Holt and Company, Inc.
Publishers since 1866
115 West 18th Street
New York, New York 10011

Metropolitan Books™ is a registered
trademark of Henry Holt and Company, Inc.

Originally published in Great Britain in 1998 by
Picador, an imprint of Macmillan Publishers Ltd

Owing to limitations of space, permission to reprint
previously published material may be found on page 330.

Library of Congress Cataloging-in-Publication Data
Ashworth, Andrea, 1969–
Once in a house on fire / Andrea Ashworth
p.   cm.
ISBN 0-8050-5762-5 (alk. paper)
1. Ashworth, Andrea, 1969– . 2. Bibliotherapy. 3. Adult child
abuse victims—England—Biography. 4. England—Biography.
I. Title.
CT788.A764A3   1998   97-46680
362.76'092—dc21   CIP
[B]

Henry Holt books are available for special promotions
and premiums. For details contact: Director, Special Markets.

First American Edition 1998

All first editions are printed on acid-free paper.∞

1 3 5 7 9 10 8 6 4 2

ONCE IN A
HOUSE ON FIRE

I

My father drowned when I was five years old. A picture of me, framed in gold plastic, was fished from his pocket and returned to my mother with a soggy wallet and a bunch of keys. The keys were to our new terraced house, which could now be paid for with his life insurance.

Outside the house, my father's mini-van sat undriven. Days before his death, he had stencilled its sides in yellow: ANTHONY CLARKE: PAINTER AND DECORATOR. TEL: 431 7677. Occasionally, newly-weds called up, wanting to have their homes decorated. My mother explained that the man they needed was dead.

On the way home from his last paint job, he had stopped to take a pee, my mother said. He slipped in the mud, landed on a rock and drowned face down in a shallow stream.

'Less than four inches deep,' she told people.

Strangers dropped by to mourn over tea and biscuits.

'Such an 'andsome young feller.' Everyone sighed at my father's photograph on the sideboard. 'What a waste!'

My mother lost a lot of weight. Sometimes she would shake all over, after a visit from my father's ghost. He would wait for her on the stairs or in her bedroom at night, she told our granny, trying to reach out and touch her.

'Oh, luvvie.' Granny held on to our mother's hand and

stroked her curly brown hair while she cried. 'You know he's not coming back, don't you?'

Our mother stared at the carpet and nodded.

Eventually she looked up and wiped her nose. 'Don't worry – I'll not do anything silly.'

She kept herself going, she murmured time and time again, for the sake of me and my three-year-old sister, Laurie (whose real name was Lauren). Stepping out through the front door, she carried a big smile on her face. Her veiny hands took us through the sooty streets of Rusholme and Moss Side, up the rougher end of Manchester, as if nothing had changed. Scuffing along the pavement, my red sandals jumped the cracks by heart. I glanced up every now and again, from the shoes of strangers who had stopped in the street to stare at my mother and her daughters. My eyes floated past hedges and chimneys to purple-grey clouds, bellies full of rain, about to bucket down.

'What bee-yutiful lasses!' ladies exclaimed over our caramel faces, gasping at our mother. 'You don't look old enough, love. You truly don't!'

Our mother was becoming a celebrity on our street. A twenty-five-year-old widow, she had long lashes casting velvet shadows around her wide, chocolatey eyes, and dimples that danced about her lips when people swore she looked like the gorgeous Natalie Wood.

'Oh no, *she's* a beautiful woman!' Our mother laughed over the compliment every time, blushing and waving it away. Her laughter sounded the same as ever, though it came out of a thinner face.

By the time I was six, our mother's stomach was swollen full of a third child. She was lucky to find someone prepared to take on a pair of orphans and save her from growing lonely, she told her friends when they showed surprise. A looming, red-faced man, quite a bit older than her, stepped into our house for tea and was introduced to Laurie and me as our new daddy.

'I used to be a sailor,' he told us. 'In the merchant navy, like, on the big ships.'

I suspected he was around to stay when huge paintings of ships, sails billowing, began to line the staircase. Our pregnant mother strained on tiptoe to hammer the winking brass hooks into the wall. A new wedding snap squatted on the sideboard in a heavy wooden frame: our mother was standing in front of a brick building (not a church) with the tall new man. Both of them were trying to smile while her dress ballooned in front.

Before the baby was born, our stepfather, Peter Hawkins, used to lug home bulging sacks of misshapen Mojos for my sister and me.

'Off the back of a lorry!' He let the sweets spill, all colours, on to the carpet. We gathered up the squashed and twisted squares, then counted them over and over into paper bags to share out in the playground next day. Pale, freckled faces, skinny black girls, short boys in turbans all chased after me.

I skidded to a halt one afternoon when the headmaster called me by a strange surname.

'Andrea Clarke-Hawkins!'

My name wagged its ugly new tail, stirring whispers behind my back until the home bell rang. My mother wasn't there to explain the name; she was in hospital giving birth to our new sister, Sarah, who came out blonde and screaming.

Sarah's eyes were sky-blue marbles. Her yeasty cheeks made me think of chewing. When my mother wheeled her home from our school, ladies stopped the pram to coo over her face while Laurie and I stood by, fingering the spokes in the wheels.

'The little angel.' They tutted and sucked. 'Looks nowt like yer darker ones, though, does she?'

'Different father,' our mother explained.

During the day, our mother stewed Sarah's dirty nappies in a bucket in the kitchen. When it threatened to rain, she rushed out into the back yard to unpeg the laundry: the clothes smelt of other people's chimney smoke; the clothes-pegs were wooden princes and princesses. Laurie and I played with them while our mother clanked pots and pans and steamed up the kitchen.

Every night, at the same time, our stepfather's keys rattled at the front door. Boots brushed and scraped on the doormat. In came Peter Hawkins, a red face sticking out of wide blue overalls smeared with car grease. Before tea, our stepfather scrubbed the oil from his face and hands at the kitchen sink. He combed his black hair flat against his skull and flicked the dandruff from his shoulders. Under the soapy scent, we caught faint whiffs of petroleum when he smacked our cheeks with kisses.

Tea was ketchup with mashed potato and things out of tins, baked beans or spaghetti. We ate it without a word while our stepfather sat chomping and staring over our heads at the telly. After tea, our mother washed the dishes, washed our faces and changed into a stiff green dress that zipped up the front. Then she folded into her car – a battered blue Princess whose patches of rust she was forever daubing with metallic paint – and drove off to look after dying people until dawn. She worked the night shift at Manchester City Council Home for Geriatrics.

'It's at night that they pop their clogs, that's the worst part,' she told Auntie Livia, describing the toothless corpses that she lifted from their still-warm beds. 'Their faces are smiling – sort of floating up – but their legs feel like lead.'

While she swept corridors and bathed worn-out brows, our stepfather was left with my sisters and me. Lulled by soap operas, his eyelids drooped over a warm can of beer. Sarah slept cradled on his dozing belly, calmly rising and falling, while Laurie and I played in silence behind the dining table. We were allowed to play with Lego, but only if we pressed the bricks together without any clicking sounds. Our heads were crammed with Lego helicopters and dinosaurs, but we put all our bricks into building ships to please our stepfather. He slumped back on the settee while the television's light flickered electric over his features, now blue, now red.

'Da-daa!'

We stuck our ship, portholes and all, under his nose. He rubbed his eyes and sat up to let a smile break over his creased face.

'It reminds me of me navy days. When I were a lad: no kids to feed; no cars to fix neither.' Our stepfather took a long look at the yellow plastic ship.

He had gone through a whole other family – wife and babies – before he ran into our mother. One afternoon, while he was at work, his old wife had rung up to tell our mother a thing or two. Our mother's face fell while the high-pitched story chunnered into her ear. She knew nothing about any ex-wives with babies to feed. As soon as she had laid the receiver back on its rest, she and Auntie Livia had to go and brew a pot of tea in the kitchen. Behind the glass-panelled door – clicked shut – they mouthed and made faces. Broken noses, affairs and drained whisky bottles whispered through.

Before he got home, our mother changed her face and wiped it smooth, her fingers tucking at the temples where crinkles might show. Our stepfather scraped his boots and elbowed at the sink to soap the car-grease from his face. A pale, hairy stomach peeked out over leather-belted jeans. Our mother smiled through his kissing compliments.

'House looks spotless, love. Me trousers dry? Fried mince for tea? Smells grand. Really grand. Christ, I had a bugger of a motor to fix this afternoon! Let's nip down the pub tonight, eh? I'll fetch the babysitter.'

Our mother said nothing about the strange phone call. It was kept in the teapot, to be tinkled out and sipped in the afternoons between her and Auntie Livia.

We ploughed through the mounds of cabbage and mince that our stepfather adored. Then, when she had scrubbed the dishes, our mother pulled on her black silk dress, blooming painted roses. It was the same dress she had slipped into every Friday night when our real father had come home from pasting flowered paper on to people's walls. With the week's house-work done, she had set her old Motown vinyls spinning under the needle and swished about hypnotically, purring into her spiky hairbrush. The songs were all about love and leaving, but our mother just smiled and smiled and sang along. Our father used to come home in his baggy white overalls, splashed with gloss paint, to whirl his hips with hers before tea.

Now our mother fastened a plain, cardboardy coat over her dress to step out into the rain with her new husband. He didn't like music, so there was no swishing, but sweet musk wafted in the hall as the door closed behind her.

Our babysitter was a fifteen-year-old called Tracy – 'a bit podgy but very pretty,' our mother told Auntie Livia. She curled up in our stepfather's favourite chair, which Laurie and I would never dream of going near, with coffee and chocolate biscuits and a dog-eared paperback.

'What are you reading?' Laurie and I fidgeted, waiting for the adverts to jingle and burst colours across the screen for fantastic, too-fast minutes, before we had to face the dull grown-up programmes again.

'Nothing for noseys,' she snapped from behind the stained cover.

Before bedtime, Tracy put down her paperback and nipped out for a smoke in the back yard. We inspected the book, splayed over the arm of our stepfather's chair. *The Moors Murders*. The words were red and dribbling, like blood, over two photos: a man and a woman, with hard mouths. You could tell they had done something evil. But the really spooky thing was the way the faces drew you in, making you peer at their lips and eyes: were they sorry or secretly pleased?

Laurie and I begged Tracy, when she came in from her smoke, to tell us the story inside the book. She rolled her eyes: 'Okay, but only after you've cleaned your teeth and got into bed. And you're never to tell your mam about it, right?'

'Right!' We scrubbed our teeth for the Moors Murders and climbed into our bunk beds. The story came out in nicotine and coffee whispers.

The man and the woman kidnapped children just like Laurie and me. They took the children to a secret place on the Yorkshire Moors where they tortured them and touched them in the wrong places. They recorded the screams and sent the tapes to the children's mothers. Then they killed the children and buried them under the purple heather out on the moors where no one would ever find them.

Tracy switched out the light and disappeared downstairs to scoff a few more choccy biscuits before our parents came home from the pub.

'Get to sleep!' she shouted up the stairs, when she heard Laurie and me shifting in our creaky beds, unable to rest. 'And no more of your blummin' whispering, got it?'

I dangled my left foot over the edge of the top bunk, so Laurie could see it from where she lay underneath. It made my toes icy, but I stuck my foot right out from under the covers, so my sister would know I was there while she was going to sleep.

*

I woke in the dark, yellow streetlight seeping through the curtains. Muffled voices squeezed up through the floorboards and swirled about the bedroom before sharpening into whole words. Bastard! Bitch! Bastard! Bitch!

I went to the top of the stairs and looked down from my hiding-place behind the banister. At the bottom of the stairs Tracy's round face was streaked with green eyeshadow and black mascara tears. I could hear my mother weeping in the living-room. My stepfather strode out into the hall, still shouting. His face was twisted red and shaking.

'Fucking clear up that shit, Lorraine!' Cold coffee dribbled down the wallpaper in the hall. 'Just fucking clear it up! I'm taking Tracy home.'

The next morning my mother spent a long time on the telephone. Tracy's mother was livid because Peter Hawkins had spoiled her daughter. But Tracy insisted that she loved my stepfather. The affair was dropped, and our new babysitter came with thick glasses and horrid skin.

Most of that summer, when I was seven, was spent with my five-year-old sister Laurie in the back yard. It was all bricks and concrete: the outdoor toilet and a half-demolished air-raid shelter (where people had tried to hide from bombs in the old days) left little room to play. During the school holidays, we entertained ourselves with empty orange crates and high bouncing balls until lunchtime, while our mother spent the days sleeping to get up enough energy for her night shift. The moment our local church gonged twelve, I unlatched the back gate, a pound note tucked into my knickers, and led Laurie down the back alley. This was filled with the pong of dog mess and rotting rubbish, but we pinched our noses and hustled all the way down it to the sweet shop, in order to avoid the road. If anyone spotted my sister and me alone on the street, my mother warned me, she'd be reported and sent to prison and we would be taken away. Every evening, when she got up to make tea, she quizzed us about what we'd bought for lunch. I told her apples and oranges: she would have been horrified to know we were thriving on Jelly Babies and Spangles.

On Saturday afternoons, Laurie and I were banished to the back yard so that our mother could take a nap with Sarah upstairs, while our stepfather put his feet up in front of the telly to contemplate the football in peace, locking the back door and drawing the living-room curtains across, to blot Laurie and me out of sight and bloody mind. Hopping about in the cold, we clambered over the rubble of the air-raid shelter, imagining bombs whistling out of the sky, but taking care to keep our voices down. Every now and then, we crept up to the window to peer through the crack in the curtains to see if our stepfather had fallen asleep. Eventually, his head would tip back on the settee. We opened the back gate without a sound, then dashed through the stinking alley to the street. There, we lifted the letterbox to spy on Auntie Jackie, who was not a real auntie, but the lady who lived next door. If we spied grim-faced in-laws under her letterbox flap, we would skulk back to our frosty yard. But if Auntie Jackie had no visitors, we would tap the chorus of 'Brown Girl in the Ring' on her brass knocker. Then she would usher us into her back room to face the electric fire with its blazing orange bars, for creamy glasses of milk and as many biscuits as we could pluck up the cheek to pick out of a red barrel that we worshipped, blue horses prancing around the gold knob of the lid.

Because Auntie Jackie and her husband, Uncle Duncan, hadn't managed to make children, their house was crawling with lazy lady cats and scrawny kittens that would be sold to the pet shop the moment they peeled open their eyes and tired of kissing their mothers' bellies. On Easter Sunday, instead of Creme Eggs, Auntie Jackie slithered a pulsing ball of kitten into my palm and Laurie's. We fell out of love with them when their ears perked up and their cushiony paws grew claws that scratched our shins, while worms of poo turned up in the carpet's shag pile. Our stepfather gripped Laurie and me by the scruff of our necks and thrust our faces close to the mess on the floor.

'I'll rub your noses in it,' he promised, 'if you let them do it indoors just one more fucking time.'

Summer gave way to rain, first spitting, then belting down. Our mother kissed Laurie and me goodbye at the school gate and wheeled Sarah off in the pram. I spent the mornings helping other children to read and to spell, since I was ahead of my year in the Wide Range Reader stories. When I was three, my mother had saved up to buy a set of Ladybird books and taught me to read from them. My father had taken a photo of my mother grinning and pointing at my head bowed over the pages.

When the bell rang for playtime, I would rush out to look for my sister in the crowded playground. We touched hands for a second, then ran off with separate groups of coloured faces. My eyes scooted along the railings: sometimes, our mother would be standing there on her way home from the shops, peering into the crowd for Laurie and me.

One time, she stopped to give us some Opal Fruits before she went home to sleep. We took the shiny yellow packets through the railings and kissed her hand before she pushed off into the traffic with Sarah's pram.

Laurie tore into hers. A flock of schoolmates swooped in, sticky palms and begging smiles. I gave up a green sweet to a red-haired girl who was taller than me. She was after a pink one, but I was saving those. The freckles gathered over her eyes when she chewed.

'Why's your mum wear sunglasses all the time, then?' she asked the playground as well as me. 'Even when it's raining.'

She took a pink sweet after all and sauntered back into the crowd, her red plait swinging along her spine.

When I got home I tried not to stare at my mother while she hoovered our trodden green carpet in her dark glasses. Rain tapped at the windows. She put the kettle on. Auntie Livia came round to show off the snaps of her new council house. In the photographs, my mother stood out like a beetle: every shot caught her smiling in sunglasses. My aunt and she giggled, but when my mother lifted the shades, her face was puffy with green and purple bruises. Sarah's dimpled fist reached for the colours; my mother winced.

Behind her teacup, Auntie Livia asked, 'He doesn't hit the girls too, does he?'

'God, no!' My mother was adamant: 'He'd not lay a finger on them!'

I looked at my mother's swollen eyes. She knew nothing about the night my stepfather had knocked me out with the back of his hand.

Sarah had made a stinking mess in her nappy. My stepfather didn't know how to change it because my mother always made sure she had taken care of everything before she went to work. He pinched his hairy nostrils and rolled the dirty nappy into a ball. When he went to fasten the clean one he couldn't find the pin.

'Where the f—?' Biting his lip, he sent me upstairs to find it.

I couldn't find the pin anywhere. The nappy was loose, Sarah was screaming, but I couldn't find it anywhere. My stepfather came upstairs, spraying spittle.

'Where is it then?'

I couldn't say. My stepfather smacked me across the face, and I fell against the door jamb. My head hit the hinge.

When I woke up, Sarah had stopped screaming, and my stepfather was crouching over me, a chocolate bar in his fist. His black hair was dripping: he had gone out in the rain to buy it. Pressing the Milky Way into my hand, he murmured, 'You're not going to tell your mum, are you?'

My throat was tight, but I ate the chocolate to show that I was not going to tell. My stepfather watched me swallow before he stood up tall again. Then he took the bright blue Milky Way wrapper and buried it in the bin, underneath the potato peelings.

'Whichever you like, Andy, love.' My stepfather ruffled my hair in front of the man who owned the pet shop, smiling and urging me to pick out my favourite fish from the gurgling tanks. At home, in the alcove of our living-room, he had installed an aquarium: a second, living TV. Laurie and I spent hours gazing at it, hypnotized by the hum of the water pump and the sight of shiny backs skittering about: silver, gold, pink, electric blue. We kept our eyes on the black shark fish. They flared red when we tapped on the glass to distract them from nibbling the tiddlers that had hatched out of splurges of eggs. Laurie was fond of the yellow-and-black-striped ones we called bumblebees. Although they seemed stupid, the pink angels were my favourites: I watched their slow, O-shaped mouths kissing, while their pearly bodies shimmered, so pale you could see something pulsing inside.

'Do fish have hearts?' I asked my mother.

'Ask your dad,' she said.

I kept quiet. Presenting me with a tub of fish food, my stepfather had made it my job to sprinkle flakes on the water every morning and night: 'It's up to you to keep the blighters from goin' belly up.'

At first, I couldn't help grinning at the honour, which allowed me to lord it over my little sisters. But I soon found my heart doing dives every time I went near the aquarium. I had to kneel down and press my face close to the glass, willing every last fish to keep on swishing its tail and wafery fins.

When she didn't look too bashed, our mother took us on Sunday mornings to see her own mother. We dressed quickly, rushing to leave while our stepfather still lay snoring in bed. Granny Chadfield lived on the eighth floor of Circle Court, a concrete tower of lonely old people in the middle of Stretford; on Sunday afternoons, kids hijacked the lifts and pelted down the echoing corridors, buzzing pensioners' doorbells then legging it, spurting giggles that ricocheted off the walls. Laurie and I played with our cousins, chasing each other until we were dizzy, then gathered for Gran's meat and potato pies. They glowed in the middle of the table, gravy sizzling through forkholes, with glazed pastry leaves whose veins had been etched in, one by one, with a knife. Wolfing down my wedge, I nodded for more although I felt stuffed to bursting. My jaw worked to make sense of the hours Gran put in, kneading and rolling, then waiting by her oven all alone, before the pies came out looking varnished.

After Sunday dinner, Gran collapsed the table's wings and pressed it back against the wall. During the week she would eat packet meals from a tin tray on her lap. She hardly ever went anywhere or talked to anyone, except for a few polite words if she bumped into a neighbour in the lift. We knew that after we had kissed her goodbye, she would sit and gaze over the city, thinking, while cars roared past on the motorway below.

'I don't ever want to live cooped up alone like that.' Our mother shook her head on the way home. 'I'd rather be dead than so alone.'

I used to imagine living with Gran's wallpaper, patterned over with orange and yellow cubes. One moment they seemed to stick out from the wall; the next they were sucking in. Once I asked, 'Do they go in or out, Gran, these boxes on the wall?'

'That depends on your perspective,' she said.

'What's that?'

Gran gave my hand a squeeze.

'It's the way you choose to look at things.'

My grandmother had been forced to look at things differently years ago, when her second husband had run off with her eldest daughter and the brand-new refrigerator: Grandad and Auntie Vera had moved north into a semi-detached cottage in Bury, where they had three children. Every week, my grandmother trudged across Manchester to take the pies she had baked for her grandchildren who also happened to be her stepchildren.

'Flesh and blood.' She had stiffened her chin when neighbours twitched their eyebrows, calling it a dirty scandal. 'They're my own flesh and blood, come what may.'

Now, after a lifetime of lorry driving, my grandfather had died of a heart attack without ever letting his children know that they were his grandchildren too.

'They'd be gutted,' my grandmother fretted, so the secret was kept from them, though I had worked it out by stringing together grown-ups' whispers and comparing all the eyes and noses in the family photographs ranged along Gran's window ledge.

My mother woke in the night sometimes, sobbing because her family had been mangled. Still, our stepfather drove us out to visit my Auntie Vera on the odd Sunday afternoon. Our car strained up the hill, chugging, then Laurie and I peeled ourselves from the sweating vinyl seats to go dashing across the back fields with our cousins. At teatime, we came in from the cold and crowded around the kitchen table, noses red, feet kicking underneath. 'Mmm!' We were all nudges and murmurs when Auntie Vera pulled a steaming sponge cake from the oven and set it in the middle of the table.

'Want a piece, Andy, love?' Her great big bosoms beckoned behind the cake. 'It's your favourite: lovely vanilla.'

I looked up at my stepfather to see if it was all right. The furrow between his brows said it was not. We were not allowed to accept treats when we went visiting with him. The cake loomed there, a heavenly pillow, until my aunt took a knife and cut eight hot slabs from it.

Plenty. I breathed in lovely vanilla, lovely vanilla . . .

When I looked up from the crumbs, my stepfather's eyes glowered black under hooded eyelids. He motioned to the door; I swallowed and scraped back my chair. The carved sponge was still steaming in the middle of the table.

'What have I told you about being greedy, you little sod?'

It felt frosty outside. I shivered.

'I wasn't being greedy, Daddy: I was just being polite.'

'You don't go shovelling down cake to make me look bad!' My stepfather yanked at my hair and jerked my head back against the stone wall. 'You want everyone to think I don't feed you properly?'

The stones of the wall cut into my head. I whispered, 'I just ate it to be polite, Dad, after Auntie Vera had baked it for us.'

He lowered his face to mine, his eyebrows meeting in the middle. 'You know fucking not to.'

His spittle was in my face. The stones were cutting in. I began to cry. My stepfather fastened his moist hand over my mouth and shoved my head back harder against the wall.

'Shut it! Shut them tears up before I give you what for.'

I shut them up behind my damp, hot face and he slid his palm from my mouth.

'Now go inside and be quiet.'

I went inside and was quiet.

It was the same whenever we went visiting with him. People wafted biscuits and cups of tea under our noses; we always said no. We had to sit still and be quiet when our stepfather was in the room, if we didn't want a good hiding when we got home.

Often my smacks came out of the blue, when I thought I had been quiet and well behaved. Sometimes I was able to work out what a smack was for, and could even tell when one was coming: a hot wave would rush up my neck and tingle around the edges of my face.

My stepfather's favourite ornament was the fat porcelain Chinaman who was supposed to bring good luck. Instead of perching with all the other glass and china creatures on the spindly display stand, it squatted in the middle of the dining table. Our mother put it there, on a crocheted doily like a magic carpet, well out of harm's way. But one awful afternoon, I knocked its head off with my high-bouncing ball. I balanced the face back on and prayed no one would notice. For days, it sat grinning over its potbelly, good as new, while we went through our meals. I stopped praying.

In the middle of stewed cabbage one night, the head fell off with a clunk.

'I'll knock *your* bloody head off!' My stepfather swiped at my face and caught me between the eyes, so that everything went fuzzy for a moment.

On Sundays we had to be super-quiet and still so that our stepfather could enjoy what he called his day of rest. He snoozed in front of the gas fire while the rain slapped a wet, grey curtain against the window. The television droned through church services or sports or black-and-white films that left Laurie and me flummoxed: men turning trembly and sweating, screeching about in cars and even grabbing their guns to sort out problems utterly invisible to us. I used to go and lie on the carpet under the dining table, reading with my book propped upside-down, so that the words would seem stranger and more exciting, running back-to-front along the lines. I was hooked on reading this way, but I could only do it under the table, where my stepfather couldn't see me. It got his goat when he caught me – 'flamin' little freak' – with my nose stuck in a book turned the wrong way up.

This Sunday, I was under the table reading the new book my grandmother had bought me out of her pension money. Fairy tales: hardbacked and expensive. I was reading it the right way up, so I could enjoy the pictures. Coming to the end of the first story, where the ugly duckling sprouts wondrous white feathers, I kept skimming forward and peeking into the next story, to see what the little mermaid might do in her watery world. Laurie was fidgeting with our plastic toy basket that bulged full of playthings being saved for our baby sister, now that we had outgrown them all. She pulled out our old red ball and teased it across the carpet to tickle my elbow. I caught it and held it, itching for a throw. I looked at the Chinaman, whose chubby cheeks had been glued to give him back his grin. I looked at my stepfather, dozing on the settee. Then I sat up and tossed the ball to Laurie. It made a small rubber thud. Our stepfather stirred, skipping a snore, and peered at us over his white belly. He spotted the ball through the legs of the dining table.

'Put that bloody thing away before you break summat else!' His face twisted, furious for a second, then he sank back into the settee's cushions.

I stuffed the ball into the basket with a sigh. 'God, I hate Sundays.'

The words escaped him, but he caught the tone.

'What was that?' He sat up.

Dropping 'God', I told him, 'I hate Sundays.'

My stepfather stood up, tightening his belt a notch.

'You said you hate me, didn't you?'

'I said I hate Sundays, Daddy, not you.' Looking up at him, I squeezed affection into the word 'Daddy'.

'You said you hate me, Andrea. Admit it!'

Behind the hardbacked fairy tales I denied it.

My stepfather grabbed the book. He was going to have to teach me a lesson. Gripping the first page in a hairy fist, he said, 'Admit that's what you said: you hate me.'

My lips opened, but nothing came out.

My stepfather ripped the page and crumpled it in his fist. He tossed the pale paper ball on to the carpet. After that I admitted nothing, because I knew the book was gone. He tore out every single page to the end, to the empty spine and the cover that still said *Fairy Tales*, though all the endings had been scrunched into paper fists and scattered over the carpet.

He stormed out into the rain, without his jacket. The door shuddered behind him. My mother made me wash my face while she washed hers. The day was in shreds. It was time for our weekly bath.

Our mother used washing-up liquid on our hair. She clipped our toenails and our fingernails and trimmed our fringes sharp and high across our foreheads. She kissed me, and I went to bed knowing that Gran would never hear where her precious food money had ended up.

When our stepfather staggered home reeking of whisky, ceramic hit the wall. We got used to the smash and the next-day stain, but eventually the wallpaper began to fade, and he and our mother decided to change it. Every wall had to be stripped of the old flowered paper my real father had pasted up before he drowned. We set to with clumsy metal scrapers.

During the decorating, our mother and stepfather fixed a date at the domestic court where Laurie and I were to be adopted by Peter Hawkins.

'A proper, legal family we'll be then,' our mother imagined. She zipped us into our matching party frocks, the ones with green and purple frills that made us feel like flowers.

At court, Laurie and I stood gripping hands, trying not to gawp at the lion and the unicorn rearing up in gold on the wall above our heads. An official woman wearing a silver badge took us into a side room for questioning. There were no windows. She closed the dark wooden door and asked me:

'Would you say that you are happy with your stepfather?'

There had been a time . . . There had been a time during the night when my stepfather slid his fingers under my blankets and touched me between the legs. Keeping my eyes closed tight, pretending to be asleep, I had rolled away, close to the wall, to stop it.

I looked at the official woman, who smelt of apples. Pearly buttons ran straight up her shirt into a dead white collar. Her pen was poised above her clipboard. The silver badge blinked on her breast.

Yes, I said, we were happy with our stepfather.

The door opened, and we were ushered into a larger room

with bright lights. Our stepfather signed some papers, and my new name was pronounced: Andrea Hawkins. We went home in our party dresses to eat spaghetti on toast. Our mother sprinkled cheese on top and melted it under the grill until it bubbled up, gold.

After tea she let me hang about her skirt while she washed the dishes. She was wearing yellow rubber gloves, squeaking and squeaking against the plates, when she asked in a low voice, 'Andy, which of your two daddies do you love best?'

My father used to croon Elvis ballads over his wooden guitar. His jacket was padded blue and smelt of turpentine and had pennies hidden in all the zip pockets. Sometimes he would let Laurie and me stay up long after bedtime, snoozing in his lap on the settee while he watched films starring werewolves or vampires; before carrying us up to bed, he would take us out into the back yard to blink at the moon, showing off its fat midnight light.

My feet shifted and I looked to them for the right answer, the one that would make my mother feel nice.

Before I could speak, my stepfather yelled from the stairway, ''Ere, Andy, chuck: come and give us an 'and with this wallpaper.'

I left my mother's skirts at the kitchen sink to join him on the stairs. He put a blunt, rusted blade into my hand and tousled my hair.

'Good girl.'

Biting my lip and making a fist around the handle, I pressed against the wall, scraping to peel off the paper and all its dead, stained flowers.

2

Laurie and I were zipped nose to nose into an itchy sleeping bag on the settee while our bedroom was stripped and decorated. Our stepfather hired a bearded man who looked like Jesus to paste up the new wallpaper, but soon caught him using our telephone to make secret, long-distance calls. He dragged the man outside and punched him in the street, shoved him into his car and slammed the door on his foot. The car dribbled off with the driver's nose bleeding into his moustache, his half-used cans of paint wobbling on the back seat. My stomach churned because I was the one who had blabbed about the calls.

It took a long time for our stepfather to paste up the wallpaper himself, but eventually our bedroom was a queasy sea green. A hollow plasterboard wall now divided it in two, with a sliding door to shut Laurie and me off in our bunk beds from Sarah in her cot. When our stepfather's mother, Nana Hawkins, came for tea, she shook her head in admiration.

'You've done a smashing job, Pete, love.' She bounced our baby sister against her bosom: 'It's nice for our Sarah to have her own room, separate from the other two, like.'

Because we were darker than Sarah, Nana Hawkins didn't consider us her proper grandchildren. When we stayed with her, she powdered her face in chalky layers before dragging us round the Bramhall shops, tutting over her purse at the extra money she was spending to feed us. Other blue-rinsed ladies, coming out of the shops, raised their eyebrows.

'They're not yours, are they, Ida?'

'They're our Pete's adopted,' she explained. 'Proper little Pakis, aren't they?'

They laughed over our heads, flashing pink dentures.

Nana's husband, Grandad Fred, had more time for us; while he was sitting in his armchair, watching the wrestling, Laurie and I would clamber over his knees on to his squidgy lap. He wore brown nylon trousers and a blue string vest that let us fiddle with the moles lurking like mushrooms under his arms.

'Off Grandad's knee!' Nana Hawkins came out of the kitchen, waving a spatula. 'Tea's ready, so sit still and shush up.'

We sat on the settee in silence, eating out of bowls on our knees. Instead of knives and forks, Nana Hawkins gave us plastic spoons to shovel up the peas and potatoes she had mashed to hide the fact that there was no meat in the dish. We watched bubbles of green gloop swell and slowly burst in Nana's lava lamp while we let our food settle quietly, the way we were told. Then we climbed back on to Grandad Fred's lap, to tickle him and whisper in his ear. He was a soft, squashed copy of our stepfather. Laurie and I were drawn to his chair and his sweet potato smell until Nana Hawkins called us upstairs one afternoon, into the bathroom.

'You see these?' She sat on the toilet's carpeted lid, holding up a packet of pink, doughnut-shaped sponges. 'These,' she said, 'are your Grandad Fred's. He puts them in his trousers 'cause his bladder leaks: it's a medical condition.'

She let Laurie squeeze one of the sponges.

'Now then,' she stood up slowly, blotting out the light. 'Don't go bothering your grandad no more, or he'll have to go back to the doctor with his bad bladder.'

We went downstairs and eyed Grandad Fred as he dozed in his armchair, before Nana's frown sent us outside to play.

Their council house huddled with lots of others – all exactly the same – in a low, grey ring around a concrete playground. When Laurie and I went to dawdle on the swings, older kids shoved us off, calling us wogs and dirty Pakis. We insisted we were grandchildren of the Hawkinses at number seven, the ones with the brass lion knocker, and tried to explain that our real, dead father had been a quarter Italian, a quarter Maltese and half English.

'Yer wot?' A skinhead stuck his broken nose into my face.

I told him I was dark-skinned because I had some Mediterranean blood in me, but that, actually, I was English just like him.

'You're not fucking English!' The pale boy backed into his crowd of skin-headed friends, swigging the beer in his fist. I was only eight, skinny, and a girl; they smashed a few bottles and took off.

When we stayed with Nana Clarke, our real father's mother, things were completely different. For one thing, Sarah was never allowed into the grubby council flat, because Nana Clarke had cockroaches and was what people called doolally. She didn't shout or smash things, but she did call our stepfather Hitler and she did accuse him of killing her son, our father. At other times, she would jab her finger at the television and insist that our father was there, alive and moving in the broken, fizzing picture. Hearts pounding, Laurie and I couldn't help peering. Sometimes it was Elvis on the screen, sometimes only the man reporting the news; you could hardly tell the difference, since a tube had exploded in the back of the set, tingeing the picture dark green.

During the day, Nana Clarke liked to wander, in spite of the pains shooting through the blue veins up the back of her legs. She was often chauffeured home in a police car after her aches made her stop and sit down on the pavement or right in the middle of the road. On weekday afternoons, she waddled about Lewis's, where she was in love with the moving stairs. A seventy-year-old in white knee socks, she exasperated the ladies on the perfume counters by demanding squirts of scent and film-star make-overs. She promised to buy eyeshadows of every colour, though her purse held only coppers and plastic trinkets got from penny machines along the pavement. Her English was broken, because (apart from being half Maltese and half Italian) she had grown up in a French convent in Egypt before she married Grandad Clarke, a British Air Force man. From Heliopolis, City of the Sun, he whisked her back to Manchester to feed four children on Social Security in a council flat surrounded by belching industrial chimneys.

'No wonder she flipped her lid, poor bugger.' Our mother explained how Nana Clarke, on her thirtieth birthday, had laid down her knitting kneedles, shaved her head and stopped speaking. When she opened her mouth a year later, only children and animals responded to her mumblings: French, English, Arabic, smatterings of Italian and German, she blended them into a mish-mash of her own. Once in a blue moon, she broke into plain English to explain that Billy the Kid had told her to shave her head, to accuse our stepfather of being the Devil, or to announce that she was heading back to Egypt tomorrow, which was why she had wrapped a knife and fork inside a pair of knickers that she kept in her coat pocket.

During the summer holidays, Nana Clarke liked to drag Laurie and me through the Indian streets of Rusholme that our stepfather avoided. His nostrils quivered every time Nana knocked on our door.

'Hi, Hitler,' we thought she said, before barging past him

to grasp Laurie and me in her surprisingly strong arms: 'Go shopping!' We were all that was left of her sweet, sweet Tony, she reminded our mother, who packed us into our cardigans and let us go, winking to remind me to keep an eye out – I was under secret instructions to stop a policeman if necessary, to steer us all back safely before dark. Laurie and I trundled with Nana along the sticky streets of Rusholme, stopping at Indian sweet shops and jewellery stores and delicatessens where flies buzzed around splits in rotting fruit too strange to buy. In fabric shops Nana stroked lengths of blood-red silk threaded with gold, and asked the woman in the sari: 'What price this? What price?'

Incense wafted out of the food shops that our stepfather refused to step into, even when we had run out of milk and there was nowhere else open. Nana led us inside one, where the lights were dim and things crawled along the shelves at the back. My sister and I held our breath among the spices while she chattered in Arabic, gripping our chins to show off our faces to the ancient Indian man behind the cash register. Nana spoke, beaming, in a language that no one could understand, but her pride was clear. The man nodded in his turban, smiling back out of his wizened-prune face. Before we left, he folded a small gift into each of our fists. When we got outside into the sunlight, our faces fell: in my palm I held a furry green fruit; Laurie had a shrivelled fungus in hers.

We went home full of the Indian streets, and the music that plinked out of tape recorders behind boxes stacked along the pavement, bursting ripe fruit from far away and mangy, withered vegetables. I twined my hands together above my head and did an Indian dance for my mother, rolling my eyes, twisting my neck from side to side while strange words dribbled from my lips.

'Stop that flamin' warbling!' My stepfather reached out to whack the back of my knees: 'You're not a bloody Paki!

'Any more of it and you'll get a clip round the ear'ole!' he warned.

But the wavering music was stuck inside my head. More of it leaked out under my breath until I got a clip round the ear'ole and then it dried up.

My ears were still stinging from my stepfather's clout when he gave me another one for out-and-out cheek.

'Mithering little shit!' he fumed, when I brought home a form requesting five pounds along with my parents' permission to go on the overnight school trip to Derbyshire.

'Why should we fork out for it?' He had a row with my mother, but ended up signing the form and stumping up cash, so that my teachers wouldn't think we were poor.

In my red vanity case my mother folded a small towel, on top of which she laid a toothbrush, a pair of knickers and a clean T-shirt. The T-shirt was my favourite, spattered with tiny Union Jacks and other, curious-looking flags that I took to represent the world, though their colours were only red, white and blue.

'Anything else?' my mother asked me.

We made room for Enid Blyton before we fastened the case. Leaving me at the school gate, my mother kissed the top of my head and pulled a packet of paper tissues from her pocket.

'Put them in your case for the trip,' she said.

'Oh, Mum!' I dashed to the bus clutching the plastic packet in my hand; I wanted people to see that I had a full, unopened set of Handy Andies all to myself.

The coach snaked through the grey terraced streets around our school and pulled on to the motorway. Factories gave way to whizzing trees; our faces pressed against the windows to drink in the greenery. Two Handy Andies and a packet of wine gums later, we reached Derbyshire. There were red-nosed walks the first day, panting across hills where we gasped at sheep and cows and birds that weren't pigeons or sparrows. After dark, we gathered in the common room to scribble poems about the Glory of the English Countryside before rushing to play ping-pong and bingo.

Next day, we visited the Bluejohn Mines. A guide led us down into the caves to show us the crystals in the hushed green damp.

'Stalactites.' She pointed a neon stick at the frozen jewels trickling from the roof. Then she asked, 'See his face?' Across the roof of the cave, she swept her eerie stick, tracing features in the shadows. Her whispery voice echoed: 'A nasty ogre.' Blood rushed to my head as I strained to see the ogre's face. I looked and looked until my legs began to sway and I had to straighten my neck. Soon we were back outside in the spitting rain, yanking our coats over our heads, buzzing about the ogre in the rock.

'Did ya see them eyebrows? Even fangs!'

I nodded and chatted with the others, although I had seen nothing but a slimy green rock with a few cracks here and there.

When my mother met me off the coach, I fitted my hand inside hers and told her about the cave and the ogre that I hadn't been able to see.

'Well, who wants to see an ogre?' My mother squeezed my hand: 'No point getting all het up over something that isn't there.'

Soon after my school trip, my parents began to speak to one another in code, spelling things backwards so that I wouldn't understand. A-D-A-N-A-C. I said nothing while I worked out that my mother was planning to visit her sister-in-law in Canada. After a treat of egg custard tarts, it came out of her mouth the right way round.

'I'm going to visit your Auntie Carla in Vancouver,' she said. 'Your dad'll look after you for a couple of weeks.'

Our mother promised suitcases of souvenirs to make up for the looks on our faces: a fortnight with our stepfather, alone! But when the black cab finally came and took away our mother and her small vinyl case, our stepfather was nicer than we had expected. Chocolate crept into our daily menu to keep us quiet, and everything was fried, fried, fried. Eggs, bacon, sausages: men's food. On the fourth day without our mother, he made a few phone calls, then handed Laurie and me a new canvas bag each. Sensing something exciting, Laurie and I rushed to pack with our stepfather, filling an extra bag with Sarah's nappies and favourite toys. I was beginning to see snow-peaked mountains and towering evergreens like the ones that arrived bashed on the back of postcards from Auntie Carla in Vancouver.

By evening, my dreams of aeroplanes had crashed back down to earth: our stepfather dumped us at Auntie Vera's house before driving off to the airport. The minute she closed the door, Auntie Vera was on the phone to Auntie Pauline.

'Can you believe it? Just like that – rushing off after her as if she can't breathe by herself! After wiping all them old biddies' bums for this one holiday of her own; she'll be furious!'

If our mother was furious, it didn't bring her home any sooner. The fortnight dragged itself out while Laurie and I played in the back fields all morning, loving the way the long grass whipped our arms and legs, but missing our school, which was miles away. Later, after we had watched Andy Pandy and Looby Loo, the Clangers and Bagpuss, Laurie was happy to stay in with colouring books all afternoon. I was fascinated to see what Mr Ben would be: he could turn into anything he liked – a spaceman, a cowboy, a clown – just by putting on the right clothes. But as soon as the cartoon was over, I went and hovered around the back door, itching for a wander. Auntie Vera made me give her my solemn promise that I would go nowhere near the main road. Then she let me put on my cardigan and disappear into the street on my own. A ten-pence piece rolled around in my pocket, swinging back and forth like a pendulum, until the church bell clanged three and I ran down the hill to the sweet shop for two ounces of lemon sherbet and a stick of liquorice – the hard kind, for sucking not chewing.

Dipping my liquorice stick in the sherbet, I trudged back up the hill and lingered around the red telephone box at the top. When the street was clear of grown-ups, I heaved the door open and slipped into the box, clogged with stale cigarette smoke. Because I had no number for my mother in Canada, I dialled strange numbers until the ringing tone began to purr in my ear. If anyone answered, I slammed down the phone while the pips were going off. After that, I scurried back to Auntie Vera's house for tea, secretly full of the sherbet and liquorice and the choking, smoky calls.

Our parents came home from Canada, breathless and full of plans they no longer bothered to spell backwards. We would be emigrating to Canada.

'As soon as we find a buyer for the house,' our mother told Auntie Livia. Clutching her cup of tea, my aunt asked enthusiastic questions about this part of green, sun-soaked Canada that my parents swore was chock full of amazing opportunities.

'The standard of living's fantastic, Liv.' Our mother's eyes lit up. 'Any Tom, Dick and Harry can afford steak for tea, Pete says, and you don't have to be loaded if you want to build your own house. Right from scratch!'

Auntie Livia's eyes were glistening with sadness, afraid that cups of tea at our house were about to run out. She patted her frizzy hair and laughed nervously. 'Who'll do my perm when you're gone?'

The playground was chattering because, although I was only just nine, I had been pushed up a year, right into the top fourth-year form, after winning the school's annual competition to wrestle as many words as possible out of the name 'Manchester'. Nibbling the rubber end of my pencil all weekend, I turned up at school on Monday with a flapping list, the longest they had ever seen:
cheat
mean
stern
stench
man
rat
ranch
ran
rant
chant
charms . . .
'Nearly one hundred words Andrea Hawkins got out of "Manchester"!' Older kids nudged elbows, seeing me through new eyes when I dashed past.

I won a green leathery book, stamped with gold letters. *The Secret Garden*. It felt heavy and exciting between my hands, but I couldn't imagine actually opening it to read the pages, because it wasn't by Enid Blyton. My teachers were always telling me that I would have to give up her tales – they talked about 'Enid Blyton' as if it were an illness. Luckily, our mother had nothing against the adventure stories, knowing how quiet they kept my sister and me. She allowed us to pack them into the metal trunk that was to carry our most precious books, toys and ornaments across the sea to Canada. They took up no room at all, considering what was inside them: secret islands, magical circus stuff, whole mountains and rivers, not to mention the Famous Five, the Secret Seven and the adventurous four – the nearest thing to all the real friends we would have to leave behind, Laurie and I persuaded our mother.

'Go on then, shove them in!' She took out her own favourite ornaments to make room when we clustered around the trunk, our arms aching full of books.

I felt woozy when I finally opened my green prize-book and found the gate that led to the garden where everything was so much more bright and shiny than in the world outside. I read those bits over and over, never tiring of creeping through the hidden entrance to discover all the flowers, trees and birds, as if it was the first time I had stepped inside. I could imagine lying on the grass, which would be thick and velvety, like the posh cushions on Auntie Livia's settee. Even the sky would look different, once you had gone through the secret gate. It might not be so bad being a cripple like the boy in the story, I thought, if only you could get into a place so heavenly, that grown-ups didn't know about. I read the book twice in a row, then once more, before I was ready to hand it over so it could be packed with everything else.

'Too late.' My stepfather stood in front of the locked trunk, which he had just finished binding in brown tape and rope. 'Rule was, anything you wanted to keep, you had to give me yesterday for packing up.'

'Not to worry.' My mother took the book from me, promising to make space for it in one of the suitcases.

'Oh no you don't!' He snatched it out of her hands – 'Rules

is rules!' – and put it on the pile of things to be sold or given away.

Because our mother was superstitious, baptisms were arranged, along with haircuts, to prepare us for our new life in Canada. Our mother took Laurie and me to the Greek barber shop where tough men swung in and out, dangling cigarettes between their lips, while the barley-striped sign spiralled red and white, red and white, red and white. We came out naked at the neck, our dark hair cropped close to the skull. On the way home a blonde girl passed us, swinging a ponytail like the ones we had just left, lopped off, on the barber's floor. Behind our mother's back she stuck out a long, wet tongue as if Laurie and I were Pakistani boys. Strangers in the street no longer stopped to coo over our faces; they saw little skinhead lads when they looked at us.

By the time we stood at the altar to be baptized, wispy curls had begun to creep back around our ears. Bright orange dresses, obese poppies lolling up the sleeves, confirmed that we were girls. Stained-glass light dribbled over the vicar's face. He dipped his cuff at the font to leave holy wet fingerprints on our foreheads, and that was that: Church of England. We went home blessed, to nibble sausage rolls and pineapple chunks speared on toothpicks. Our mother had spent all morning chopping hot dogs and cheese for the relatives we were about to fly from.

'Lovely spread you've done, Lorraine.' Fat aunts complimented her buffet through mouths full of egg mayonnaise, watercress straying at their lips.

'Well, you have to go the whole caboodle – don't yer? – when you're leaving so many people behind.' Where others nibbled sandwich triangles, my mother clutched a burning cigarette, the smoke swirling about her cheekbones. Suddenly, she stumped it out and grabbed my hand.

'Tell you what,' she bent so that her hair fell silky in my face, 'why don't we put on a bit of Motown and have a quick dance?'

The records started spinning and people relaxed, smiling, tapping their feet. My mother loved to dance, swirling her skirt in circles, sashaying over the carpet: shy hip swings and clever, hopping toes. She led me by the tips of her fingers, whirling me under the arch of her arm like a tree, a weeping willow whose branches sway down to meet you.

'Lorraine!' My stepfather called my mother away to refill people's glasses.

By now, I was hot behind the ears and down my back, twisting my hips into small, smooth circles like my mother's.

'That's enough dancing, Andrea,' my stepfather told me.

'Oh, let her twist, Pete.' Auntie Doris laughed, tipsy. 'She's doing no harm.'

The music was still playing; people's feet were tapping in time; my sandals twisted and shuffled against the carpet's dull green until hot breath whispered into my ear: 'Upstairs!'

My stepfather's anger was hidden from the party under the music, the flushed chatter and clinking glasses.

On the stairs, he pressed a large, cold hand against my back, shoving me up into the bathroom. Inside, he locked the door and twisted the taps until the water gushed into the sink and was sucked, belching, down the plughole. The cascade drowned out the sound when his hand came down to slap my face.

'Don't you dare defy me!' My stepfather's lips moved while my ears rang full of the slap and the water and the party downstairs. Behind his head, I saw my own face in the bathroom mirror, red and blotted where steam was rising from the taps to mist over the reflection. I went to say, 'I won't, Dad,' but the words were muffled under his hand, pressing down to stifle my tears. Faint petroleum seeped from his palm, choking me.

When my eyes bulged, my stepfather peeled back his palm and washed his hands before twisting the taps shut. Everything stood still in the bathroom. The mirror was steamed over, reflecting nothing.

He took a flannel and wiped my face with a shaking hand.

'Now then, go on downstairs to the party.'

The party was still brimming with smoke and chatter and spilling drinks. Bubbling with wine, people asked me to twist for them. I pressed my back against the wall, smiling out of sore eyes.

'I'm tired of dancing,' I told them. The music sounded flat and tinny. I stayed close to the wall.

When people finally gathered their coats to leave, some of them were in tears. 'You'll be thousands of miles away,' the wine reminded them.

'Good luck, love. Take care!' Car doors slammed. Aunties, uncles, friends – everyone we had ever known – chugged off down the street. At the corner, yellow indicators winked before the cars turned and were gone. I finished waving on the doorstep, then climbed the stairs to wash the tears and lipstick kisses from my face. Our bedroom light went out at eight o'clock, but I read by the light of the streetlamp, then rehearsed my twelve and thirteen times tables, flustering to grasp the fourteens, until I fell asleep.

'Wake up, Andy: it's today,' my mother whispered in my ear and I opened my eyes. Her face was lowered to the pillow, close to mine. My heart always speeded up at the scent of her face cream.

'Shh! Let's not wake the others.' My mother planted a smoky kiss on my forehead and handed me my clothes for the trip: flared green corduroys and a red velour sweater that snuggled around my neck. Downstairs everything was still: a mug of coffee let off fine wisps of steam at the table; strewn around it lay old letters and love poems from me. The poems were full of birds and water and flowers and rainbows, the loveliest things I could think of, but really they were all about my mother.

'I'm sorting my papers out,' she told me. 'Some of them'll have to be thrown away.'

'Not this one.' I picked out a makeshift envelope I had tried to seal with spittle. Inside, my love letter began, *Dear Mummy, I love you more than God.* It went on to insist that I loved my mother more than mashed potato, more even than Auntie Livia. The previous Sunday, when I had written it at the dining table, my stepfather had snapped, 'Don't be so soppy!' He had reached to rip the page out of my notebook, but let me finish it when my face threatened to crease up and fold.

My mother read the letter again, laughing at the word 'georgeous', then slipped it into the hidden pouch of her wallet.

'No!' she smiled. 'Not this one.'

Then she slid her hands across the table and took up both of mine in her warm palms. Stroking my fists, she unfolded my long olive fingers against the laminated white of the table. We sat quietly together, my mother tracing around each of my fingers, pausing at the knuckles, until the milk van came rattling bottles outside the window to break the spell.

Our suitcases bulged at the locks.

'All our worldly goods!' Our mother laughed. Later, while we waited for Auntie Pauline and Uncle Bill to drive us to the airport, she cried on the telephone, squeezing in a few more goodbyes to Gran.

'I'll write, Mum.' Sobs came up from her chest. 'The minute we land I'll write to you.'

I was glad when Auntie Pauline and Uncle Bill pulled up and our mother had to dry her eyes to face them; her tears made me feel dizzy and small.

At the airport, our stepfather stood at the window with Sarah in his arms and Laurie by his side, watching the planes take off into the night. My mother and I sat at a red plastic table, sipping Coke in tall glasses through straws. She reached her hand across to squeeze mine tight, whispering: 'We can always come back, Andy, love – any time you say so, if you get frightened or homesick or anything.'

Before then, it had not occurred to me to feel frightened or homesick or anything.

I whispered back: 'I'll tell you, Mum, if I'm not happy.' Then I puckered my lips around my straw and sucked at my Coke until it was time to pass through the metal detectors and board the plane. An air hostess buckled me into my seat, and I sat looking out of the window, mulling over what my mother had said, over and over until the engines roared, my stomach shot up into my mouth, and Manchester dropped out of the picture.

3

It was like being shut up in a spaceship with our stepfather, pressing our faces out at the world. Not in the clouds, where smiling air hostesses hovered under helmets of hair and made us suck mint after mint out of crinkling silver wrappers, while he sat strapped into his seat licking their legs with his eyes. Not in the clouds – but from the moment the plane nosed down, and our stepfather unbuckled his seatbelt, clutching the passport with all our names in his fist. He slipped the passport into his shirt pocket, and a look shimmered across his face, like a glass door sliding shut. No more Gran or aunties to keep their eye out or stick their oar in.

Down a long tunnel, as cold as a fridge, Laurie reached to grip my mother's little finger: 'My legs've gone funny.'

'Move it.' Our stepfather grimaced behind the trolley full of luggage.

Suddenly, a sea of faces surged in front of us. One of them was Auntie Carla's; she came rushing out of the crowd with our cousins, Robin and Rosalie, followed by her new husband, Uncle Wayne. He was even taller and wider than our stepfather, whom he clapped on the back and called Partner.

'Damned heatwave,' Uncle Wayne drawled when we came out into the glare to load into his truck. He bent to lift Laurie and me into the back with the suitcases. 'Sun musta knew you were comin'' – he winked – 'put his hat on, special.'

The air boiled in slow waves, making the air ripple up off the tarmac and the grown-ups' smiles slip and slide over their faces. I wanted to ask my mother if she remembered that summer in Manchester when the ladybirds landed and landed on our arms, then crawled drunkenly through the hairs, sucking the sweet sweat. But her face was fixed over my head in a happy mask set to spoil if I tugged on it.

While our stepfather swore, wrestling with suitcases, and our mother mopped up Sarah's tantrum, Auntie Carla slipped a jar of something weird into my hands.

'For you and your Laurie.' It looked like golden glue oozing with light.

'Honey!' Auntie Carla laughed. 'Out of a beehive.' She explained through her grin how the honeycomb had been ripped out of the beehive and squashed into the jar with the lid screwed down.

'Oh.' Inside, at the heart of the honey, glistened a world of boxes that bees had spent their lives building out of the faces of flowers. I balanced on the back of the truck with the suitcases and Laurie, letting her stroke the glass but gripping the lid jealously in my fist, to keep the sweetness from spilling.

Even after dark, the air in Canada was warm and thick with smoky, rum-laced stories of the good life. Uncle Wayne's voice was music, murmuring sentences like songs, while crickets clicked and purred in the dark behind him. It was only when my sisters and I were sent in off the verandah and the door banged shut on the flowing night noise that I could imagine it all evaporating into one long airy promise, like Auntie Pauline had muttered – that afternoon in Manchester, behind our stepfather's back, with the trunks already sealed up for shipping.

No going back.

When it came to the crunch, our mother now admitted to me, Auntie Carla and Uncle Wayne were our only hope.

'The only souls we've got to rely on,' she sighed, when they invited us to make their bedroom our home. We had to sleep locked in as a family while Auntie Carla and Uncle Wayne squashed up in the living-room on the settee – the cream-coloured velvet one that Laurie and I had watched our cousins sprawl over in front of the television, while our stepfather scowled at us to keep the hell off, forcing us to sit cross-legged on the floor. I hid my face under the damp heat of the covers, my tummy sweating against Laurie's, until our stepfather's snores lulled full in the dark and my muscles slipped out of their knots into sleep.

While we were waiting to find a house of our own, we kept our lives squeezed up against the walls in plastic leather holdalls too crammed to risk opening properly. Our mother unzipped just a corner, and whatever she pulled out we wore.

'The buggers'll never shut back up,' she said when Laurie and I urged her to hunt out the twin red dresses whose halter necks would let the sun melt down our backs. She chipped her nails shoving stockings and dumb woollens back through the zip jaws.

'This is bloody ridiculous!' We saw the half-moons spoiling and stopped clamouring for our favourite clothes.

Some nights, after the whitest-hot days, our mother let other things spill out behind the bedroom door. She pulled us to her and buried her salty face in our hair, crooning horrible but delicious, *It wasn't meant to be like this, it wasn't meant to be like this*, until our stepfather sozzled in off the porch, and her eyes dried up.

'Don't fret, Lol.' He patted her thigh and fell into bed, slurring, 'We've wads of cash. Have our own pad in no time.'

Before the end of our first week, our stepfather had blown a wad of cash on a fat red Cadillac that he screeched us about in to see the sights. Laurie, Sarah and I clung to the back seat, watching years of Auntie Carla's dog-eared postcards spring to life, gulping pine and soil and sun-grilled grass as it smacked through the windows to fill our faces and set our hair screaming. Our mother sat in the front seat, her face dead under dark glasses, as mountains whizzed by.

At night, she soaped the days off our faces with a warm flannel. We watched our stepfather and Uncle Wayne tuck into steak and white bread dipped in steaming gravy, while we chewed rubbery hot dogs out of tins. Our jaws cycled slowly, taking care not to scoff, until the men jerked back their chairs and left the table to bite the heads off cigars. The doors slammed on our stepfather's red Cadillac, and they growled off in search of bars.

Something fisted in my belly when Auntie Carla scraped off the plates, forking chunks of still-warm steak into the dog dish. Our mother helped her rinse blood and gravy off the plates, then they boiled up some milk and bowed their heads close at the table. Their perms mingled into a single frizzy bush as they whispered over two milky coffees. Whatever they had on their minds was drowned under the miraculous splash and whirr of Auntie Carla's new dishwasher. I stood next to it, *Wishwish-wishwishwishwish*, gobbling bits about jobs, big houses, bruises and the bloody fortune just blown on that damn car.

A month of sunsets rolled by and we were still living out of holdalls up against the wall in Auntie Carla's bedroom. 'Just for the interim,' our mother kept saying.

The day trips dried up.

'Seen one mountain, seen 'em all.' Our stepfather shrugged when we begged him to take us shooting along the freeways again, where totem poles flashed past, tossing thrills across the back seat.

Now he was busy chasing opportunities – fast money he heard of from strange men in bars.

'See you later, doll.' He pecked our mother's cheek, revved up his car and was dust.

I hung about my mother's chair, milking her for after-dinner kisses. When my stepfather was out she would give me her cheek – Ponds spiced with Craven A. She let me twist her newly permed curls in springy tubes around my thumb. But her smile snapped when I tried resting the tip of my little finger in the fleshy groove where her eyebrows met.

'Enough, Andy, love. Enough.' My mother dug her knuckles into the small of my back. 'Go on now and grab some fresh air. It's a whole new world out there.'

I sulked with Laurie down the darkening road, blinking at the whisks of dust stirred up by cars speeding past us, heading for the horizon of ice-cream-tipped mountains. Occasionally the cars would have kids in them, kneeling on the back seat. Then Laurie and I would smile and wave like mad until the faces dissolved in the dusk. We were bursting to make friends, because the summer holidays had only just started and it would be ages before we went to a new school and met anyone our own age. Our cousins were prepared to watch TV with us, but, at eleven and thirteen, they were too old to play with us or even to be seen with us outside the house, since I was not yet ten and Laurie was only eight. We hung around them as long as we dared, letting their watery Canadian accents wash over us, soaking up new ways of saying things. Crisps were 'potato chips', tea was 'supper', 'pizza' was a squelchy, cheese-and-tomatoey thing that you ate by itself, with no vegetables on the plate. Robin and Rosalie couldn't believe that we had never seen, let alone eaten, a pizza before. We let them tease us about how much we didn't know, until their jibes began to turn nasty. Then we made ourselves scarce.

My sister and I snailed along the road, inhaling heady grass smells, scouring the ditches for empty beer bottles. At the end was a shop – the liquor store – owned by a pudgy-faced man named Chad, who let us swap any bottles we found for what he called candy. 'Ready to trade?' he would ask us when we clinked into his store with our booty. There was nothing as good as the Arrow bars and Mojos and Refreshers that we used to get in England, and we knew better than to choose chocolate, since the stuff here tasted so odd it gave us the shivers. Usually Chad would press us to take liquorice laces. We had to smile into his jowly face knowing they would be wiry and stale. Sometimes, though, the weeds turned up enough bottles, brown-gold with red labels, to persuade him to hand over a box of Crackerjack. On the packet, a sailor boy billowed in blue over red writing: *The more you eat, the more you want!* That was true; but it made me feel lost, squabbling with my sister over shards of broken toffee and popcorn kernels in the bottom. We trundled back in silence, squinting against the dying light to spot more bottles glinting in the grass.

It was like wearing cosy, invisible sleeves, with the sultry evening air pressing on our skin. But all the warmth drained away and the sky suddenly looked dark, as if it were frowning, when we ran into a posse of boys clutching sticks like rifles. Laurie and I shivered. These were not nice boys, like the ones we had been expecting to find in Canada, after seeing Tom Sawyer and Huckleberry Finn on TV.

'Get your fucking shoes off!' One of them jabbed his rifle stick into my chest.

Laurie glanced up and down the dim road, thirsty for grown-ups. I agreed to take off my sandals if my little sister didn't have to.

'Get 'em off!' The smallest boy stood up to my nose, ketchup rusting in the corners of his lips. He winked at his beefier friends, a crowd of horrible grins. Then he bent and thrust his stick into the grass before swooping it up to my face. On the end, a swollen worm was flailing, frantic to lay its belly down.

'Grass snakes!' The boys sniggered.

The snake's pale belly glowed in the last of the light. Then, with a mad writhe, it flew off the stick and dropped, wriggling invisible, into the grass.

My toes gleamed, naked as slugs, in the weeds next to the ditch. I stood my ground, my throat clenched against crying as I spoke up: 'Give us my sandals.'

'*Give us my sandals, give us my sandals, give us my sandals!*' The boys pounced on my Manchester voice, tossing it between them in a sick sing-song mixture of home and here.

'Stuff you!' I lobbed my full-blown accent from home. It had been getting wet around the edges, as if it were beginning to dissolve. Now the old words were flying out of my mouth as sweet as they were filthy. I came as near as I dared to swear words, then grabbed Laurie's hand to storm off, barefoot, along the gravel side of the road.

Our mother would hit the roof, because the sandals had cost two dollars at K-Mart, but Auntie Carla might hum her car back along the ditch to rescue them from the dark before our stepfather got home.

'English trash! English trash!' The sandals walloped our backs.

We scooped them out of the dirt and ran full pelt.

Our adventure put Laurie and me in the limelight for the night. We sat shining in front of our cousins, feeling as fascinating as television. Our fingers throbbed, clutching icy glasses of cherry Kool-Aid which sped pink and stinging into our mouths after scooting through rollercoaster straws.

By midnight it was over. The house had clenched up, tense, all eyes on the telephone. Uncle Wayne and our stepfather had not staggered home at their usual hour.

'Bloody fools!' Auntie Carla kept saying in a high, scratchy voice. 'Bloody fools! They could have been knifed, or shot even, the dives they end up in.'

Our mother rasped a match to light one more cigarette, half closing her eyes at the first puff, then flicking her other wrist fast to snuff out the match's flame. She met the tip with a slow pucker, and her thoughts were her own.

When gravel crunched in the drive, she stubbed out her smoke in the ashtray brimming with dead dimps. They came in laughing, my stepfather and Uncle Wayne, holding one another up in a stinking cloud of cigars and spirits. We scattered as they fell on to the settee, muddying the velvety cream.

'Lolly, love—' Our stepfather gagged on his own tongue. His face kept twitching and twisting, trying to sort tears out of the drunken, queer laughing that had taken over his insides.

'Lolly, love,' he got out, 'something...' Then his face let go and there was an avalanche of tears, worse than sick. We froze, fascinated.

'Lol.' A bloodied hand groped for my mother's. 'It's me car. The Cadillac. Down the ditch, an accident – tell them, Wayne.'

I saw my stepfather's wide, red Cadillac smashed in the murk of a ditch, back wheels dead in the air. A truck had come steaming round the bend – lights too low, no bloody horn – and there was nothing for it and that was that, one almighty swerve and they were lucky to get out alive, goddammit and sweet Jesus.

Our mother boiled up some coffee and made our stepfather sip like a baby to still the trembling and stop the tears. He moaned low into the mug, slurping, 'Lolly, Lolly, Lolly.'

But you could see through the steam it was his smashed-up Cadillac he had in mind.

The next night the men abandoned the dirty dishes like always, staggered back slit-eyed and singing like always. Before midnight this time, no blood. A whiff of disappointment streaked through the air when the door swung open on their songs. Our stepfather lurched in, deep pink from drinking, sagged on the velvet settee and yanked our mother into his lap to pass on the hard whisky promises Uncle Wayne had been making all night.

'Wayne's found work for me, under the table, like.' He spoke with bright wet eyes. 'Few months is all it'll take me to get me act together, then we can think about building our own place, Wayne says. How about that, then?'

His hair reeked of smoke and whisky, but our mother smiled straight into the face of our stepfather's dreams. If frowns wrecked her forehead she kept them well under her perm.

'Smashing, love.' She stroked our stepfather's hair. His black curls sweated at the roots, limp from alcohol and the muggy midsummer night.

'A pad of our own,' our stepfather sighed. 'How 'bout that, Andy, love?'

It was bloodshot but rare, the smile my stepfather tossed me. I saw the Cadillac nearly killing him and thought of kissing his hands where they sprawled on his tired denim knees. The knuckles lay hairy and grooved, resting, I imagined, after a lifetime of hoisting sails and fixing cars. Under the nails lurked ancient oil stains and dirt out of nowhere.

'We'll have a garden, won't we, Dad?'

His fingers flexed, promising to pull a house out of the ground: ironed lawns and a white wooden fence all around.

'Yes, love,' my mother whispered. Our stepfather had slipped into one of his drunken snoozes.

'There'll be a huge garden,' she said, as he began to snore.

There was a huge garden. A huge, leafy jewellery box sprouting yellow melons and golden squash. Pumpkins perched like swollen footballs, a crowd of strawberries crawling tendrils and pouting ruby kisses along the fence. Canada. Our eyes devoured it all, while our mother and stepfather retreated for a moment out of the sun. They had to leave Laurie and me on the verandah with Mr Singh, the owner, while they stepped inside to make their decision. In private.

'We'll take it.' Our mother smiled hard, as if she had been slapped, when they came back out.

'Very good,' the Indian man said, touching his turban. 'Very good.'

Our stepfather shuffled green paper into the man's hand. It fluttered in the breeze. Rent.

'Just a month for now, mind.' He frowned at the man's bright purple turban. 'We'll be buying our own place any day.'

'Very good.' Mr Singh made a fist of the money. Then he waved it over the garden: 'This not included, you understand?'

He left us on the verandah, held up on stilts, over the empire of fruity colour.

Our stepfather borrowed Uncle Wayne's truck and led us around flea markets and garage sales on desperate quests for furniture. But we sloped home without the mirrors or pictures that might have made the walls seem more friendly. The

46

curtains, from the cheap end of the rack, were a dull red-orange, like a rotten sunset. To ease our mother's migraines we had to pull the curtains tight and put up with the putrid orange light seeping through them. Otherwise, the sun shot straight in like a guillotine and it was headaches all round, hot and hammering behind the eyes.

'The heat here can be cruel,' our mother wrote to Gran on postcards of shiny mountains or pioneers smiling in front of forts. I could almost taste the beads of sweat glistening on her lips where she sucked the end of her pen. She scribbled the last of her love and rinsed a flannel ice-cold under the tap. I watched her dabbing against her temples and in the hollows of her neck, where the clavicles stood out proud and arched, like jewellery. Her bones were so fine people often ended up staring.

Going to play her favourite record one morning, my mother found it curled up and melted on the turntable under the window.

'Why didn't you pull the curtains?' She gave me a look and yanked them across so that the room swilled orange and my tummy turned over. I watched her cursing the sun and weeping over the shrivelled black disc. A woman used to sing, 'Don't cry for me, Argentina', teasing hairy tremors deep into the back of our necks. Our stepfather would skulk off and leave us to ourselves – my mother, my sisters and me, alone – in the music. Now the song was dead.

Nobody had warned me about the wrong kind of sun. In England, it made you feel more alive, glimmering out from behind the clouds and then slipping back in before you'd had enough. In Canada, it made you think of dying.

The moment I saw it shining to kill, I went to lie in the shade of the porch, resting my face on the cool stone steps. I closed my eyes, and the sun was a different yellow. Under my lids, the old, Manchester sky bulged full of purple clouds, like bruises, swinging in sooty circles over slate roofs and chimneys and concrete lamp-posts. There were horses in the clouds and strange faces, like God's. Like Gran's.

Hauled out of the ditch and mended, the battered red Cadillac still clogged up the drive, its front end a mangled silver smile. I went inside where the house sat sweating behind its sour orange drapes. My stepfather slouched asleep in the only armchair. His head lolled back, baring his neck white where the sun never ventured.

I held my breath to keep him like that.

He had woken once, when I wandered into the dark orange room, and pulled me into his lap.

'Here, Andy, give us a kiss.'

I brushed my stepfather's bristly cheek and went to get out of the chair, when his denim knees gripped. Holding my head like a melon between his hands, he slid his tongue into my ear. A black shudder went through me, all down one side.

'Now, you kiss me.' My stepfather turned his face away and pushed back greasy curls: 'In my ear.'

My bony thighs were bruising between his knees; I stopped wriggling and looked into the ear.

'No, Dad.' Hiding panic under a giggle. 'It's too hairy!'

Nails scratched my face when my stepfather grabbed my hair, 'Come on, Andy, love.'

'No!' My voice threatened to break out of its whisper, with all the clobbering inside: 'I've got to go and wake up Mum, Dad – Mum's asked me to wake her up.'

The knees slackened and my stepfather shoved me off his lap, 'Go on, then.' *Little bitch*, he added under his breath – 'Go on, then.'

The clock, plastic gold, was ticking and echoing, ticking and echoing down the hall.

I wanted to go to my mother. I knew she would be lying in her room with the covers fastened over her face. Our house was baking, baking, but still she hid under her heaviest blankets. She had to have her sleep. There had been fights – screaming and smashed ornaments – over money and booze and indolence.

'Sheer bloody indolence!' our mother threw at our stepfather.

To get to this hell-hole she had sacrificed her trusty blue Princess and the red terraced house our real father slaved for until the day he died. The house and the car and the furniture – the whole flaming shebang! – had not been shrunk into dirty green notes just to stuff his pockets and swell his potbelly with spirits by the bloody gallon. Our lives were fluttering in the wind, for Christ's sake, while he lazed good-for-nothing on his bastard backside all fucking day.

'I wouldn't have to laze on me backside all fucking day' – our stepfather gritted his teeth – 'if I were legal to work. I can't do a flying shit with no papers, can I?'

Now he got so worked up his jaws unlocked and he broke out of his laze to lunge at our mother.

'Nagging bitch!' He grabbed the collar of her housecoat in his knuckles, shaking and knocking hollow and hard, as if he might crack open her chestbone.

'Peter!' Our mother's head whipped back like a doll's. 'Not in front of the girls!' She shrieked slightly, choking, but our stepfather's face was swelling. He kept up his strop.

'Outside, girls,' our mother gasped. Her voice wobbled, but her eyes looked quite set: 'Outside!'

We went outside while they got on with it indoors.

'Wanna play frisbee?' the kids next door yelled from their yard.

I shook my head. They had a paddling pool and a trampoline that we were dying to bounce on. But our stepfather would go mad if he caught us in someone else's yard; he was afraid we would go blabbing our mouths off, letting strangers know his business. We would have to wait for summer to end and school to begin before we could start chatting and getting friendly with them.

For now, my sisters and I had to sit on the verandah under the neighbours' stares, watching the sun slink down. Across the back way, two fat birds hung upside-down, dripping, on a pole. The man with the gammy leg liked to slip into his green jacket and drive off with his guns on a Saturday afternoon. When he got home, he trussed up his catch and slit the necks. Every Saturday night they came out, tied up by their toes, dripping in the dusk, while we tried not to notice.

Just after dark, our stepfather would slam out and rev up his car to go drinking. Tyres screeched under him before his patched-up Cadillac clanged and sputtered down the drive. We crept back indoors for an evening of orange gloom. Our mother disappeared into her bedroom, where she shut herself in with her cuts and bruises. The knob clicked once and there was dead quiet behind the door. I boiled up the kettle, stirring mugs of sugary coffee to wheedle my way in.

'Coffee, Mum.' My ears strained to make her breathe through the wood.

Sometimes, a muffled groan rose from the blankets. My mother was conscious and might let me in to grip one clammy hand while she sipped from the other, trembling one. More often, a murky silence seeped under the door and I had to balance the coffee back down the hall without spilling. The cup sat on the television, waiting for her, until a cold stink slithered out and we had to pour it down the drain.

Laurie pestered me to do jigsaws on the carpet. To stifle our three-year-old sister's tantrums, we let her suck the bits of cardboard before scattering them in fistfuls over the floor: 'Make them fit!' I used to win Sarah's and Laurie's awe by grabbing at a glance how the shapes locked together into livid green landscapes and blue skies. But I shuddered each time a picture was on the verge of coming together: I had a secret horror of the holes where pieces had gone missing.

Worry muscled and cramped in my calves, kneeling over the puzzles. I left my sisters and tiptoed back down the hall to my mother's door, where a sly twist of my kirby grip slid open the lock. Her face was buried under the blankets. I had to peel them slowly back, holding my heart down.

No splits or gashes. All the bones where they should be.

I let myself breathe. Around her eyes the skin puffed veiny blue with bursts of purple, then sagged, yellow-green and hollow, under the cheekbones. Her dimples were shadowy holes, carved deep into the cheeks.

I bent to kiss the smell of my mother's messed-up face. It was comforting, when her sores made her look a bit like a stranger, to find the same old scents. Woody perfume came from her hair, rich with hours of sipping coffee and huffing on cigarettes in her pink housecoat and green fur slippers.

'Andy, love?' Her eyeballs shifted under bluish skin lids.

I hovered – *wake up, wake up, wake up* – over the closed eyes.

My mother's head lolled in the damp pillow. I bent closer to catch her murmurs, before they faded and slowed. She sank back into bruised sleep, and I let her be.

When our mother was what she called recuperated, the door would creak open. The toilet flushed and gurgled. She flapped down the hall in her slippers to cook tea. In place of meat we had mashed potatoes. Stiff mountains with no milk and only the meanest idea of margarine to soften them up – not squishy and delicious like they used to be in England, but dry, so that it was like eating sand. Ketchup would have worked wonders, but our mother declared it disgusting and bad for our health. She insisted on a smattering of frozen vegetables, to add colour and nutrition. Peas like pebbles and stony cubes of carrot hit the bottom of the pan in a bullety hail; after boiling they tasted of nothing but the tin insides of the saucepan. We trudged through our plates, chomping green balls and orange cubes.

'Mommy, your face is funny.' When Sarah threatened to cry, our mother held her and let her stroke around the fragile features, so that she would be less afraid of them. She stood at the window, smoking and staring out over the garden swelling ripe in the dark. The Singhs never got round to plucking things before they burst. We saw melon after melon puking pink seeds through cracked bellies, while grapes blistered black on the vine.

My mother stumped her cigarette and slipped the hot stub back in the pack for later – she liked to grind every last breath out of her cigarettes. Letting out a long, smoky-blue sigh, she drew her fingers over her face, then wound her sleeves up tight to do the dishes. I hovered close to her hip, wiping plates hot and lemony out of her hands, trying to swallow the bitter orange pill she made us suck on a Saturday, to be sure of our vitamins.

When the phone rang, her face frowned painfully, and she fumbled to kill the bubbles between her fingers.

'Hello?' Nobody ever rang us in the evenings. People were too busy feasting in families over tea and television.

It was a stranger at the other end, making our mother sing cheerful, tight as a wire, down the line.

'Yes, that's us,' she said, then folded into a chair to chat. Laurie and I stood by, riveted. We watched her shoulders melting, lines unravelling out of her forehead into the phone.

'We'll be waiting.' Our mother laid the receiver in its cradle and plunged her elbows back into the bubbles. We knew better than to ask who had called. 'Curiosity killed the cat,' she would have tutted. It was bad manners to pry. Eventually she pulled out the plug and sent the suds burping down the sink. She wrapped the dishcloth like a scarf around the hot tap's neck and twisted her wedding ring back on, over the swollen red knuckle.

'Well, kiddlywinks' – she touched her face round the edges – 'we've somebody coming to see us. Tomorrow, first thing.'

We went to bed with jam butties inside us instead of water. We had a name, too, to chew on. Auntie Penny, distant cousin of Great Auntie Agnes in Manchester. It's lovely, I wanted to tell my mother, when your stomach lets you lie down without that hole squelching full of water while you're trying to sleep.

When we woke up, our mother was a new woman. She threw the curtains back wide and drew a slick of lipstick glossy across her mouth. Instead of her exhausted pink housecoat and green slippers, she came out in royal blue slacks, seams pressed sleek up her legs. We marvelled at curls springing out of their rollers, where yesterday her hair had been dead brown straw clinging to the skull.

'You look absolutely gorgeous, Mum.' I admired the Precious Plum kisses her lips printed at the end of every cigarette and on the rim of her mug.

She let Laurie, Sarah and me press our noses against the nets to look out for our visitor. We were glued to the glass when a wide silver bonnet purred up our drive.

A lady's Cadillac.

She stepped out glazed, her skin tanned: Auntie Penny.

Gold earrings dangled money around her face. I kept my eyes on them, trying not to stare where her eyebrows had been plucked to death then pencilled back on, too high, in skinny wings of surprise.

'You're all so pretty!' she laughed, though her eyes skated politely to avoid the colours bruising our mother's face.

She was tall, and her knees made delicious cracking sounds when she stooped to give us kisses and biscuity stars baked out of gingerbread, dipped in pink icing. Where once I would have burned to wipe it away, I let the lipstick kiss linger, sticky, a pearl on my cheek.

4

Auntie Penny gave us ice-cream and barbecues and a garden growing wild – grass under our soles and pine trees to look up to. She wanted to be sure we made the most of the sun before it got tired and it was time for us to put on long trousers and start school. Her silver Cadillac whisked us to a white wooden house only a blink from the sea, with an outdoor pool that made our mother gasp: 'Azure!'

Life was too short, Auntie Penny had discovered over the years, to be anything less than sweet.

We stripped off and skinny-dipped in the blue, before sinking our teeth into beefburgers that burnt our eyes: smoked over charcoal, sizzling cheese, oozing spicy tomato relish out of sesame seed buns.

'Little gannets!' Auntie Penny laughed. My throat seized up in the sun.

But he was miles away – we had left him buried, snoring, under the covers.

She smiled over us. 'Tastes better with your vests off, doesn't it now?'

Afterwards, Auntie Penny stuck us under her Power Shower and let us loose with her perfumed soaps in the bathroom full of mirrors and fancy bottles. I could have stayed in there forever, water pummelling my back, steam rising behind the swirled-glass door that you could lock, without a sound, from the inside.

'It won't run out,' Auntie Penny insisted, when I worried about the water.

At our house the tank never heated all the way, so the taps gurgled lukewarm before gushing out icy. The electricity cost a fortune, and we had to conserve all our hot water for dirty dishes and for our mother's long, silent soaks, locked in the bathroom with cotton wool and pink ointments after another bloody to-do.

Auntie Penny pressed a white furry towel into my arms, and rubbed my toasted back.

'Little wings.' She traced my shoulder blades. 'Little wings, sticking out to fly.'

'Get summat on,' our stepfather tutted, after his car growled up and he caught us spurting cherries and spitting bloody stones in our Fruit of the Loom knickers.

My arms folded over the nipples, suddenly prickling.

'No.' Auntie Penny spoke as if she were royal. 'It's good for them, a lick of sun on their backs.'

Our stepfather's eyebrows met in the middle, but his mouth sat still.

'Now, Peter, honey' – Auntie Penny's nails shimmered, bronze lacquer, against a green bottle – 'what would you say to a beer with your burger?'

Our stepfather left us bare-bellied under the sun, to run in white knickers through the sprinkler's rainbowed webs. But things were beginning to cloud over, and my mind was on my vest. The wildness was gone.

Under Auntie Penny's influence, our mother marvelled, her Pete was a reformed character. Instead of sponging up game

shows and days full of soaps, he heaved out of his armchair to
face the mirror over the sink.

'Time for a shave, methinks.' He slit his eyes and peered at
himself, lost in the lather.

Laurie and I stood by his side, scrubbing our teeth in
harmony, watching the razor in the mirror. Up his neck, it
rasped. Slowly. Slowly again. Slowly, with never a nick.

He slapped his face when it came out of the foam, gleaming.

Our mother looked up from her lipstick.

'Street angel, house devil,' she muttered, without losing her
pucker.

Our stepfather sped us like lightning to Auntie Penny's garden,
where he could preside over the barbecue, talking money and
motors with her rich but shrunken husband. Uncle Charlie
was the shakier side of sixty, his hair white and his words few
and slow. His skin made you think of apples rotting, but
there was something pure trapped in his flossy hair. He and
our stepfather stood across the garden, spearing steaks and
making men's talk in the curling, meaty smoke. I kept my eye
on them – swigging gold beer from green bottles, while the
sun slid down – and wondered how long the barbecues would
last.

Although he still smelt of smoke and men's spirits, our
stepfather was not unpleasant to be near, now that Uncle
Charlie had secured him work fixing the odd motor here and
there. 'Soon adds up, the odd job does.' Every morning, instead
of dozing the day away on the back verandah or brooding over
the white peaks of the border, our stepfather got fully dressed
– covering his usually bare chest and pulling on socks and
shoes – to go off to work while the sun was still struggling into
its stride. At night he came home stained with engine oil that

my sisters and I helped him to scrub off at the kitchen sink. We squirted washing-up liquid along his arms and soaped up the hairs while he boasted about cash.

There was no crowding around the sink the night he came home grinning and pressed his oily palms over our mother's eyes.

'Outside, you.' He pushed her out on to the porch in her pinny. My sisters and I tripped over our heels behind them, to get to the front door and peek into the drive.

'A Pinto!' Our mother drew in her breath. 'A Pinto, Pete.' She found herself smiling at the sky-blue sports car gleaming, just for her, in the drive. 'You rum bugger, you! What in the devil's name are you like?'

We looked the other way while our stepfather put his face over our mother's, nuzzling her purply swellings where they were aching to die down.

'Lol, me love.' He kissed our mother as if we didn't exist.

Some nights, our stepfather swaggered home with iced dough-nuts in boxes and passed pink sugared almonds and stray green notes into our mother's hands. Other nights, he staggered home empty-handed, carrying only sick whiffs of whisky and dirty, clinging smoke. If he had no engines to fix, he went prowling to kill the hours. On the rampage, our mother called it. Empty days brought him home sagging, though he might puff himself up on tales of wild cars and vile men toting guns in back alleys. On the most awful nights, he turned up in mad debt, having squandered a fistful of cash on a telly or a stereo or some other dodgy deal. We were torn between biting our lips for our mother and smiling for our stepfather when he tried to pass off his drunken disasters.

'Here, kids' – it could be anything from a bashed-up bike to a radio that nearly worked – 'I got this for you.'

Our mother ranted and wept, but there was no getting the cash back.

'We've sod all to eat, and you're still frittering it away!' She clenched her jaw. The sinews stood out like knives in her neck. 'What in Christ's name are you thinking of?'

'Shut it, Lol,' our stepfather slurred. 'Just shut your flamin' gob, why don't yer?'

One night, he lifted his hand as if he were going to give her a smack, then pulled it back and clenched it into a fist that he thrust against his own forehead, grinding the knuckles. Our mother wrenched his knuckles away from his head, then gave him a funny, painful-looking hug to steady him as he crumpled in her arms. She bit her lip and turned her face to one side, so that she didn't have to breathe in the fumes from his mouth. Instead of blowing up, our stepfather cried and was sick, and our mother dragged him like a dead man down the hall to bed, while I helped her with the feet.

'Monsoons,' our mother gasped, when hulking black clouds came wheeling in off the Pacific to dump the ocean in silver sheets.

'I never thought I'd miss the rain,' I told my mother.

My sisters and I pressed our faces with hers at the window, watching the heavens ripple and explode.

'Me neither.' She let Laurie and me drag her out on to the verandah for one magnificent drench before our Sunday night bath.

It was a special bath this week. Our mother squirted in washing-up liquid, frothing bubbles around our shoulders to soften the blow.

School.

*

Because George Greenaway was what they called Progressive, the playground was dotted with children who were special: deaf or limping or smiling without seeing out of eyes spaced wide. Killing time before the bell, older kids gathered around the puny ones to make freaks of them in the crowd.

'How many toes do you have?' they asked, day after day. Or, 'What makes your face that way, huh?'

I stood silently on the edge of the circles, hoping not to be shown up as a freak before the bell rang.

In class it was impossible to be invisible. My voice turned heads.

'Cockney!' the older kids decided, ordering Laurie and me to sing after school like those kids in the Pink Floyd song. 'We don't need no education,' I sang in Cockney, without understanding, until the pock-faced Garth brought in his album to stick the cover under my nose: 'There you go, English!'

A bloody machine dragged in children at the top, grinding them up and oozing pink mincemeat out of a hole in the bottom.

'Gross!' I laughed and pushed the picture out of my face to leg it home with Laurie.

But at night, when I closed my eyes, there was the bloody machine: grinding slow circles, making bright pink mincemeat out of English schoolchildren.

It was all phone calls and kerfuffle and paradise flashing under our roof.

And then it was gone, before you could stop it.

Every morning was the same, opening the door on the wet world outside and having to swallow – not sadness, but a hole where happiness had been – before stepping into the road. Gran had been there, under our roof, with Auntie Pauline and Uncle Bill and our cousins, Ben and Sasha and Becky. They had come on a plane and slept in sleeping bags on the floor just to be with us. We had photographs to prove it. Mount Seymour and Mount Vernon, we had all visited: White Rock, Peace Arch Park, Fort Langley, Chilliwack. Our stepfather had insisted on taking everyone around 'his town', showing off corners of Vancouver that Laurie and I had no idea existed, including the planetarium where we saw shooting stars through 3-D glasses, and Chinatown – a world of tortured ducks, glistening and revolving in sad slow dances in all the windows. He had even paid to take us and our cousins panning for gold in a creek near Brittania Bay, rubbing our hair, not a glimmer of anger, when Laurie and I failed to scoop any nuggets. He bristled, embarrassed, every time it turned cloudy or rained; when the sun came out, his legs fell into a swagger of pride. In the evenings, he stoked up the barbecue on the back verandah, treated our mother as if she were a princess, and regaled Gran, Auntie Pauline and Uncle Bill with his plans to make it big in the building business. Shuddering at the fake North American accent he put on to dress up his ideas, I looked daggers at Laurie to keep her from giggling in front of the grown-ups and giving our stepfather away. We basked in the glow of his slapped-on smile while our mother snapped away with her Kodak instamatic.

As soon as he waved everyone off at the airport, our stepfather was at our mother's throat. Auntie Penny was off defying the wet weather and cruising the Caribbean with Uncle Charlie and his arthritis. The neighbours refused to see anything.

'Howdy!' They kept everything packed behind their eyes, in fat looks that I strained to weigh up.

The only person to share our mother's bruises was Auntie Carla, who had a face full of her own – something odd was happening in her house, the huge one Uncle Wayne had built out of raw timber with his bare hands, to show the sheer size of his love. They sat like twins, sipping coffee, looking livid.

'Go and play, girls.' Our mother dismissed us upstairs with our cousins, while she and Auntie Carla whispered fast, gripping hands.

'Man, I hate my dad!' My cousin Rosalie backcombed furiously.

'Does he hit you?' I held my breath.

'Sure.' She hissed hairspray. 'My dad's a bastard.'

Though I could never pass it over my own lips, it was good to hear the word bastard.

'So's mine.' I slipped my cousin a kiss, just inside her wrist.

Three weeks later, Uncle Wayne was dead.

'Stone cold dead.' Our mother could not believe it. 'Of a brain tumour, so they say.'

Auntie Carla came to our house to heave through the days.

'I thought it was just the booze,' she sobbed, 'and his godawful temper. How was I to know?'

She wept through eyes still puffed blue-green in the wake of Uncle Wayne.

'Shh, love.' Our mother laid Auntie Carla's head on her bony chest, stroking her devastated perm. 'You weren't to know, Carla. Who could have known?'

I was desperate to ask someone about brain tumours.

'Do you get them from drinking?' I wanted to know. 'Are they catching?'

I thought of all those nights our stepfather had strolled off and rolled back, shoulder to shoulder, swaying and singing, with our dead Uncle Wayne. I caught myself in the mirror and it was written all over my face – what I was thinking – ready to sell me down the river the minute I opened my mouth.

By the time Auntie Penny came back from the Caribbean, Auntie Carla had stopped whimpering, but our mother had taken to her bed with her own worries. Fights in the middle of the night made her too tired to get up during the day. She had even lost the urge to visit the fleamarket, where she used to love to go pouncing on bargains.

'I can't make it this week,' she mumbled from her pillow when the phone rang. I heard myself donated to Auntie Penny: 'Oh aye, our Andy would love that.'

When Auntie Penny picked me up in her silver Cadillac, I tried to flash things at her out of my eyes. My stepfather would kill me if I breathed a word, but I tried to let on, without words, what had been happening inside our house while she was away on a luxury liner.

'Okay, sweetie-pie?' Her eyes danced between me and the rear-view mirror. 'Everything okay?'

At Auntie Penny's it was just me and the TV: she cooked things up in the kitchen while Uncle Charlie lay in bed, looking to put some life in his bones. There was nothing I might do to help her – no dishes or polishing or sweeping up or anything.

'In this house we relax,' Auntie Penny declared. 'You just sit back and don't fret, till I call on you to appreciate my cool-a-nerry talents!'

With nothing to look out for over my shoulder, I let myself sink into the cushions and watch the screen. It was time, a gravelly voice echoed, to enter the Twilight Zone.

A skinny man in spectacles had an addiction to books: he had to read them all the time and his wife hated him for it. He would smuggle books into the bank where he worked, then hide during his lunchbreak in the vault with the gold. There, he could read to his heart's content, before real life took over and he had to go home to his wife nagging in the house. He was ugly and old and he wore glasses, but something put you on the skinny man's side.

He read and read in the vault with the gold, where nobody would think to disturb him, until one lunchtime a bomb hit the town while the skinny man was locked in with his book. When he finished his chapter and came out to face work, the whole town had been wiped out, including his wife. Despite all the rubble and everybody being dead, it was paradise, because he found doughnuts to eat and then stumbled upon the library – still standing, with majestic white stone pillars, crammed with books just waiting to be read. You could feel the music lifting you up, like the man, inside, thinking of all those books and no one to stop you.

The skinny man went dashing up the library steps. Then he tripped and the music changed. The screen zoomed in on his spectacles – smashed on the steps. He was groping for them, blind, when the picture faded and The End came up with the tune, which now sounded more scary than exciting.

I shifted among the cushions, feeling hot and nervous, as if I were guilty.

'What,' I asked Auntie Penny when she popped out of the kitchen, 'was the point of the bomb, then, blowing up his wife and everything, if his glasses were going to end up smashed?'

'Oh, that's just the way it goes on TV, honey.' Her mind was stuck on roast lamb.

*

It was between *The Twilight Zone* and Auntie Penny's antique dinner table that the sensation came over me.

I had to go home. I had to get home to my mother and Laurie and Sarah, all stuck in our house without me.

'It's asparagus, honey,' Auntie Penny smiled, when she saw my face chewing strangely.

'It's lovely,' I said, but I couldn't bring myself to swallow the third grassy finger.

Hiding it under my tongue, I looked at Auntie Penny and asked, 'Can I be excused?'

In the bathroom I let the mush out of my mouth and flushed it down the toilet. It was divine, the white-green taste under my tongue, but I had to spit it out. My mother and Laurie and Sarah, my stepfather and the insides of our house, had all seeped into my mouth and spoilt it.

Black stars crowded across the bathroom, blotting out the mirrors.

I called, 'Auntie Penny.'

It was like nothing before. Smashing and thudding yanked me out of sleep and I sat up in bed at the same time as Laurie. Something hot and edged ran up my spine.

'You bloody bastard!' our mother was screaming in the kitchen.

'Get out of the fucking way!' We heard our stepfather shoving to get past her into the hall. 'Where is she, the stirring little bitch?'

Laurie reached for my hand in the dark.

'You keep away from them,' our mother was saying. It came out twisted, as if through locked teeth. Then a clattering metal smash and she screamed, 'Peter!'

We leapt out of bed and ran down the hall, blinking at so

much white electric light after the sleeping dark. In the kitchen, the table had been knocked flat on to its back, smashing dirty plates, oozing cold gravy with peas. Under the sink, he had wrestled the cutlery drawer off its runners and on to the floor. The silver lay skewed and glinting against the tiles.

'Dad!'

In his hand, our stepfather had the carving knife, shining, with its varnished wooden handle and the long silver blade edged fine for slicing beef. Our mother was standing against the wall, her back pressed into it as if it might swallow her up, away from the beef-knife hovering and gleaming along her cheek. Her eyes looked through the blade into our stepfather's.

'Put it down, Pete,' she said softly, over the trembling. 'Put it down, love.'

My stepfather shifted his eyes at me.

'You let that little bitch feed people a pack of lies about me.' He jerked the knife, pointing.

'This isn't about the girls, Pete.' Our mother's voice was like a lullaby. 'Let's put down the knife and talk about it, why don't we?'

Our stepfather was sweating.

'Get rid of the fucking kids, then.'

Thick, whitish drops welled, shivering, in his nostrils.

Laurie and I held hands in the hall, barefoot and glued to the carpet. Our eyes glanced to take in food spurted up the walls, plates smashed against the tiles, then went back to the blade.

'Back to bed, girls,' our mother whispered. 'Go on.' She slid steel into her voice when we failed to move. 'Back to sleep, the pair of you.'

We stood for a moment, swaying and saying nothing, then turned and padded back in the dark to bed.

5

My stepfather forbade me from fainting outside our four walls, and put a flaming end to those luxury weekends – swanning off as if I was somebody in that silver Cadillac.

'Spoiled fucking brat!' He used his words as well as his hands to bring me down a peg or two.

Instead, Auntie Penny came to us, and our mother let her in whatever the state of her face. Although we tried not to get up our hopes, she was often there, complete with just-baked surprises, when Laurie and I loped home from school.

I became convinced I had psychic powers, predicting night after night which Cadillac would be waiting in the drive when Laurie and I came around the corner from school. I took the corner hard, concentrating over the pounding in my chest to conjure the right number plate. When it was silver we saw, our hearts rose up and ran; they weighed down with slow blood whenever it was the battered red.

Our stepfather would be in his armchair, glaring at the walls, cracking his knuckles into the quiet.

We weren't to waste precious electricity on mindless friggin' TV, and there was frost stabbing across the yard. So Laurie and I took to smuggling eggs out of the fridge as soon as we got home from school. When no one was looking, we took one and went to squat with the tools in the shed. Our twin winter anoraks kept us warm: zipped into sponge-filled blue nylon, with snorkel hoods, pockets lined with a white fur that was perfect for incubating eggs. We held hands in the windowless black, chanting the Lord's Prayer and humming old hymns from England, to make the egg hatch. Then we had to smuggle our warm secret back into the fridge, before our mother got out of bed to cook tea. It was pot luck whether our egg would be picked out and cracked on the edge of the frying pan. We held our breath every time, until the shell broke out yolk into the sizzle, and not mangled bloody chick.

My sisters and I stuck mostly to ourselves, since our mother and stepfather didn't like us to invite anyone into our house. We had lots of friends at school, and they all had a habit of visiting each other's houses, even staying over for pizza and pyjama parties that they would chatter about in the playground. Laurie and I sometimes felt a bit left out. But when it came to Halloween, our mother let us go out trick-or-treating just like everyone else. We waited by the front door, nearly suffocating in our plastic pull-on costumes. Laurie was a witch, under a cardboard pointed hat and a hooked rubber nose with warts; I was a skeleton, whose skull and bones were guaranteed to glow in the dark; Sarah was a pumpkin that we left behind the door when our friends finally gathered in the street and we took off in a gang of devils and witches, vampires and werewolves.

It was knocking on all those doors that made Halloween thrilling. Some people muttered and shoved Tootsie rolls into our hands, just to fob us off the porch. But other doors meant glimpses into warm strangers' lives, peering at the ornaments in their lighted hallways, while they fussed to make sure we got one of everything from the bowls of boxed candy they had lined up ready.

'What cute little monsters!' Older ladies had a fondness for our faces and our sweet English accents, they declared, when Laurie and I lifted our masks to say thank you.

'Here, take these, honeybunch.' We let them pat our heads and press extra candy into our hands while we drank in the paintings off their walls.

After promising for weeks, the sky let go of its snow. We broke up from school and waved goodbye to our friends, knowing we wouldn't see them until the holidays were over and it was a whole new year.

Christmas came. The tree wobbled under tinsel and glittery globes, Bing Crosby and Val Doonican spinning in the background. The fireplace was crowded with cards sending Season's Greetings Across the Miles. I tore into silvery wrapping paper, smiling and smiling so that my mother would never guess I had no tingles of excitement.

Only when we went out into the night and passed other people's windows decked in red and green lights did I feel Christmas go through me. And later, when our stepfather took us sliding in the snow, my heart jumped out of my anorak on top of a white hill.

He fixed me between his knees on a battered tin tray and whooshed me into the night.

'Bombs away!' I smelt whisky laughing into my neck, car oil worked into the jeans clamped about my face.

'Bombs away!' I shouted with him.

We flew for a moment, on the tin tray. Then we hit a rock and skidded off. My head landed on something sharp under the snow, digging in while the weight of my stepfather crushed my arm.

'Dad.' I sat up, dazed, and saw blood dripping black in the snow in the night.

'Bloody hell!' My stepfather eased himself up and stopped laughing.

'Bloody hell.' He made a fistful of snow and pressed it over the cut. 'How's that?'

Blood kept coming. My stepfather was terrified I might cry.

'It doesn't hurt.' My head was numb with packed ice, and with the thrill of blood spilled by accident, laughing, in the snow.

My stepfather put a kiss over the cut – hot whisky, with nothing nasty in it. My insides warmed and turned over. But afterwards, when we piled into the car and he wailed with his whisky, 'Show me the way to go home,' my throat packed up in the back, having to sing along.

We went back to school and a new decade was declared along with the new year.

Mr Farrell scraped *1980* on the board. I looked at the white chalk numbers looping against the black and my head began to throb where it had hit the rock.

What's happening?

I had been forgetting to breathe on the way to school. Sometimes I had to stop on the sidewalk to remember which way was forward, which back. It was dread in both directions: stifling up the house, waiting for me at school.

'Okay, people.' Mr Farrell was ready to roll. 'Start of the week – news quiz.'

He pinned down the blinds and we sat at our desks in the dark, all eyes on the huge school-sized TV wheeled in to enlighten us.

Earthquake-missiles-coldwar-crisis-bombs-secession-Quebec-floods-famine-exchange-rates slapped across the screen: flashing pictures with words too fast to fit.

The blinds shot up. Lights blinked back on.

'Okay, people . . .'

I swallowed frantically. I thought I might be sick if anyone asked me how the world worked.

While Monday mornings made me queasy, Friday afternoons came close to heaven.

Ice-skating. It meant blisters on my heels, but it was worth it for cold speed: gliding like a bullet. I flew in circles, breathing hard, chuckling in my chest, until the speed got too much and I had to crash into the barrier and start again. I imagined the cold smack of a fall, when the wobbling came on, and the *schwink* of someone's boot-blade slicing off my fingers as they looped on by while I lay on the ice.

It was giddy hot and cold, shooting.

Then it was weekend.

'What've you got there, love?' My mother showed a glimmer of interest when I came through the door lugging a huge atlas under my arm.

'Mr Farrell lent it to me.' I opened it on the kitchen table, flicking straight to Europe.

'Look.' I put my finger on England.

'Mmm.' My mother saw green blobs in blue space, through the veil of her cigarette. 'Lovely.'

I carried the book to our room and laid it on my bed, tracing the shapes and crayoning them in purples and yellows to make a map of my own that I folded under my vest. Then I hid the atlas under the mattress, where no one could find it to ruin it before I carried it back on Monday.

Also under my mattress was a book I should not have had, because it came from the twelve-year-olds' shelf in the school library. I zipped through the books for ten-year-olds, scribbling reviews of them on yellow slips, almost always winning a gold star. I would lick each star and add it to my reading chart in the corridor, hoping the librarian might notice the cluster of gold and decide it was time for me to start on the books for older kids. But she just sailed on by the charts and never said a thing. I was too afraid to ask, because she wore specs with fiery red frames and lenses tinted dark, so I couldn't see her eyes.

I knew I was two years too young for the book I wanted, but I slipped it, sweating, under my coat: *Are You There, God? It's Me, Margaret*, by a lady writer called Judy Blume. About the terrors and triumphs of being a teenager, it said on the back. At home, I locked myself in the toilet and read great chunks at a time, learning about breasts and blood between the legs and how to pray to bring them on. If I could develop some breasts, I calculated, they might reduce my risk of being picked out as a freak at school, where the grade system had thrown me two years ahead of my age. In with the big kids: while I sat puny, gathering my gold stars and winning the spelling bee each week, the older ones loomed over me, with fully formed boobs, underarm hair, and weeping cheeks of acne.

'Milk-fed,' my mother called Canadian kids. 'I swear they put something in the milk that makes them grow so bloody fast.'

Anyway, she believed, my period was on its way and boobs would come with that. Spotting blood on the toilet tissue one bedtime, when the bowl failed to flush, my mother had perched me on the side of the bath and locked my hands in hers to pass on ladies' stuff behind the closed door. Once a month, she told me, in time with the moon, women get menses: the eggs that might have been babies leave their wombs and come out with a bit of blood, just a teaspoon, though it might seem like much more. Once a month and just a teaspoon and when it happens, she told me, you put this in your knickers and come straight to me.

'Thank you, Mum.' I prized the huge white pad, stuffed with something light like tissue, smelling heavenly, of women.

'I'll come,' I told her, 'when it happens.' I kept the sanitary towel in the drawer with my knickers, knowing my period was not about to happen. I hadn't the heart to tell my mother that the blood on the tissue was coming out of my nose, night after night, from nowhere.

It was not my lack of breasts, but the boy next door who finally branded me as a freak in the schoolyard. One stormy afternoon, the boys in my grade launched into their taunts at him:

'Michael de Monkey! Michael de Monkey!' His real name was Michael de Mano, but his lips stuck out rubbery and thick so that bigger boys could use them against him.

While the other kids taunted him, he turned on me – standing to one side, watching and saying nothing.

'What about you?' the boy next door shouted. 'Your dad's a drunk and an outta work bum, ain't he? We hear him shoutin' at night, way over in our house. Your mom screamin' too, so we don't get no sleep.'

A slap out of the sky. I stood behind the smile caught on my lips, waiting for my feet to unstick, to run me home through the thundering rain.

That evening the mother of Michael de Mano knocked on our door, carrying a huge cardboard box in her arms.

'For you and the little ones,' she said to our mother. 'Mr de Mano, he gets them free from his work boss.'

Inside the box were thirty-six packets of macaroni cheese.

'Kraft!' My eyes widened at the famous blue and yellow boxes after the cheap no-name labels our mother had to stick to at the superstore.

'No, no, I couldn't,' our mother protested, while we crowded around her skirt, willing her to say yes.

Mrs de Mano pressed the box on her: 'For the little ones.'

She had a straggly, black moustache, but she smelled miraculous, of meat simmering in peppers and tomatoes. I stood at the window after she left and watched her bottom swaying wide, from side to side, before disappearing back into the de Mano house for dinner.

Our stepfather refused to touch the macaroni.

'Bloody nosing-in charity!' he fumed when he spotted the boxes' blue and yellow. 'Tell them to bloody well shove it.'

Our mother hid the boxes on the cupboard's top shelf, where we had to scrape up a chair to reach them.

'Not under his nose,' she said, and we knew what she meant.

One evening, before our mother had finished her nap, Laurie and I had decided to take care of ourselves and our Sarah by creating a marvellous macaroni cheese tea. Laurie snipped the corners off the cheesy powder packets; I balanced a pan of water on to boil; the front door rattled and in he strolled.

'What's all this bloody nonsense?' Our stepfather found us alone at the stove, with Sarah perched on the counter to watch.

'Lorraine!' he bellowed. Our mother came flapping down the hall, fumbling where her housecoat flashed open on shy, dull-pale skin.

'What's up, love?' Her eyes were red and watery with sleep.

'What's all this shit?' he wanted to know. 'Where in Christ's me dinner?'

'I'll make it now,' our mother trembled, rolling up her sleeves. 'You're back early, love.'

'I bloody well am, aren't I?' Our stepfather smashed the heel of his hand into the table. 'Got the kids cooking behind me back now, have we?'

Just out of bed, our mother's creased face screwed into a pale question mark. It jumped, frightened, from the great pan of water gurgling on the stove, then back to Laurie and me.

'We were meaning it as a surprise, Dad,' I said. 'Mum didn't know.'

'Shut it,' he said. 'And don't you be defending this slag – she's a bad mother, she is, lazing on her arse when she should be up and cooking.'

Our mother stiffened her shoulders. 'That's bloody evil,' she gritted. 'What've you done for them lately, you greedy sod, except guzzle the food money so's I can't feed them like I should?'

He lunged to slap her.

'Cheeky bitch!' He missed her face, but tore the silver butterfly earring out of our mother's lobe.

She winced and put her hand over the rip.

'Get to your bedroom, girls.' She spoke without looking at us, eyes fixed on our stepfather.

They stood facing one another, anger simmering in each of their faces, like a mirror.

Our mother was flaming livid. Our stepfather was flaming livid.

'Get to your bedroom,' she said again, in a strange, mannish voice.

Thinking of punches and slaps and the beef-knife flashing in our mother's face, my stomach churned to leave them alone. My voice cracked when I dared, 'But we've not eaten yet.'

'Get into your room and lock the door!' Our mother screamed when our stepfather grabbed the pan of boiling macaroni off the stove, swinging around to face her. I stood frozen, gripping Laurie and Sarah by the hands, until my mother shoved me.

'Get to your room. Call Auntie Penny, then lock the door,' she said.

We stood our ground. The pan was bubbling and spitting in his fist. Our mother looked naked in the face of it.

'No, Mum,' I found myself crying. 'Please, Dad, you're frightening us.'

Laurie and Sarah took on my tears: we had all three of us seen our mother's face smacked scarlet, punched blue-purple, but the water was something else.

Simmering. Scalding.

Our stepfather looked at us, then turned away.

'Oh, Jesus!' He flung the boiling water and macaroni behind him into the window, letting the pan clang into the sink. Pasta slithered slowly down the pane and over the sill.

'Christ, what am I doing?' Our stepfather grabbed his hair in his fists and scrunched his face tight red. His eyes were wet slits. He opened them and looked at us all, crying.

'I'm sorry. Jesus, I'm sorry.'

In the light of next morning, our kitchen window looked sorry for itself. Macaroni tubes had congealed on the panes in the night, the flowery sashed curtains were stained cheesy yellow. Our stepfather sat with his head in his hands over the toast and eggs our mother had fried in lard as usual, to soak up his hangover.

'What you goggling at?' He looked up, bloodshot, to catch Laurie, Sarah and me staring across the table while he lobbed salsa into his yolks. He tutted when our mother let a glass slip through her shaky fingers while she was washing it, so that it splintered against the tap. 'Pathetic bloody cow: pull yourself together!'

It was almost worse when our mother pulled herself together and acted like everything was fine and dandy while scabs streaked her cheekbones, bleeding when she caught them with her hairbrush. We missed having her cry in our hair – holding our heads, kissing and moaning into our crowns.

'Go on and play.' She brushed us off when we tried stroking her hands or kissing her on the temples. 'Take your Sarah and go on.'

We left her lost in her cigarette and went to our bedroom, baffled.

Fluttering, tissue-thin letters were as close as we could get to Gran and Auntie Pauline and anyone else on the other side, since the price of a transatlantic call was astro-bloody-nomical. Our mother lingered over the telephone, then resolved to sit down and write – boiling the kettle, stubbing her cigarette, shoving the dirty ashtray out of the way. We had to leave her be while she gnawed the end of her biro, writing and ruminating for hours. At the end we were allowed to sign our names and crayon fast flowers, before licking the bitter edge of the envelope to seal it with all our love. Then our mother hid the letter like a magician, until she could get out to post it.

'There'll be fireworks if he gets his hands on it.' She crinkled her forehead, in search of the safest hiding-place.

There were fireworks when our stepfather discovered a bit of blue tissue lurking in among his dirty underpants and socks. The envelope was addressed to our Gran – Mildred Chadfield, in Manchester, England – but he tore straight in to see just what our mother had to say about him. Our mother was too careful to write anything bloody, but the letter gave out how homesick she felt – enough to sell up and go home.

'What do you think you'll sell, smart-arse?' our stepfather demanded. 'We've got nothing, so you keep telling me.'

I looked at my mother, wondering where on earth the money might come from to get us back over the Atlantic, home.

'It's just pie in the sky, Pete,' she sighed. 'Wishful thinking's all it was. We're not going anywhere.'

'Dead right you're not.' Our stepfather grabbed our mother's face between his fingers and thumb, twisting the skin the wrong way and ruining the Cupid's bow of her lips. His grip was so tight she could only speak with her eyes through his fingers.

'You're not going anywhere without me.' He slid the words, with bits of spittle, straight into her ear. 'Don't get any fancy ideas, Lorraine. You're not leaving me, bitch!'

Our mother snuffed out the light in her eyes and, when our stepfather let her face go, she said in a dead flat voice, 'Don't worry, Peter, I've got no fancy ideas.'

But the snuffed look in her eyes let on differently. Behind them were some very fancy ideas that no shouting or beating were about to wrench out of her.

Our stepfather drew back his hand and brought it slamming into her cheek. The skin gave a quick shout then turned a deep, slow red, but our mother's face stood still.

He booted a hole straight into the wall and stormed out.

I ran a facecloth under the cold tap; my mother let me press it against her cheek.

I touched her hair. 'Don't you want to cry, Mum?'

A tear welled and ran from her left eye, but it came from the slap, not from inside.

'No.' She stopped my patting hand and held it still in hers. 'There's nothing to cry for now, Andy. Nothing at all.'

My mother gripped my hand hard and I went to bed. Jammy Dodgers and iced Bakewell tarts sifted into my dreams. Custard creams, teapots and drizzly days.

Every night I got jammed in the same dream, finding a path that led to a bridge that looped high over the water to Manchester. If morning hadn't come, I could have walked all the way back to Gran's flat, direct to the eighth floor. Fluffy scones crouched in her oven: hot raisins hiding, juicy black, in their moist hearts.

My ears would burn when I woke up and realized I was still in my bedroom in Canada. They heated up just as painfully whenever I thought of telling my mother where I was going in my sleep. She and I would spend ages, just the two of us, whispering about wishes and dreams, even sharing our fears about my stepfather. But we always steered away from the subject of England, which set off a little tic between her nose and her left dimple.

Finally, one morning, when we were alone folding the laundry, I couldn't help asking her,

'Is that the only way to get back to England, Mum – in a plane?' I tried to stamp my voice flat, as if I was just wondering.

'It's the only way I know of,' my mother said, without smiling. 'The only way, I'm afraid, so don't go getting your hopes up.'

Breasts dropped out of my prayers, to make room for bigger stuff.

'If you're there, God,' I took to repeating under my breath, 'please get us home to England. Soon. Without You-know-who.'

*

By the beginning of spring, Laurie and I had to accept that our stepfather was not about to drop dead from a brain tumour. Despite a sinking feeling, it dissolved the guilt we had been carrying, in case his outbursts were caused by an illness. We had hesitated over our hate.

Now, when our stepfather went for our mother and we had to pant down the hall to call Auntie Penny and lock ourselves in, there were no doubts and no excuses.

Laurie and I hid behind our bedroom door, rocking Sarah between us, singing into her ears – cramming them with lullabies to block out the thumps and screams. We swore at the grin on our clock, willing the Mickey Mouse hands to move it, to flicking well *move it* – to make Auntie Penny's car zoom, to get her into our house before it was too late.

'Is there no way back without flying?' I worked up the courage to ask my mother again.

We were alone, polishing the fireplace with baby oil. She put down her rag.

'Not a word.' She lifted a ball of newspaper out of the hearth that cost too much to light. Wrapped in the faded news lay dangly diamond earrings, a ruby ring, and an old, old watch wrought in dull gold.

'They're your Gran's,' she told me. 'She's said to sell them to get us all back.'

A blue tissue letter was folded up in the chimney; my mother pulled it out to show me. From miles away, in gorgeous loopy writing, Gran was begging Mum to sell up and fly.

'Can you, Mum?' I tried not to get my hopes up in front of her.

'They were supposed to be heirlooms.' My mother sighed and looked at the jewellery in the murky print. 'They're all we've got.'

'We can get more heirlooms, though, can't we?' I pressed my palm against hers. 'In England?'

To keep her eye on the cost, our mother set the clockwork oven-timer ticking when she picked up the phone.

'Hello? Mum?' She spoke loudly and quickly over the ticking to squeeze in all the details before the bell went off. The timer was set to ring in twelve minutes, and everything seemed sorted, when our stepfather sauntered in from his afternoon revels.

'What the . . .?'

Our mother went white on the phone. Our stepfather saw it all.

'You scheming bitch!' He lunged at our mother and tore the phone cord out of the wall. The line to Gran hung dead in his hand, dripping bits of plaster.

'Peter!' Our mother shielded her skull when our stepfather raised his fist.

'No, Dad!' I ran to my mother and wrapped myself around her. Laurie and Sarah hurried to do the same. The four of us stood clinging to one another in front of our stepfather.

'Christ!' he screamed. 'What are you trying to do to me? Out of the way, girls,' he told us, but we all three held on to our mother. I felt her ribs sticking out brittle where I had seen them kicked by a boot on the bathroom floor, late at night under fluorescent white light.

'Move!' He grabbed the teapot, steaming full, off the table. It was fat and round, with a sharp ceramic spout curving out to pour. He held it up to throw.

'Daddy!' Sarah began to cry and our stepfather's arm stiffened.

'You bitch,' he said to our mother, very quietly. His pupils glowered and grew. 'You fucking bitch.'

He looked our mother deep in the eye, then brought the teapot and its spout crashing into his own temple. Blood and tea trickled down his face, oozing out of the hairline, past his ear, into his collar. Staring at our mother, he pulled back the teapot and smashed again, this time cracking off the spout, howling.

My mother peeled my fingers from her arm and shoved me towards the back door, keeping her eyes on our stepfather.

'Fetch the police,' her voice was hoarse. 'Run.'

I pelted into the street in my socks, heading for the house on the end where the family with a pool table and a stuffed moose head lived. Their car was gone from the drive. I panted back the other way to the old couple who gave us white chocolate on weekends. The curtains were pulled tight. There was nothing for it but to knock on a stranger's door.

I came back with a policeman and the man with the gammy leg, who had agreed to make the call.

My stepfather was sitting on the kitchen floor, in all the exhausted chaos, holding his face in his hands, moaning. When the strange men came in from outside, he looked up and wiped his nose. Blood was beginning to crust in his hair.

'That's my dad,' I explained.

My mother moved out of the corner where she had been sheltering Laurie and Sarah, braced behind the table for his next move.

'I'm sorry, Officer,' she said. 'I'm afraid we've wasted your time. We're working things out for ourselves.'

'Well, folks, if you're sure . . .' I watched the two men turn and shuffle to get out of our house, clearing their throats and forgetting things fast.

'Go call your Auntie Penny.' My mother gave me a dime. I ran back into the street, this time in my sandals.

Auntie Penny and Uncle Charlie turned up with age sagging in the ripples of skin under their eyes. In front of them, our mother and stepfather looked like children, lost and dirty, with rips in their clothes and their hair sticking out.

Auntie Penny shook her head at the bloody mess spewed across the kitchen and down my stepfather's face. Her gold earrings rocked.

'This has got to stop.'

No words, only sniffling, came from our parents.

'You can stay with us,' she told my mother. 'I'll help you and the girls till you get back to England, if that's really what you want.'

'It is.' My hand grasped Auntie Penny's leathery one, loaded with sparkling rings.

'It is,' my mother said, looking at my stepfather and his bleeding head. She moved to bathe it, but Auntie Penny caught her arm.

'Help the girls pack, Lorraine.' She held my mother gently by the wrist. 'You've got to make up your mind what you're taking with you, and what you're leaving behind.'

6

My mother said goodbye to our stepfather and her sky-blue Pinto. The heirlooms got us on to a Boeing 747 that seemed to hum in the sky for days, before it shuddered down in Manchester in the dead of night.

Auntie Vera was ready and willing to put us up while we had nowhere else to go.

'You's can all snuggle in my bed,' she declared at the airport. 'Like sardines!'

A black cab sped us north to Bury, through sleeping streets, up the dark hill to her house. It was tucked in a stony row of brooding chimneys, next to the giant industrial ones that rose up like kings and queens on a chessboard, though most of them were destined to be demolished and would never puff again.

Auntie Vera struck a Swan Vestas match and set her battered kettle wobbling over the blue hiss of the gas. It screamed its old tin whistle, as if we'd never flown away and then had to fly back fast, a world of cuts and bruises and mountains in between. The same stink of rotting rubber insides whiffed up when she filled the hot-water bottle, its mouth gasping and sputtering like an old man.

'Nighty-night now.' She smothered us in talculm-powder kisses and gave us the bottle with God-blesses, to battle the cold at the bottom of the king-sized bed. Between the marble sheets, I tried to kill shuddery thoughts of Grandad – lying with Auntie Vera, dying when his heart crashed – right there where we laid our heads on the pillow under the purple satin headboard.

My mother, Laurie, Sarah and I huddled under the old blankets. Our feet mingled while our chests rose and fell, rose and slowly fell, in time. Blankets and blackness. After shattering nights on the other side of the sea, I slid into sleep, though I sometimes slipped off the edge and hit the icy linoleum, its ancient pattern muzzy with green ghosts.

Sun slithered through the curtains. In my faded rainbow nightie, I tiptoed downstairs to help Auntie Vera get up the fire and to sit with her over her cup of tea.

'First brew of the day.' She took a smacking sip. 'Sets you up royal.'

Then she stuck her head full of blue curlers into the fireplace, kneeling on the cold hearth tiles to scrape out yesterday's cinders. I shivered and scrunched pages of the *Daily Star* into airy balls that wrinkled to black nothing the minute the flames tongued up.

My mother came down to a glorious fire, crackling to roast the front room and its jungle of brass animals. Everything but the settee was swamped under porcelain, china, crystal and brass – smiling figurines, dogs, plaques and pearly vases. Although our mother declared they were ugly, Laurie and I agreed that there was something nice about the crowd of ornaments. They made you feel safe. Auntie Vera took her orange feather duster to them at dawn, rearranging them day in, day out, to face the milk man and gabbing ladies and the Reverend Father when she strong-armed him in for a bit of Battenberg cake. Also polished to high heaven, dark wooden crosses stood out on the walls: crucifixes off the market, drooping gold plastic Jesuses. Next to the telephone, a black leather-bound bible lay open with Christ's words in red ink, so you could spot His Truth at a glance. It put God in the room with all the knick-knacks.

On Sundays, Auntie Vera fastened Laurie and me into the poppy-patterned frocks we had nearly outgrown, and marched us uphill to let the neighbours know we were holy, no matter how often our mother had been married or where our devil of a stepfather had got to. She forced our arms into our dresses and zipped them tight up the back, while we pulled faces at the prospect of church ladies congregating in posh coats on the crest of the hill.

'Lovely lasses!' The flowery headscarves clucked when Auntie Vera turned up with Laurie and me, looking right pretty in spite of our swarthy skin.

'What divine little faces.' They smiled through tight lips, shaking their heads to one side. 'You need the Lord, you do!' Then they muttered between themselves: 'Poor little blighters.'

Inside, Laurie clutched my hand. We swayed between the pews while the preaching droned on. Only the Lord's Prayer sent a shiver down my spine, when we bowed our heads to whisper it over our sandals: *Our Father, Which art in heaven, . . . Those who trespass against us, Lead us not into temptation, but deliver us from Evil . . . For ever and ever, Amen.*

Later, after a Sunday tea of boiled eggs and Vimto, I asked: 'What does God do for you, Auntie Vera?'

She was bending to pull a rhubarb crumble from the oven, flashing the tops of her knee stockings.

'The Lord looks after His own, Andy, love.' She stood up and wiped her brow over the steaming crumble.

'I know,' I said. 'But what does He *do*?'

'He answers your every prayer.' She closed her eyes to send a smile into the ceiling.

'All of them?' I asked.

Auntie Vera fiddled to straighten the knot in her apron strings.

'Eventually,' she said.

Every morning, our mother set off to find a job and a house for us in the heart of Manchester.

'It's a bugger of a bus ride into town,' she insisted, when Laurie and Sarah clung to her coat. 'I can't take you with me, loves.'

We had to stay behind with Auntie Vera and the brass animals, fidgeting the day away. Sometimes she would take us up the hill to the market, where we strolled past stall-owners belting out sing-song prices, before we lugged home muddy vegetables and prize chunks of meat bleeding out of waxy paper. I begged for the honour of carrying the cabbage, heavy as a head in newspaper, between my hands. Back home, while Auntie Vera baked and Sarah napped, Laurie and I hunkered down in the back yard, tormenting red lacquer ladybirds with grass spears. We raced them like clockwork cars down the aisles of a broken cutlery tray, or trapped them in a drained Vimto bottle, then peered through the glass until they gave up fluttering and crashed on their backs. Clouds cleared. We dashed up the road to the cattle grid, where we balanced on muddy metal poles.

'You'll break you's bloody necks!' Old people shook brittle fists when they saw Laurie and me trembling to keep our balance, or when we let ourselves hurtle down the cobbled alleys on a single roller skate each.

'Someone's definitely gawn to break they's neck.' They shook their heads as they puffed their way up the steep back alley, heaving string bags of tinned mandarins, cat food and minestrone soup. They had to stop and stop again, to put down their shopping and give their hearts a rest, while we raced past.

It could be my neck. I closed my eyes for a moment, daring my bones to break.

When we belted home for tea, we found our mother in front of the oven, easing her swollen feet out of blue shoes stained white with rain. She had trudged miles in her heels and put on her best voice, but still no job to show for it, and no house fit to be called a home.

'What in God's name's got into you, Andy?' She sighed and bent to dab Dettol on my stinging knees, where the scabs would never get beyond the cornflake stage before I knocked them off into new bleeding. It was worse than a slap, the disgusted look my mother gave me when she was bone tired:

'You'll be the death of me, you will, with all your bloody gallivanting.'

It was decided I should go to my cousins' school for the last few weeks of term.

'But it's nearly summer,' I protested. I had skulked past the school and seen rough, red faces burning through the railings at my brown skin and scabby knees.

'I know, love,' my mother said. 'I know. But you've got to sit your Eleven-Plus exam – it's the law.'

I slipped into my anorak and zipped it so it bit under the chin, the snorkel hood drawn tight around my face.

'I won't be long,' I said. 'I'm just off for a bit of sherbert.'

When I was out of sight of the house, I broke into a run and went flying along the cobbled streets that Auntie Vera told us never to go down. Where the posh people lived, with their wonderful front windows: gleaming nets with precious ornaments in the middle of the sill, like a twisted crystal vase, glitter sparkling in the glass, or a miniature tree dotted with tiny oranges. In one window was a fox, caught and stuffed in the middle of a stroll, a walking stick in his paw and a round glass over one eye, spying out at you sideways.

Where there were no lights on, I lifted the flap of the letterbox to breathe in the scent of the strangers' house. You could smell the fancy wallpaper in their hall and all the braised lamb dinners they'd ever eaten, caught in the carpet. They had modern, gas fires down these streets, so there was none of that inky blue-black stink that took over Auntie Vera's kitchen when the coal man came. He would turn up during breakfast on Tuesdays, a full sack on his shoulder, green eyes darting out of a sooty face, looking for something – even after Auntie Vera had given him his money and the empty sack from last week. A bright green eye would wink right into mine, as if we shared a secret, in the middle of toast and marmalade.

I lifted my last letterbox flap, inhaled another life, and ran back to tell my mother how tangy the sherbert had been.

Monday came and I was left stranded inside the school gates. I squinted through the rain at Laurie and Sarah, holding hands with Auntie Vera, shrinking uphill to market.

'Welcome Andrea Hawkins,' the teacher told the class, and the faces chimed, 'Welcome.'

I sat down to do geometry but, after being top of the class without having to think twice in Canada, now I had to stare into the protractor, swallowing hard. My head throbbed where my mother had scraped my hair high into an elastic band. I saw sums swimming in a sea of blue squares.

At last the bell rang. Chairs screeched; the class crumbled. We pelted out to race in zig-zags across the playground.

'You're not from roundabouts, are you?' asked a freckle-faced boy. A circle gathered to ask questions about my queer Canadian accent and the darkness of my skin.

'Not a Paki are you?' They narrowed their no-colour eyes.

'Course not,' I said, and a bunch of girls stuck out sandpaper hands to grab mine.

'Good,' they said, "cos Pakis means germs.' They tore off across the tarmac, dragging me with them.

By the end of the week I was a star. I streaked through the playground: running, running, until a skipping rope came up and my face went down and smashed into the ground. Peeling up off the tarmac without tears, I wore the eggy lumps on my forehead as trophies of my speed. I played hand tennis with myself, palms stinging to whack the ball against the school wall, until I was fast and fancy enough to face the others. On Friday the sun came out to shine on the hand tennis tournament. I went home with a red rose of Lancashire safety-pinned to my jumper, having won the tournament and the hand of a lad called Roddy, who liked girls who were like boys.

In the living-room, Laurie was waiting for me to lie on my belly for *Blue Peter* and the cartoons. I missed our daytime television and the haunting half-whistle of *The Clangers*, hiding in moon craters, singing circles to each other through the big black – echoing, without words.

'Here, Laurie.' I let my sister have the paper rose off my chest.

Propping my chin in my hands, I tried to lose myself in *Loony Tunes*, while my legs throbbed against the carpet. The bones felt long, gawky and long, growing.

Eleven, just turned. A real live lad had rubbed the warts on his palm against my own palm, behind the electricity generator in the back fields.

I kept my eyes on the screen while my chest niggled and I felt something leaving me, draining out, like water dashing through my fingers to disappear, blinking, down the plughole.

The next week I came home sporting a glorious bruise under my right eye.

'What was it for?' my mother wanted to know when she got home.

'Just this lad bullying,' I told her.

She pulled me close to inspect the damage. Her eyes scrutinized the swelling without looking into mine. 'Little swine!' she cursed the culprit. 'We'll have his guts for garters.'

My mother creamed cool Germolene under my eye and let me go.

I sat in front of the television, caressing the marbles in my cardigan pocket. Two gold-swirled globes got from the corner shop, plus five smaller ones won, scooting, against the school yard wall. When I wouldn't give them back, the boys had turned nasty.

'Bloody foreigner,' one lad had started. 'Bloody Paki!'

Bloody Paki, bloody Paki, bloody Paki, and when my shoe shot out to shut him up, his dirty fist smacked into the side of my face.

Not one tear spilled and still seven marbles clacking in my pocket: glassy tiger eyes winking under the scratches, after skidding across the tarmac to be lost and won and lost and won and plunged into the best pocket at the end of the day.

While I scooted marbles and swapped football stickers with pasty-faced strangers, Laurie took to biting her toenails in front of the telly. She was able to twist her foot right up into her mouth to nibble at the nails.

'Doesn't it hurt?' I frowned, fascinated by her contortions.
She looked at me, chewed her toenails, and said nothing.

When Auntie Vera spotted her twisting her feet up into her face, she told my mother:

'She's got talent, your Laurie. A proper little Houdini. She should take up ballet or some such.'

'Aye,' my mother sighed. 'But the lessons cost the earth.'

Before long, Laurie started to sleepwalk.

Our mother zipped us into our tight Sunday frocks, folded a vinegary pound note into my palm, and sent us up to the church hall for the Thursday Dance Extravaganza Night. Inside, the lights went down and a silvery ball started twirling, slowly, on the end of a wire. Slushy music crackled out of the walls; everyone slipped off their sweaty anoraks. In a sea of bare shoulders, sequins and fantastically high heels, Laurie and I stuck out as if we were naked, in our nylon poppy dresses with their strangling collars and cuffs that cut into our wrists. Our sandals left us shorter than everyone else, all tottering about on strappy satin slippers.

'This isn't ballet.' Laurie tugged me off the dance floor. 'Let's not.'

We turned the pound note that was meant to buy us tangoes and cha-cha-chas into Caramacs and Quavers and a curvy bottle of Coca-Cola, shared through two stripy straws. Then we pressed against the wall with all the mothers and little brothers, guzzling in the dark, while the sequins spun around and around in glittering silver circles.

'They're lovely, they are.' Laurie was mesmerized by the dresses. 'But it's not ballet.'

We were lying on the rug in front of the fire one Friday night when the telephone rang next to the bible.

'It's Himself,' our mother whispered to Auntie Vera. She

strangled the wire to stretch it across the room into the kitchen. Murmurs seeped under the door to mix with the fire's crackling and the hollow telly laughter.

By the time our mother came into the room and slipped the phone back in its place, the laughter had died, and a sad-looking man in a tie was reading the news. Her face looked hot and flustered.

'Time for a bath, girls,' she said.

I looked up from where I lay on my belly next to the fire.

'What – tonight, Mum?'

Only on Sundays was the boiler clanked on to heat up the water for our bath. Then the whole house hopped in and out of the ancient tub – two at a time, oldest first – to make the most of the water before it turned cold.

'Yes, madam – tonight.' Our mother waited for us to haul ourselves off the carpet, drowsy with the warmth of the fire. 'Your father's paying you a visit in the morning.'

Laurie, Sarah and I folded into the tub, a crush of pink and brown elbows and knees. Our mother washed our backs and scrubbed our hair with the block of household soap that Auntie Vera used on Fridays to rub stains out of knicker gussets and ground-in grey collars.

'What's he coming for, Mum?' Laurie stuck her neck out to ask.

Our mother was ruthless with the green soap brick. 'Don't be silly now.'

Laurie peered over the bath rack at me. I squinted back through the lather. Our mother pulled the plug, and we clambered out, shivering wet, smelling as if we had been carved out of green carbolic soap.

Sarah was done up in pink, cherry bobbles in her white blonde pigtails, and matching cherry socks. She sat where she had been plonked in front of the telly to watch cartoons, giggling and looking shiny, like someone else's sister. There had been a time when kissing her was like eating. Laurie's cheek had been egg custard until Sarah turned up milkier and more yeasty. But now it was Laurie I was hungry for again, since Sarah's skin tasted like boiled cabbage, or processed peas out of a can.

'Keep your mucky paws off!' Our stepfather had always warned us when he caught us playing with our baby sister in Canada. He had drawn a line around her, spiky as barbed wire.

Our mother let Laurie and me wear the matching lemon cardigans that Gran had knitted to help her get through wet and windy nights in her lonely high-rise flat.

'My tummy hurts,' I said.

'Shh.' My mother rubbed the muscles over my stomach and smoothed back my hair. 'Don't go getting the collywobbles – your dad'll be here in a minute and it'll all be hunky-dory.'

She sent Laurie and me to stand on Auntie Vera's gleaming red doorstep, where we could wave at our stepfather the minute he came chugging up the street.

He looked taller than ever, stepping out of his van.

'Hiya, kids.' Our stepfather hugged us with tears in his eyes. His collar let off sly whiffs of Brüt that battled with the green carbolic armour scrubbed into our skin.

'Hiya, Dad,' we muttered to please our mother. 'Hiya.'

Above his ear, where we had seen the teapot's spout smash into his skull, a white half-moon scar curved gently along the temple. He had combed streaks of brilliantine through his curls to keep them under control. We gave him quick, prickly kisses then stepped back, shrinking to get lost in the clutter of Auntie Vera's crystal and brass.

'Give your dad a proper hug,' our mother insisted, when he pulled us on to his lap, then rustled a white paper bag into each of our fists.

'Sarsparilla!' My bag was crammed with red lozenges. Laurie's held tons of pear drops. A week's worth of sucking on our personal favourites.

'How did you know?' Laurie inched out of his lap, looking at the boiled sweets as if one would never get past her lips.

'Oh,' our stepfather smiled at our mother, pleased with himself, 'a little birdy.'

Laurie watched our mother smiling back at him over the sweets.

She freed herself from his knees. 'I'm going to have mine out the back.'

Our stepfather let Laurie go, since she was known to be odd. Because I was supposed to be normal, I stayed squashed up with Sarah in my stepfather's lap, sucking sarsaparilla after sarsaparilla, so as not to rub him up the wrong way. Eventually he got up for a heart-to-heart with my mother, behind the kitchen door. I slipped out into the back fields to find Laurie.

She looked like a lemon, stuck up the tree near the telemast, where we were forbidden from playing since old men were wont to wander around with their zips down, flourishing something awful in the long grass. Clouds rumbled and darkened. I took off into the grass, tearing through it to get to her.

Pear drops were pinging out of the tree, as if it were crying. I climbed right up to the top to join my little sister. We swayed in the highest branches, daring them to crack while we looked out over England: millions of chimneys huddling together under a bad-tempered sky.

Rain came, sudden and heavy, whooshing down to drench us. We tried scrambling, but neither Laurie nor I knew how to get out of the top branches. It was all snagging cardies and slimy wood sliding under our sandals. The grass was a long way down – worlds away. We had to sway in the sky, tasting petrol in the rain, until our stepfather spotted us and came storming out of the house. We watched him striding closer and closer, until he snarled up through the branches, swearing at us to jump.

'We can't,' I shivered. 'We're stuck.'

His forehead glowed in the rain. 'Get the fuck down this second!'

Laurie and I grabbed hands and jumped and crashed our knees into the ground.

In the warmth of Auntie Vera's kitchen our stepfather belted Laurie and me across our backsides before we were allowed to dry ourselves in front of the oven. A terrible prickle ran down my back and clawed into my bottom before the whack.

You can't do that any more, I wanted to tell him. *You're not our father, you know.*

But my legs were wet and livid with stinging. I bit my lip and swallowed salty blood down the back of my mouth until it was time for tea. Then we sat without speaking around the table, while our stepfather cracked God jokes right under the nose of the crucified Jesus, and tucked into toad-in-the-hole. We watched him losing himself in sausages and Yorkshire pudding.

'Nah, don't bother.' He wiped his mouth and waved his hand when Auntie Vera offered to stick the kettle on for one more brew. 'I've got to be getting back, like.'

My mother's face fell while ours rose inside.

'Bye, Dad.' We lined up for the last bristly brush against his face. 'Bye.'

*

In the wake of his visit, our mother couldn't keep from wittering on about Canada.

'Paradise, it was.'

Auntie Vera let her muse over mountains and the sea and the Seattle Space Needle, where our stepfather had paid extra to whirr our mother up to the restaurant at the top. Steamed mussels and proper, real champagne, they had, revolving over North America.

'It was another life, Vera,' she sighed, stuck in her reverie.

'What about all that funny business, though?' Auntie Vera shifted in her seat. You could almost see her mind fidgeting, full of the gory details Auntie Pauline and she often gossiped about on the phone during the day, while my mother was in town. 'It can't have been worth it, Lorraine.'

My mother pursed her lips over the other world in her cup. 'You don't know the whole story.'

She was convinced that a part of Auntie Vera, and of Auntie Pauline too, had danced a little jig of triumph when she came scurrying back with no money and her tail between her legs, leaving the dream stuck in the mountains.

'The thing I could never get over,' my mother stared into the dregs of her cup, 'was how such ugly vile things could be happening in such a beautiful place. All them mountains and the sea so close.'

I held my mother's hand, thinking of the one white peak that never moved, that was always waiting like some fat lady god on the horizon when you pulled back the curtains. No matter what had gone on the night before.

'Any road up,' my mother snapped out of it and gave my hand a lively rub, 'we lived to tell the tale, didn't we?'

I found myself falling in love with the edge of Auntie Vera's toast, where the crusts were always slightly burned and butter caught without melting, so you got a glob of it on your tongue.

'I love you,' I told Auntie Vera while my mother was out, traipsing after a job and a house. I knew it was a sort of betrayal, but I wanted never to leave her kitchen where the fresh laundry dangled, like floppy angels, over our heads on the rack. Thick towels baked close to the ceiling too, letting off lavender when the door opened and stirred the air. Then there were potatoes, bubbling night after night, to be drained out of their milky water and mashed. Everything: vanilla and Dettol and ashes you thought of eating, even the spike of inky coal that pricked your nostrils. Our hot-water bottle had its own drunken gurgle, different from the others, when Auntie Vera filled it up for bed.

'I love you,' I confessed over my crusts.

When she took me on the bus to face my Eleven-Plus exam, my mother let me sit on the top deck and held my hand all the way. I had to do the test by myself in Bury Town Hall, since all the eleven-year-olds in Lancashire had done theirs while we were in Canada. My mother and I hurried past the dozing guard and down long dusty corridors to a room thick with smoke and tired ladies' perfume.

'There you are, luvvie.' A secretary handed me the stub of a pencil that someone had got their teeth into before me. On the wall above me, the Queen was smiling without looking happy under her crown and lots of heavy-looking fur. I filled in all the spaces and gave the pencil back, not even stopping to nibble the chomped end.

'Good gracious, that was quick!' The lady smiled. 'Little Einstein, are we?'

*

My mother looked at me with tears in her eyes when the results came through the post.

'You're to go to Lancashire Grammar.' She smoothed the creases out of the letter, caressing it as if the results were her own: 'Passed with flying colours.'

I munched the celebratory pink marshmallow biscuits, then bolted down to the cattle grid to balance back and forth along the poles, dreaming, the sun on my neck. When my cousins came legging up to slap me on the forehead, teasing me about my brains, I went to crouch on the edge of the quarry. I stared down into the yellowy pit at the rotting sheep skull that had made me heave the first time we stumbled on it.

'Don't be mard.' Our cousin Joe poked my chest with the same stick he used to poke the skull. 'It's only piddlin' nature.'

We watched flies buzzing in the eye holes, holding our breath at the stink, wondering where the rest of the body had got to. The neck was hacked, shrivelled flesh and bits of windpipe drooping in the dirt.

'That's not nature,' our older cousin Patsy decided, after a closer poke. 'That's people, that is.'

Every night, after washing my hands, my mother let me slip the white letter out of its long brown envelope for one more gander in front of the fireplace. I went to bed full of the ancient brick grammar school and the blue-and-gold tie I would wear. There would be French, Latin and algebra every day, and at night, with my books backed in brown paper, I would dash home in patent leather shoes to balance along the poles without scuffing.

In the middle of shepherd's pie one night, our mother cleared her throat.

'I've found myself a job,' she said, and we all stopped chewing. 'At my old nursing home. Looking after the old crumblies again!' She sort of laughed.

'Trouble is,' she laid down her knife and fork, 'it's in Manchester, so you know we'll have to leave the countryside.'

Auntie Vera looked at her plate. Laurie looked at me.

I gulped my peas. 'Does it have anything to do with grammar school?'

'Well, Andy, love,' my mother took up her knife and fork to carry on eating as if nothing was up, 'it'll be too far to go to the grammar.'

'But they've got one in Manchester, haven't they?'

'Actually, love,' my mother shook her head, 'I'm afraid they've no grammars where we're going.'

My tumbler of water trembled in front of my face. 'No grammar whatsoever?'

'No grammar.' My mother chewed while she spoke. 'But they've loads of comprehensives to choose from, Andy. It's all new-fangled, like, in the city.'

I bowed back over my shepherd's pie, grinding bits of gristle that had got into my dreams, with gravy, under the mashed-potato roof.

7

We clambered on to the bus with all our belongings, then waved goodbye to Auntie Vera, who soon shrank to a funny-sad smudge. The green world withered, and a grimier one shot up. Blocks of curved towers loomed, with shirts and stockings dripping out of the windows. The Bull Ring, our mother called it, crammed with skinheads and pensioners and dark-eyed families flown in from far away. We gaped at smashed glass and graffiti shrieking Fuck Off Wogs, Paki Scum Go Home.

'Don't worry,' our mother muttered when we wondered what the flats looked like inside, 'we'll not end up anywhere like this.'

Lost black ladies, boys in turbans, bald men dangling fags, all gazed into the clouds or down on to the pavement. I imagined living with them, everyone baked in at the windows like currants in a concrete cake.

'Don't you worry.' Our mother turned her back on the high-rise estates and fixed her eyes on the road ahead. 'We're not that bloody desperate!'

Everything we owned was stuffed into our single surviving suitcase and a pile of plastic bags whose handles gouged our fingers, making raspberries of the fingertips. We got off the bus in the centre of Chorlton and dragged our things down strange streets. When the strap of the suitcase snapped off, we had to shove it over the pavestones, stiffening our backs so as not to seem common, while its hinges screeched and its flowery sides bulged like a fat lady with bellyache.

'Seventy-two, Denton Road.' Our mother muttered her way down the shabby street. We would be staying with Auntie Jackie, the lady who used to live next door to us on Thornton Road when we were little. We scoured doorways for what was to be our future.

Door-window-door-window-door-window-door, with the odd house boarded up. There were no spaces between them, unlike the ones at Auntie Vera's, which were built out of blond stone and clumped in twos. Here, the sky stood still, over streets blessed with nothing that could be called a garden: splurges of dusty hedge and the odd clump of dandelions. Our eyes dived into front room after front room.

'Enough nosing,' our mother panted, pausing in her wrestle with the suitcase to prise our gazes away from bedraggled curtains and twitching sooty nets. Chorlton would be posh, she had promised, while we were packing at Auntie Vera's.

'Where do they keep the trees?' Sarah asked, sparking giggles that slumped into silence. We followed our mother's frown down the road full of lamp-posts, where there were no leafy branches swaying against slate greys and brown brick. My eyes fell back to earth, snagging on dog turds and gutted fag packets. Flaps of newspaper strewed busty ladies along the broken pavement.

'Here we go.' Our mother halted. 'Seventy-flamin'-two!'

Black paint flaked off a door whose window panes had been smashed into glass webs. Someone had stuck them together with Sellotape, which had rotted to the colour of wee. We hauled our things through the whingeing wrought-iron gate.

'It'll only be making do, mind,' our mother whispered after ringing the bell. 'Just for the time being.'

*

The door groaned open on a plump woman, about the same age as our mother, with wiry, copper hair. A gang of marmalade-coloured cats arched against her shins, glaring at us with silver-black eyes. Her own eyes squinted through glasses as thick as milk bottles.

'Lolly!' she cried. 'And the little monkeys, no less!'

The woman folded us into her cardigan. 'You remember yer Auntie Jackie, don't you?'

Her skin was sticky as suet pudding and puffed up, as though someone pretty had been absorbed behind the glasses. I remembered her by smell.

'I know you,' I mumbled. 'You used to live next door to us on Thornton Road, with Uncle Dunc and all those cats and kittens.'

'Din't we just!' Another kiss smacked me around the nose. 'We used to 'ave you little 'uns round all the time before your mam upped sticks to Canada, din't we, Lolly?'

'Aye. Spoiled 'em rotten, you did.' Our mother tutted to show how generous Auntie Jackie and Uncle Duncan had been, all those years ago, while the nursing home had swallowed her nights and written off her days. I remembered Saturday afternoons when I was seven: Laurie and me round at Auntie Jackie's house for fancy biscuits, spoiled by the cat-hairs that crept under our tongues and clung to our cardigans. We used to cradle the nibbled hearts of Jammy Dodgers in our fists, while the cats bristled and clawed and curled up to sleep in our laps. Basking in the orange glow of her electric fire, we would gaze at the telly – at Doctor Who and the Daleks, then Bruce Forsyth and all the prizes sliding by in front of our eyes – while the afternoon purred into Saturday night. The cats always sprang off our knees, snarling, as soon as our stepfather clacked on the knocker.

Now, standing in this strange, dingy doorway, Auntie Jackie lowered her lips at the corners: 'They've all popped it now, me old moggies.' Then she let her mouth spring back into a grin: 'But we've an 'ouse chock-full of toms, so you'll not be lonely!'

The smell of chips, socks and fur bulged out of the hallway to usher us in.

On Friday night, our mother sighed home in her blue zip-up dress.

'Twen. Tee. Five.' She counted out notes from a brown packet, the best part of her wages, and laid them on the mantelpiece under a fiery painting that glowed full of wild swans and naked, wet-looking men and women. *Horizons*, Auntie Jackie called it, when we asked her whether it was a picture of heaven or hell.

In exchange for our mother's money, Auntie Jackie let us live in her attic. 'As long as you like, Lolly, love.' She offered the dank room under the roof as if it were a favour from the heart. But I watched her fist rustle notes off the mantel, after my mother had chewed her lip to lay them out under the picture of fire and flesh.

Grubbing around in her purse, our mother came up with pocket money to keep Laurie, Sarah and me out of her hair. On top of pennies for sweets, she sent us to buy a tennis ball and a rainbow box of chalk to go with the skipping ropes that Auntie Vera had given us, with handles that used to be bobbins, shuttling cotton in old mill-buildings. She lined us up after breakfast, to give out the rules about where was safe to play and where was bloody well not. Mostly we stayed in the square opposite the house, watching grown-ups step in and out of the red telephone box – some laughing, some whispering, some shouting – while we kept our distance so that no one would think we were noseys. I hopscotched myself stupid and skipped with Laurie and Sarah, until local kids crowded around. Then I bounced my ball against the wall in snazzy arcs, whistling, while my little sisters carried on with their hops, skips and jumps.

'Where you lot from, then?' Kids with sticky jumpers sized us up in our old-fashioned cardigans, swirly buttons fastened up to our necks. Our mother had scolded us into woollens that made our movements stiff, like robots: 'I'm not having you traipsing about looking poor.'

'We've just come from Rawtenstall.' I spoke for the three of us. 'And before that we lived in Vancouver – it's this place in a corner of Canada, across the Atlantic Ocean.'

We stood in the centre of the scruffy kids' circle, letting them mull over our cardies and Canada, giving them a go of our ropes with the bobbin handles. They squinted at our sharp 't's, the rasp of our aitches and the way that our 'g's rang at the end of words like having and singing and running, where theirs had fallen off.

'Think yer posh, don't yer?'

Running clear of the accusation, Laurie and I beat them at tag and spurted the odd loud 'Oi!' although we knew we would have to pay for it over the baked beans at tea-time. Our mother would let out an end-of-her-tether sigh at our shame-less flaming antics, our screaming like banshees and acting proper common for all the world to witness.

Tucked up with my book on the settee, I could be free of my little sisters for half an hour before tea every day. I would study my mother's face over the pages, swallowing guilt at the cash she had stumped up the day she took me, just me, to John Menzies, where I picked out a prize for passing my Eleven-Plus exam. She stood over me with her snakeskin purse, while I lurked along the bookshelves, gripping my hands behind my back. 'Go on, Andy, love!' Her smile never wavered, although the cost mounted up – and up and up and up – as I slid out *The Twins at Saint Clare's*, the complete set by Enid Blyton, then hurried, clutching them against my chest, to the cash till.

I read them to death, one by one, then one by one again, dreaming of a boarding school brimming with brainy girls. I saw myself plucked up and plopped into Saint Clare's, in the light of my affinity for spelling and sums, but squirmed at the ruse I would have to pull to get into such a school. Since I hadn't been blessed with rich parents, I would have to pretend that there were no parents at all. If you were an orphan, it seemed to me, pity would persuade people to spot your talents instead of your clothes and shoes, and no one would mind if you had no money.

'Can't we do anything about them?' I fought back tears in front of my mother when welts sprang up along my arms and burrowed, burning, into my neck. The fleas on Auntie Jackie's cats seemed to ignore everyone else, making a meal of me.

'What can we do?' My mother dabbed pink calamine lotion, chalky and cool, over the livid flea bites. 'They're your Auntie Jackie's pride and joy, those cats. And it won't be much longer now, Andy – don't be whingeing.'

As if to show just how soon we would find our own house, our mother slept on a spindly folding bed next to the mattress where Laurie and I huddled with our Sarah on the floor. It was magical, lying low, hearing her breathing above our heads. A slight squeak sang out when she turned over in the night, sighing. A car might glide by, shooting light through the crack in the curtains, up the wall in a wave. Otherwise silence pressed in, purple-black, coloured by crying. Our mother sobbed through her knuckles.

I wanted to cry too, to keep her company, but I had too

much grub grinning inside. Auntie Jackie packed us to bed full of pizzas and glistening vinegary chips: Auntie Vera thought fried food was wicked, but Auntie Jackie swore it was sacrilege to eat potatoes unless they'd been chopped into chunky fingers and plunged in bubbling gold lard.

During the day, while our mother was mopping up old folks, Auntie Jackie left us to our own devices and sprawled across her bed, posting After Eight mints into her mouth, sinking into paperbacks about blood-spattering crimes, eventually nodding off. Downstairs, Laurie and I built Lego dream homes and spaceships with Sarah, straining to keep her quiet when she started mithering and crying for our mother. I rocked my five-year-old sister in my lap, cooing and blowing into her eyes, tingling with pride and relief when her frown unfurled into sleep in the middle of the afternoon. Then I laid her on the settee, covered in one of Auntie Jackie's cat-hair cardies, and crept up to the attic with Laurie – for a fondle of the photographs that our mother had declared out of bounds.

We prised open the biscuit tin with *Family Selection* on the lid. At the bottom, in black-and-white, lay the only surviving photo of our real father: smiling out of his work anorak, more gorgeous than Elvis under a crest of glossy, brushed-back hair. Then there were the jagged colour polaroids of Canada that our mother had taken the scissors to one night, after a dose of rum and Coke and crying to Randy Crawford. *One day I'll fly away.* We watched our mother's face cream up, then curdle. *Leave your love to yesterday.* 'Bastard!' She sheared through the glare of every family snapshot. 'That's the bloody end of that buggerin' bloody shit.' Silver blades snipped. Our stepfather's face fell out of the picture.

*

'Nosey gits!' Auntie Jackie snorted, looking strangers smack in the eye when they stared at us as we wandered around Chorlton shopping precinct. But I caught our reflection when we stopped to gaze in the toy shop window. My sisters and me with our podgy Auntie Jackie – all curious sizes, and faces that didn't go together.

'We're not a proper family, are we?' I asked her on the way home through the rain.

'Yer what?' Her glasses steamed up against the drizzle. 'What's all this "proper family" nonsense?' We watched her fume. 'Your mam bloody well adores you three. Three gorgeous girls! That's a proper bloody family if you ask me.'

I thought of Auntie Jackie's creaking house, crawling with cats instead of babies, and kept my lips zipped.

After five twelve-hour shifts in a row, our mother would come home with a headache that squeezed all the prettiness out of her face. She glugged down aspirins and sat in front of the telly with Auntie Jackie, waiting for her jaws to stop grinding. Then she went upstairs with watery eyes to sleep.

Other evenings she came home and put on loud, jangly records like Earth, Wind and Fire, dancing around the living-room and laughing, prickling with energy that made me nervous. By bedtime she would have collapsed on the settee, moping over her umpteenth cigarette, murmuring about patching up our family, giving it a proper go.

'Bollocks!' Auntie Jackie was unimpressed by our mother's theory that Laurie, Sarah and I needed a father to watch over us. 'You need that bastard' – she had made our mother promise never to contact him again – 'like you need a hole in the head.'

*

Auntie Jackie rummaged through her eye shadows and showered her bosoms with scent out of a spray can labelled Seduce, before stepping out with Uncle Duncan one Saturday afternoon to lay bets and drink beer at the greyhound racetrack.

'I'll come back dripping in diamonds,' she winked at Laurie and me. 'I can feel it's my lucky day!'

We waved at them from the doorstep, watching them get on to the bus across the road. As soon as it turned the corner, our mother came inside and stood in front of the phone, looking at it and looking at it, finally picking it up. I knew, from the way her fingers hovered over the dial, whose name was going to come out after she had cleared her throat.

Our stepfather was waiting for us at the end of the road, where Laurie, Sarah and I clambered into the back of his van. We drove through streets we didn't recognize, before he pulled up outside spiky iron gates at the entrance to a park.

'Abracadabra!' He had brought smoky bacon crisps and Curly-Wurly bars to make a picnic on the grass.

He lugged something big and flat and oblong, wrapped in brown paper.

Before our mother could finish her crisps, he leaned forward to kiss her: 'Close your eyes, Lolly.'

Then he tore open the paper. My toes curled inside my sandals at the sight of a picture of a miserable clown, one big, blobby tear glistening on his cheek.

'Don't you like it?' Our stepfather's grin slid to the ground when our mother told him there was no way she could accept it.

'Jackie'll go bonkers,' she explained, 'if she finds out we've seen you.'

Our stepfather smiled a funny smile. Laurie, Sarah and I

watched chocolate melting between our fingers, unable to swallow our Curly-Wurlies. Suddenly he hurled down the picture and stomped on it so that the glass cracked. Then he grabbed our mother's arm and yanked her up off the grass, banging her against the nearest tree.

'Don't play with me, Lorraine!' He thumped her in the stomach and ribs. She held on to the tree trunk, gasping for breath.

I got up to run to my mother, but my stepfather moved towards Laurie and me and made us clear the smashed picture and our half-empty packets off the grass. His eyebrows gloomed over us as we piled back into the van: 'One word and you're dead, got it?'

When he dropped us at Auntie Jackie's, our mother lay down on the settee and closed her eyes. I wrapped a packet of frozen fish fingers inside a tea-towel which she let me glide over her ribs, while Laurie and Sarah held her hands. Then she sat up and made us put on smiles before Auntie Jackie and Uncle Duncan came home, tipsy, joking over the bad luck that had emptied their pockets at the racetrack. We watched our mother laughing along, hiding winces in the corners of her eyes.

Towards the end of summer, she took us to a jumble sale at the local church and hauled back a black bin-liner of wrinkled trousers, skirts, and jumpers woven with strangers' smells. Our mother set to with pins and needles, twinkling silver between her lips, tugging at waistbands and hems, scrubbing and ironing out other people to make the clothes our own.

By Monday morning, Laurie and Sarah had been buckled into tartan kilts with immaculate pleats, then toggled into duffle coats like a pair of Paddington Bears. They held hands and looked at me (trapped in pink nylon flares) with the same torn expression across each of their faces: sorry for themselves because they were being sent to primary school; more sorry for me because I was still stuck at home, waiting to be assigned to a place at a Secondary Comprehensive.

'Keep your pecker up!' Auntie Jackie tickled me under the chin when I moped back from the primary school across Oswald Road, having watched my sisters dissolve behind the railings.

I held my breath each day in the dusty front room that had no light and was completely empty except for a hulking wardrobe whose feet were wooden paws. It had a keyhole and a long iron key that allowed me to climb in and lock it from the inside, where I dreamt of a lion-and-witch world like the one in the book they read on *Jackanory*. I tucked my legs under my chin, pressing my thumbs into my eye sockets to set colours bursting behind the lids. Showers of red arrows, yellow peacock eyes snowing, roses blooming and blooming blue – my thumbs rubbed rapid circles to keep the colours coming.

Whenever Auntie Jackie was lost in one of her daytime naps, I would sneak out the back door and wander around the streets, sometimes slipping into shops where the owners were nice and didn't hang up 'NO CHILDREN' signs to frighten you off.

A lady with a tiara of lacquered, silver curls hovered behind her cash register in the art shop.

'Well, if it isn't our Michelangela!' She cracked complicated jokes, whenever I swallowed my shyness and stepped inside. Although I couldn't quite grasp them, it was fabulous to be compared with beautiful things around the globe: Nefertiti I was christened one day; Venus Something-or-other the next. 'Take as long as you like, ducky.' She liked the look of my clean face and cardigan: 'I know you're not one of them ruffians.'

Posh music oozed from the walls, making you feel like you were in a film. I loitered among the shelves, and caressed my cheekbones with the dreamy tips of paint brushes – made of something silky called sable, squirrel hair or goat hair, even wolf hair from China, the labels said. Goosebumps teased my skin. Humming down aisles lined with white and silver tubes, my head swelled with the names, like a list of superstars.

Jaune Brilliant, Raw Sienna, Aureolin, Vandyke Brown, Viridian, Mars Violet.

Purple Madder Alizarin.

It would be a long time before I would be able to buy anything like proper paint. Lining up at the cash register, I counted over my coins to check that I had enough to pay for pipe cleaners, glue, and two tubes of glitter.

I strode back down the street a cowboy. Pink flares swishing, fists plunged in pockets, I nursed the pipe cleaners and vials of glitter like guns loaded in their holsters. I marched to Oswald Road School, pacing circles outside the gate until the home bells drilled the air and my sisters burst out from behind the railings with clusters of other kids. Jealousy coiled in my chest.

The council had made a cock-up, my mother discovered, and had failed to assign me to a secondary school. She slammed down the phone: 'Clerical error!' It had all the dazzle of a car crash, none of the pain or broken bones. Yet, after ten days with no one of my own age to talk to, I was beginning to feel not quite real. No matter what you thought of school, it kept you in step with the rest of the world.

I stashed mopey feelings under my vest and whipped glitter out of my pocket to impress my sisters.

*

A mob of angels sprang to life on the mantelpiece: pipe cleaner halos perched over loo-roll tube bodies, wings of tissue doused in red and gold glitter.

'Divine,' our mother groaned, when they greeted her after work.

'Dragons.' Auntie Jackie squinted, when we held them in front of her specs. 'Dragons, I thought they were.'

Rain started spitting, then blasted the pavements in slick, dark sheets. I was kept off the streets by my dead-beat sandals, whose soles had worn through. Cutting floppy foot-shapes out of a plastic bag, I stuck them in the bottom of my shoes. But they crinkled and hissed and still let the damp sneak through, making my socks soggy and staining them blue. I pressed my face against the window pane, watching wind-bashed brollies shuffle past like birds with broken wings, spat out of the sky.

When they weren't weeping, the skies sulked. An inky gloom seeped across all the rooms. I snooped around the house, on the scent of something to read. Something to set my blood singing, instead of clotting around my heart, turning treacly in my toes. I flicked through our old Enid Blytons. *The Sea of Adventure, The Island of Adventure, The Mountain, The Valley, The Castle, The River*. Once upon a time, I would have killed to be locked in a room with nothing but Enid Blyton, and maybe a drink of milk. Now I wondered how Laurie could still be drawn in to such silly things. It was as if someone had come along and given the books a good shake until all the fizz had fallen out.

I pulled yesterday's *Sun* from down the arm of the settee, where Uncle Duncan always stuffed it after filleting the sports pages.

'Don't be reading that stuff!' My mother snatched it out of my hands and into the bin. 'It's all filth and lies, Andy, love.'

I was thirsty for filth and lies. Girl, 10, Sees Parents Killed. Fire Destroys Family of Five. Yorkshire Ripper Strikes Again. My eyes bumped against hammers and knives, sex attacks and stabbings. Fear fingered the back of my neck: there were more details in the pages than you got on the telly. You couldn't avoid finding out that a man was going around killing young ladies – nice ones, not just the kind Auntie Jackie called floozies – doing shuddering things to their dead bodies, cutting bits of their insides out. The Yorkshire Ripper wasn't buried in one of Auntie Jackie's books. It wasn't a story, and it wasn't history – it was right now, down our streets after dark.

How to build a bridge between Enid Blyton and Auntie Jackie's grisly paperbacks? Circling the entrance to Chorlton library, I had visions of being carted home in the back of a police van if I dared to step inside. Libraries were for grown-ups and posh people, not for kids who should be at school. I went back to Auntie Jackie's and threw myself into bashed *My Guy* annuals, dumped on us by her younger sister. My soul sank, discovering that the most recent issue was from Christmas 1978. I decided that faces were different from fashions, and didn't fall out of date. Skin type, shape and shade: memorizing all the laws, I was ready to make the most of my assets, the moment I laid hands on some make-up of my own.

In a pouch patterned with washed-out flamingos, my mother treasured a pair of tweezers and a blunt kohl pencil, squelchy mascara and a wine-coloured lipstick, whose gold lid I slid off whenever she was out. I swivelled it up and down, up and down, snuffling its waxy scent, without putting it to my mouth. My mother would know in a flash if the oily wine tip had touched any other lips.

At night, when the front room was in blackness, Laurie and I were able to stand at the window and spy on the street without being seen. Girls lurked with older lads around the phone box over the road, circling a cigarette that flared out of each face before being passed along.

'Right common,' our mother declared when she spotted them huddling in the rain. Bare white legs, the girls had, sticking out of minuscule skirts, stitches straining where they had sewn them tight against their thighs. Patent heels bit their ankles, making them walk with a wince.

'Ridiculous!' Our mother shook her head. 'They must be flaming freezing.'

If the girls felt the cold, their faces never let on. Chatting to lads, they folded their arms to bulk up busts under their jackets, seeping smiles and sticking one foot out to sway on the stiletto. I studied them through the smeared glass, noting the heels I would wear, the black eyeliner and lip gloss, the most luscious variety available, the minute I turned twelve.

8

A brown envelope whooshed through the letterbox and skidded on to the linoleum in the hall. Although Andrea Hawkins was of no fixed abode, the local authority was in the process of assigning her to a Secondary Comprehensive. The situation would soon be rectified; we would be notified without delay.

A second letter finally followed the first. Andrea Hawkins's place, the authorities were pleased to confirm, was now secured at Whitbrook High. Out of the same Manchester City Council envelope fluttered three green coupons.

'For your new school rig-out.' My mother scrutinized the small print. 'We'll have to go over to Moss Side Precinct and see if one of them Indian shops'll be daft enough to take the flamin' things.'

Wetting under the arms, I let the lady in the sari twist me into a pale blue shirt that we could all see was too small.

'It does not work.' She tugged at the sleeves as if to make them longer, before rubbing my wrists to tuck them under the cuffs. Her grimace deepened when my arms refused to shrink. 'It does not work with your arms.'

'You've always been lanky.' My mother jabbed an accusing look at me.

'I'm eleven.' I pointed at the tag inside the collar, flashing 9-to-10 years. 'I need something for eleven to twelve years.'

My mother frowned along the racks, searching for my size, eyes pinned on the price. My throat closed over tears that tasted like pennies when she came back clutching three shirts, all with propellor collars.

'Are they the only ones, Mum?' I sweated.

'Yes, madam, they're the only ones.' My mother gritted her teeth, refusing to acknowledge the crazy collars. 'The rest are nearly another quid each.'

I had to smile at the lady in the sari, to keep her sweet so that she wouldn't kick up a stink at the sight of green coupons instead of cash. Stepping in and out of grey nylon skirts in front of a warped mirror, I watched myself being zipped into an A-line monstrosity, nodding through misty eyes to say that it would do. I fumbled back into my clumsy pink flares, feeling friendlier towards them after the shock of grey nylon. My only hope lay in the council coupons. If they created a crisis at the till, we would have to put everything back and try again in the shop across the way, where the clothes were more expensive, but also more up-to-date. My mother unfolded the vouchers and explained how they would work. The Indian lady gave them a long look, gave our faces a long look, and decided to trust them.

'It will work.' She smiled at my mother's smile. 'It will work lovely super, never you worry.'

'Give us a twirl!' Auntie Jackie lined up with Laurie and Sarah to get her eyes on the whole shebang.

Sky-blue shirt, collars tamed under a royal-blue jumper, V-neck framing a maroon tie. A grey tent brushing my knees, which gleamed mahogany after a summer on the street, above blinding white socks scooting down skinny calves to my shoes, brand new from the Happy Feet sale rack. Although, at size 5, these looked enormous, they stuck out as my saving grace:

maroon leather court shoes, peppered with dapper holes, like proper, grown-up brogues. Goodbye to my soggy blue sandals.

My mother perched me on a chair over the *News of the World* and took the kitchen scissors to my fringe.

'You look a treat, Andy, love.' She stood back, hands on hips, to admire her handiwork.

'Mmm.' Auntie Jackie agreed over a mug of warm lager. 'Dun't she just?'

They swung me down off the chair and sent me upstairs to our mattress, my head crowned in noisy kisses. I shifted into a hot, uneasy sleep. The uniform hung on the back of the door like a headless ghost, murmuring *Monday morning, Monday morning*.

A tall black girl, her skull snaking magnificent plaits, was the one to keep an eye on. A pale lad had charged across the schoolyard to put me in the know. 'Right,' I thanked him, and shuffled along the railings. Hands flaking with eczema, his voice whinged out of a wiry neck. You could spot them a mile off, the ones that attracted the bullies. A skinny Indian girl stared out of deep swimming eyes, while white silk trousers billowed like pyjama bottoms beneath her uniform. Her grey skirt was stained with grease and creased – obviously second-hand. For someone like that, things could only get worse. You might sneak a hello through your eyes, but it was best to steer well clear. Especially if your collars flew out too far from fashion.

ChRomATogRAph, the science teacher chalked across the board in a mixture of capital and little letters that I copied, like everyone else, along the top line of my blank first page. Squeezing my pipette, I teased a trembling globe of ink on to the filter paper circle, unfurling a galaxy of shades that made my insides gasp. Fuzzy halos of purple, green and yellow bloomed out of the plink of black ink. My eyes widened, but quickly narrowed when they met mean looks on the loose across the lab. Behind the teacher's back, some of the brittle-boned kids sniffed fumes from brown bottles, giving their gazes a thicker glaze.

Bells clanged. Faces crowded along corridors. Black, brown, mustardy, sock-white and milky pink. Only the eyes stood out, during the first week, in two darting sorts: sly ones slit and on the lookout for a touch of softness to rough up; round ones, blinking wide, nowhere to hide. Break times were exhausting: trying to look tough but not terrifying, straining to check the smiles that would provoke slap attacks by lads and lanky girls who stalked down the corridors, scowling at the world. It was like being dropped into one of the wildlife programmes that used to hold my stepfather spellbound in his armchair: fierce cats lurking behind bushes, muscles poised to pounce on knock-kneed deer.

I had to turn my shakiness inside-out, letting it tremble under my skin. If I had started school on time, I could have panicked with everyone else; now there was nowhere for nerves to blend in. All the other first-year kids, who must have been as wobbly as me a fortnight ago, had been stapled into their fates. Coming from local primary schools, everyone could boast someone who belonged to them, whether they liked them or not. Coming from Canada, carrying traces of a watery accent, I had nothing but curiosity on my side.

'Go on, say summat!' Porridgey-faced kids sidled up at an angle, to avoid catching the disease that made you stick out like a sore thumb.

'Don't be soft!' I roughed up my 'o's, yanked my 'a's flat,

and stretched my 'i's as wide as they would go. Ripping the bottom out of my 'u's, I uttered everything from my guts. 'I'm from flippin' Rusholme, I am.'

Boys walloped my back, challenging me to arm-wrestles in the dining hall.

'Been eating your spinach!' They were as surprised as I was, when my arms put up a Popeye fight. Olive Oyl was my first nickname, on account of my wiry, olive-skinned arms and legs. Occasionally, I was picked out for teasing, with no nasty intentions, as a kind of mascot for the biggest black kids, whom the rest idolized or feared. Their glamour rubbed off on my skin, replacing the garish 'new girl' gleam. I foresaw a time when I would coast across the schoolyard, clear of catcalls and whistles, beautifully invisible.

I carried my exercise books in a man-sized camouflage bag, picked up for 99p from the Army Surplus store, and had covered them to protect against wear and tear, according to the school rules.

'You must be taking the mick,' Mr Butcher, the maths teacher, sneered. He held up my book by the tips of his fingers. 'This is a classroom, not a fan club.'

Since my mother refused to fork out for brown paper from the Post Office, I had backed my books with pictures ripped out of our old *My Guy* annuals. Long-haired men writhed in skin-tight trousers, streaks of red lightning around their eyes. In order to explain how they got there, I would have to confess that baked beans and cigarettes came before brown paper, in my mother's bloody book. The backs of my knees throbbed above the tight elastic of my socks.

'I thought it would be all right, Sir.' I decided to keep my mother and the question of money to myself.

He squinted over his beard. Truth or trouble? I saw him hovering, impatient to tip me into one of his boxes and slam down the lid.

'You'd better be rid of those louts by Monday morning.' He turned to chalk up the day's problems on the blackboard. 'That's just audacious, that is.'

Is this algebra? It was impossible to unlock my lips, to confirm that the precious stuff was finally before me. *Audacious*, the covers churned. *Audacious.* I was sure it was something to do with being common or rude.

'You don't go messing with the Butcher man!'

That break-time I was celebrated by good-looking but lazy black boys from the back row, their ties dangling outside their jumpers in low-slung knots like medallions, clamouring as if I'd stepped out of a boxing ring. I shivered, daring to meet their eyes for the first time. Oblivious to the charms of algebra, they were wise to Butcher's talent for wiping out insolence by hurling the blackboard cleaner at smart-arse skulls, suppressing the curses which coloured the air in other classes. I sat in the third row back, with kids like Winston and Vanessa and Nardia, who weren't too cool to mix with whites. Although white kids were on a lower rung of the ladder, they might scrape a smidgen of influence if they were hard or funny or good-looking. Or just plain lucky, like me.

'Sister underneath, ain't it?' I was knighted nearly-black, on account of my dark skin and big eyes, along with my ability to hiss 'Ras it!' without sounding too big for my boots. In front of our matey row, silent Pakistani girls huddled with bow-legged boys under the teacher's nose, where they could avoid being bullied until the bell. Finally, right at the front, Chinese boys scribbled with their heads down, noses glued to their pens, alongside white girls who smelled of soap powder and fiddled with plaits arranged by their mums. Whenever they stuck up their hands, I sensed arrows of scorn aimed at their heads from the depths of the sulky back rows.

As soon as I got home, I fished behind the settee for the battered dictionary that my mother had carted around with her for years, since Gran had given it to her one Christmas. 'All the words in the world,' my mother had laughed when she opened it: 'No wonder it's so bloomin' heavy!'

I hurried to 'A' for audacious. Octopuses glooped in the margins, tentacles dancing under blobby brains where I had felt-tipped them in during wet days alone, imagining myself at the bottom of the sea, surrounded by words fascinating as seashells. My mother had landed a slap on my forehead after Uncle Duncan had been wrestling with a crossword and 7 across brought the creatures to light.

My fingernail slid along the octopus arms: aubergine, aubrieta, auburn, *au courant*, auction, auctioneer.

auda'cious (-sh*us*) *a.* daring, bold; impudent.

My chest drummed on the verge of pride, at the heroic-sounding words. I flicked to 'I': impuissant, impugn, impudicity . . .

i'mpud/ent *a.* shamelessly presumptuous; unblushing; insolently disrespectful.

I wondered why the definitions had not been designed better, to help you work out whether a word was a compliment or an insult.

*

Friday night was still Friday night, in spite of a whole week at secondary school: Tia Maria for Auntie Jackie and our mother, toffees and telly for us kids, Uncle Duncan out chucking darts. Starsky and Hutch burst out of their car as usual, jerking their heads this way and that. On Saturday, when Auntie Jackie took us to Chorlton Precinct and we lugged back potatoes and tins, my chest stuck out proud, while my maroon shoes sailed down the street. But Sunday night brought on a bout of panic that nibbled away in my bones. I had spread my naked school books across the carpet and was preparing to cover them in perfume adverts that my mother had unstapled from her women's magazines. She got out the ironing board and turned up the radio so she could croon to the Top 40 while she was steaming out wrinkles.

'Why the face like a wet dishcloth?' she asked, when the number one had finally come and gone. 'So long as they're covered in *something*, what's it matter?'

My hands shook over the Sellotape, getting the strips in a twist, sticking my fingers together.

'I can't.' I looked at the pictures and saw my fate. I could not walk into school with my books wrapped in the pages of *Woman's World*.

'Don't be giving me grief, Andy, love.' My mother groaned. 'Not while I'm ironing, eh?'

But after the worst tears of the week, my mother gave in. Scrumpling the offending pages, she picked up the phone to Auntie Pauline.

'Listen, love.' She explained my dilemma as if it were a life-threatening disease: 'Our Andy's been told to back her exercise books in summat sturdy, like. You haven't got any of that wallpaper lying around from when you were doing up your front room, have you?'

I thought of the dark blue leaves tumbling across Auntie Pauline's walls, and crossed my fingers in both fists.

'Could your Bill drop it off on his way to the Depot?'

My mother clicked down the phone and picked up the iron, which steamed out a snort. 'Satisfied?'

'Thanks, Mum.' I blinked up at her through red eyes, from the wreckage of Sellotape and shredded magazines.

'Come 'ere, mardy pants.' She rested the iron on its haunches, freeing both arms. Locked in a delicious circle, I leaned, dizzy, into the warmth of her chest.

'What yer like, you?' My mother kissed the top of my head; the dread of Monday dissolved.

'Seconds?' Stacey, the girl who was dinner monitor on our table, balanced an enormous spoonful of slop over my plate.

Cabbage and curry, wafting pongs out of silver tins, was dinner on Mondays.

'Go on, then.' I let her slither lumpy yellow stuff over the remains of my mashed potatoes. Saying yes to seconds was not a matter of choice. Stacey was tall and tough and just like a boy, but for her long blonde ponytail, which nobody, but nobody, ever dreamt of giving a yank. Lads were afraid of her; steely-faced girls in the upper years left her well alone. If she offered an extra dollop of curry, you took it. It meant she wanted you on her side, and that she would be on yours.

Stacey was feeding me up so that I would help her with her English homework behind the coats in the cloakroom. Mrs Chappell scribbled subjects on scraps of paper which she shook in a battered top hat on her desk, asking one of us to pluck out a slip. Before next class, I had to perform magic tricks for two, pulling poems like silk hankies out of nowhere, for Stacey as well as for me. I made up rhymes about wrinkly roads running through elephants' skin, and described the schoompf of steam engines down tunnels, although I had seen no elephants outside the telly and had never set foot on a train.

Aeroplanes were like flying toothpaste tubes, I was able to boast in front of the class, since no one else had ever left England (unless you counted Wales).

While poetry felt like a game, and spelling was a piece of cake, grammar exercises were torture to me. Dismantling sentence after sentence, I fumbled with verbs, objects and nouns as if they were Lego bricks. I clicked them into what felt like the right order, without knowing what was really what. It was nailbiting, waiting for the results, knowing Stacey would be miffed if I gave her any clunking mistakes.

'Done it again!' She broke into a grin, elbowing pride when the grammar exercises came back, as if the nineteen out of twenty was really her own work. 'Blue merit badge before you know it!' Only Stacey could wear a merit badge without it doing her any damage. For the rest of us, it meant a thwack that sent the fastener spiking through your jumper and shirt into your chestbone. A gang of girls with jutting chins made it their business to inflict bruises on brainboxes.

What I got out of our partnership, apart from a gloriously unfair cut of cornflake tart come Friday at half past twelve, was protection from being called a Pakistani.

'Oi! Shut yer cakehole!' Stacey's shoulders bristled if anyone suggested it. 'Andrea's half Maltese and half Italian, yer spasmo! Definitely not one bit Paki.'

She was known to yank V-necks out of shape when her words didn't get across first time, pulling noses right up to hers so that their owners didn't dare breathe: 'All right?'

'Malteser!' The yard landed on a nickname that kept us all happy, scoring a joke about my chocolatey skin colour, but making the point that I was not Pakistani. 'Oi! Malteser! What colour knickers you got on under that tent, then, eh?'

'It's all that foreign blood, in't it?' Lads scrabbled to explain why a French accent happened on to my tongue when Mr Warburton asked me to stand up and pronounce bits of vocabulary for the benefit of the class. The words hummed off my lips, although I knew I would never see the country they came from. French was a cinch compared to the languages you had to leap into the second the bell rang for break. One for the lips, one for the legs. Strolling down the corridor without swaggering, you had to speak as if you were chewing gum, slurring all the usual words, tossing a few filthy ones in.

While Stacey's broadcasts saved me from having to explain about my skin, I still felt the need to lock myself in the school toilets from time to time. By the end of the dinner hour, my face was dying for time off.

'Wot, no titties?' I had to laugh rather than cry when lads rubbed my bee-sting breasts, after reaching to ping my bra strap and discovering that I hadn't grown out of my vest.

'You starting?' Hard girls shoved their chests against mine.

'Oh aye!' I squared my shoulders too, shuffling in sweaty circles while keeping up a smile.

The worst strain was on Wednesday afternoons, when you had to put on a brave face to get through the games period. Badminton sessions were the most scary: if you got beaten, you'd shoot to the top of the list for bullying; if you beat the girl on the other side of the net, she would be tempted to clonk you one afterwards, to get even and save face. Often, someone would be tempted to clonk you one anyway, if they didn't like the look of you. When the pretty but miserable Michelle gave me the thump she'd been saving since she first saw me, I had to hit her back straight away, grip her in a choking hug, and wrestle her flat on the tarmac, before I could get up and walk away. Kids droned like flies while we threshed on the ground – arms locked, wriggling legs – looking more like lovers than enemies.

'You want to watchit!' Thugs mingled with cowards, joking

about the strength lurking behind my smile and in my scrawny limbs. 'She can be mad 'ard when she wants to be, that one!'

After the fight, I had to go and hide in the loo, where I sat tight until I could be sure that all the red blotches had drained from my cheeks, that the dew had dried off my eyelashes. Then I flushed the bowl and breezed out, wearing the same grin as went in.

My mother spotted the maroon leather singed black in the scuffle. 'What happened to your new shoes?'

I looked down at the scar as if it was news to me, what went on around my toes.

'It must be from when I slipped this morning, running for the bus.'

My mother shook her head at the sight of my knee-length socks, shoved down to sag around the ankles, the way all the tough girls wore theirs at school.

'You'll watch where you're going in future,' she gave me one of her glares, 'if you know what's good for you.'

I glanced both ways along the corridor, then pulled my socks back up to my knees to show respect, before passing through double doors engraved to demand SILENCE. The library was more awesome than church, and unless you had a gold merit badge, awarded for 100 merit marks, borrowing books was not allowed.

AVIATION. I eased out the book, and squatted in the aisle. Curious clock faces within clock faces, endless switches, levers and dials ticked and flashed between the covers. Seven years, the print predicted, at least seven years it would take to train your brain to remember what every one of them did. I eased the book back into its dusty gap.

I would have reclining seats installed next to the cockpit, for Laurie, Sarah and Mum – not forgetting a see-through floor so that they could contemplate the ocean – after I had framed the pilot school certificates and launched my high-flying career.

In the middle of my fourth maths lesson, something marvellous occurred. Answers began to slide straight into my skull. I knew what it must feel like to sit in the front row, shooting your hand in the air to declare everything you happened to know.

'Two x plus y, going to three x minus two y,' Mr Butcher's breath panted, while his arm flourished chalky magic.

In a flash, without unpacking the formulae on the page, the solution zinged to my lips.

It was all I could do not to blurt it out. Trapping my fingers under my thighs, I sat on both hands until the urge died down.

Next lesson, I couldn't resist.

'Five x plus three y, Sir.'

Up shot my hand, out flew the words. No hisses from the back row.

'Seven x minus two y.'

Once could be passed off as an accident. Twice was something else.

'Three x plus y.'

A column of mustard and milky necks twisted to throw frowns over their shoulders from the flummoxed front row.

My eyebrows did a little waltz.

'Ras!' A wave of rasping and clucking washed across the back rows. 'Da bitch knows how to stick it!'

*

Our Humanities teacher, Miss Craig, rattled in a dinosaur of a telly on wheels, married to a mean-looking machine – a video – designed to record educational programmes off BBC2 and play them back at any time. Bending over in her men's slacks to plug this bit into that, her bottom presented its width to the world. Miss Craig was so far from pretty that you left her class brooding over what you would do if you woke up one morning to find that you looked like that too. But when she spoke, facts and figures poured out from across the universe, putting you in awe of her magical mind. The video whirred, splashing salmon after salmon upstream to lay millions of gungy eggs. Crashing against the current, these creatures would go to lengths that might seem insane, Miss Craig explained, sometimes killing themselves in the struggle to protect their species from extinction.

After the salmon, the lady from the family planning clinic came in. A few things to do with the birds and the bees were about to be made clear, she joked in a shaky voice. Then the screen sprang to life, and teemed with the naked bodies – the completely naked bodies – of plump and skinny girls and boys holding hands around a pool. Our faces burned in the dark, having to watch them standing there starkers for what seemed like light years. Eventually, they all sploshed in together. In the middle of a satiny bed, a man with a beard stroked the bare shoulders of a lady with a big nose while the word LOVE popped up in the corner, prompting a burst of hisses and boos. The screen blinked to produce an expectant mother, rubbing a huge belly beneath a huge smile. My hairs stood on end when a bloody head began to squidge its way out between legs spread across the screen.

Sperm and egg. Penis, vagina, womb. We broke out of class to go our separate ways, more than usually grateful for the end of the day. The film had injected X-ray vision: it was impossible to look at your schoolmates without seeing straight through their clothes. From the top deck of the bus on the way home, I gazed through the grimy windows at people scurrying along the streets. It seemed a wonder our own species had not become extinct, considering what had to be put where in order to keep it going.

Beverley was the bionic black girl everyone was scared of, having witnessed her tossing javelins and putting the shot on Wednesday afternoons. She strode like a god across the schoolyard, her brown frown scattering kids like the parting of the sea. Even teachers looked the other way while she conducted her break-time business, selling single cigarettes.

'Mash ya face!' She took a shine to my high cheekbones, giving them a good pinch.

I got used to having my face tweaked so that my eyes watered. Tall girls hit me with friendly filthy names, in Rasta lilts that slipped when they got flustered, flat Mancunian falling out instead. 'Ras ya cunt,' they might be laughing and clicking their fingers, until some lad landed them a thump, and 'Oi wanker!' shot up from deep down. I learnt to cuss in different colours, before stiffening to match the polite voice I put back on to talk to teachers and dinner ladies.

Blacks were ready to like me and whites were ready to like me, because they saw me as in between. I found myself walking a tightrope, balancing in both worlds as long as both would have me. Only on the way home, when the bus dropped me at the junction, did any funny stuff flare up.

'Fuckin' stinkin' Paki!' White girls in gold and brown uniforms pelted pebbles at my head. I had to walk face down, aching to break into a run, pretending not to notice the stones and jeers. Across the zebra crossing, and my face was saved.

Socks, cats and cold lard greeted me at the door. Piccadilly Radio provided company for Auntie Jackie in the kitchen, *John Craven's Newsround* bored on in the back room. Laurie and Sarah were discussing John Craven's jumper, and looking out for rhinos and pandas that sometimes turned up at the end of the programme.

Locking myself in the bathroom, I peered into the mirror over the sink. I tugged and tugged at the cord to persuade the lightbulb to glow in spite of the dodgy connection where wires spilled and flakes of plaster fell like dandruff from the loose fitting in the ceiling. I strained to stand on tiptoe. The mirror was rusted and warped. The light kept flickering and dying. A fishy stare loomed in the gloom.

I took the stairs two at a time, to find my mother in bed in our attic, where the curtains had been pulled tight.

'Mum.' I burst in and clicked on the light. 'Tell me the truth: do I look Pakistani?'

Slumped under the covers in her camp bed, her eyes were a world away.

'Don't be mard, Andy.'

I lifted her hand off the bedspread. 'I do, don't I?'

But she hardly responded. Her fingers sagged, a bag of bones in my palm. 'Are you all right, Mum?' Rubbing her knuckles between my fingers: 'Are you poorly? Is it to do with money?'

Auntie Jackie had begun to let out gusty sighs, pining for more notes to cover the rent, on Friday pay nights.

'I just need a bit of sleep.' My mother shrank under the blankets. 'Stop fretting, will you?'

Something sour in her voice kept me from reaching out to

trace the hairs along her eyebrows, mussed up against the pillow.

'Put the light out, there's a love.' I switched off the light, but crouched by her side in the dark. By the time I had worked up enough courage to kiss her hands or stroke her face, my mother's chest was heaving to its own, unfathomable lullaby.

Our mother lost her job while she was under the weather. The doctor typed a certificate to explain her nervous condition, but the geriatrics' home couldn't wait for her to get better. Sick note or no sick note – while she was snoring under sweaty covers, old folks were in bed too, dying for someone full of life to come along and feed them, to sponge their bums, change their knickers and tease out their teeth at night.

'I feel as ancient as that lot,' our mother moaned. Auntie Jackie tried to jolly her along, reminding her she had not even hit thirty-two. Was thirty-two young or old? I wondered. All I knew was that my mother's eyes were dull and the springiness had gone from her hair.

'I'm no use to anyone.' She sank into her pillow. 'Not fit for human consumption.'

I thought about the letter that she slept on, inside her pillow case. Our stepfather had written it outside the door one windy night, after driving all the way from Bramhall to see his lawful wedded wife. When Auntie Jackie wouldn't let him in, he sat on the step and scribbled. Laurie and I peeked from an upstairs window to watch him grimacing over the scrap of paper and chewed-up biro that Auntie Jackie shoved into his hands. It was the first letter we had ever seen our stepfather write. He slipped it into the letter box before growling away in his van. Our mother read it to herself in front of us, shuddered noiseless tears, then buried it under her pillow and never mentioned it again.

'Go on downstairs.' She shook off our stroking hands and shrivelled under our kisses. 'Go on now, and leave me in peace.'

'What is it?' I asked Auntie Jackie when she and I were alone, peeling potatoes.

'Yer mam's a bit depressed.' She turned down the radio to explain. 'But the doctor's prescribed her some tablets, like, and she'll be right as rain in no time.'

'Just with the tablets?'

'Aye, and plenty of shut-eye and tea.' Auntie Jackie chop-chopped at the potatoes.

'D'you think she's missing him?' I whispered.

'What? Yer dad?' She sneered under her specs. 'If that silly arse tries any of his famous bloody performances, he'll have *me* to answer to.'

I breathed in, savouring the suet of Auntie Jackie's skin, while she flourished the kitchen knife.

'He's waltzed his last waltz, that one.'

Silver flashed, swooped and sliced through raw spuds.

9

'Dance, ah-doo-doo-ah-dance!' Auntie Jackie set our mother's favourite record, *Boogie Wonderland*, blaring across the room, making everything shake. Ornaments shivered in time with the music, as if they were itching to dance.

Our mother swished down the stairs on silvery high-heels, wearing a silky red dress whose skirt slinked over each step. Laurie and I had dug her old disco sandals out of our suitcase, then mended the wrinkles and cracks in the plastic straps using clear nail varnish. Auntie Jackie had sent for the dress out of her catalogue, so that our mother could look lovely now and pay later.

'Do I look all right?' Our mother bent to kiss us.

'Scrumptious,' Laurie breathed: 'Truly scrumptious, you look.'

'Do I?' She kept glancing from us to her reflection above the sideboard, plucking cat hairs out of nowhere. 'Do I, Jackie?'

'Stop faffing!' Auntie Jackie stuck a cigarette between our mother's lips, rasped a match and held the flame against the tip of her fag until it burst to life. 'You look the business, Lolly.'

A car honked a tune from the street.

'That'll be your blind date!' Auntie Jackie grinned.

Wavering in front of her reflection, our mother stole a last glimpse. 'I don't think I should go.' She frowned at the lady in the mirror, as if she didn't deserve to look so lovely.

'You're going out for a bleedin' good time, Lolly.' Auntie Jackie shoved our mother's tired blue handbag under her arm: 'And that's the end of that.'

Getting home from school lost its gas-fire magic; our mother would be preoccupied, getting ready to go out on dates that Auntie Jackie had set up. On school nights we ate burgers and tinned spaghetti, sat through *Emmerdale Farm* and *Coronation Street*, then padded up to bed. Stray honks in the street or the squeak of the front gate catapulted us to the window in our nighties, squashing our noses against glass to take in the top of strange men's heads. Faces got lost in the dark, but we peered closely to watch the way the man walked. Laurie and I liked him to open the door and help our mother like a lady into his car, while she hung on to her handbag and swept up her skirt. One horrible night, her red dress got caught in the slam of a strange car door and she rumbled off without a clue. We slumped back to our mattress, knowing sleep would be slow to come.

'Medicinal' was how Auntie Jackie described our mother's nights out. Something was certainly making her feel better, after all those days when she had been sagging in bed with tired hair, looking hopeless and wrinkly around the eyes.

Now that she was back in the land of the living, she took to margarining our toast again. My importance shrank overnight: I gave up all the jobs I had secretly enjoyed while she had been ill in bed – taking charge of the marmalade, skimming it over each round of toast, nagging Laurie and Sarah to straighten their socks and lace up their shoes for school. But it was worth it, because now my sisters and I got out of bed with a bounce, instead of shivering and wishing we could stay under the covers, close to our mother, all day. She would be up and about, looking gorgeous in spite of her shabby pink housecoat, fussing around the kitchen, singing along to the latest songs on the radio. We felt spoiled when she paused between the tunes, turning to call us by old nicknames like Kiddlywinkles and Angelbabes, even making up new ones just for the heck of it.

'Off you pop, then, my Sugar Puffs.' She stood on the front step, clutching the neck of her housecoat against the cold, waving to my sisters and me as we went our separate ways.

'Now we are trees,' the PE mistress declared. Arms sprouted into branches that swayed above our heads to the airy lilts of Simon and Garfunkel. Tree, tree, tree: I strained my shoulders, elbows and wrists, imagining bark in the place of my skin.

'Now, slowly, lose yourselves in the song.' Miss Halliwell turned up the cassette recorder and left us to it.

'I Am a Rock'. Crouching to meet the pong of my pumps, I closed my eyes and wrapped my legs in my arms. The song swept over me – all about a rock feeling no pain – until titters let me know that my navy knickers were on show for all the lads at the back.

The knickers flashed again on Fridays, when PE was in the gymnasium and we had to hurtle over the leather horse or try to scramble up the ropes. My legs let me down when I tried working my way to the top and they were seized by stabbing pains. I slammed back to the stinking blue mat, then heaved on the rope again, eventually snailing all the way up using the muscles inside my thighs. Dangling in my own world, close to the cobwebby ceiling, I looked down on all the others buzzing against blue. I squeezed the rope between my thighs, loving the sweet heat that seeped inside my navy knickers.

I hobbled home rich, cradling cramp in curious places, hoarding friction burns.

Laurie and I began to feel restless and lonely after school, even though we had Sarah and each other, and our mother had now stopped going out at night. A tiff had taken place after Auntie Jackie caught our mother on the phone to our stepfather, filling her ears with his fantastic pleas. Auntie Jackie had actually shouted: 'You must be a bloody masochist! That bugger's got you on a string, hasn't he? Like a flaming yo-yo.' She flicked her wrist as if she was playing with one: 'Up and down, you're always going. Up and bloody down!'

Our ears tingled whenever the phone rang.

Upstairs! Auntie Jackie jerked her thumb at the ceiling, ushering Laurie and me out of earshot while our mother slid things into the receiver in a low, trembly voice. We crept back down as soon as we heard the jangle of the phone being hung up, and watched our mother whoosh smoke through her nose, like a horse. She stubbed her cigarette, grinding it against the glass of the ashtray long after it had stopped glowing.

We weren't allowed to bring schoolfriends home, our mother told us, because it wasn't our own house. I couldn't imagine inviting anyone like Stacey or Nardia or Winston back to Auntie Jackie's anyway. They would be shocked at how dusty and messy everything was, and it would be a catastrophe if any of them got bitten by a flea off the cats. I turned dizzy at the thought of the whole school knowing what my life was like. More than that, I didn't want anyone to see my mother now that she was looking so exhausted again, carrying all her worries on her face.

Drained by phone calls, our mother grew thinner and thinner, until the bones pressed against the skin on her face and jutted across her chest. Her shoulders sagged, her feet dragged. She stopped picking up the phone. She stopped dressing us for school. She stopped getting out of bed.

One Monday morning, when my uniform still lay crumpled and unwashed in the basket, I fished it out and set up the iron, trying not to touch the wires splaying out of its frayed cord. The plug had fallen off, so you had to stick the copper strands straight into the socket, then shove in the plug of the kettle to make the connection, praying there would be no sparks. Unfolding the ironing board slowly, to keep its hinges from squealing, I steamed over my shirt, tie and skirt. My hands chased to get rid of the creases that would make me look like one of the poor kids at school, before Auntie Jackie could awaken and kick up a rumpus over such a risky thing.

'What yer doing?' She discovered me dribbling tap water into the iron's spluttering nose. 'Does yer mam know what you're up to?'

'It's a surprise.'

Auntie Jackie gave herself a look behind her glasses, then shrugged and left me to it.

I took to getting up before light, to iron all our school things in the secret, silent bit of the morning. When Laurie and Sarah bounded upstairs to show off their immaculate seams and cuffs in front of our mother, she twisted in her pillows.

'You mustn't be doing that,' she moaned. 'You're only eleven. It's dangerous, Andy, love.'

'But I'm dead careful.' I spoke out of rigid collars, clammy-necked at the threat of my triumph being taken away from the start of every day. 'It's easy, Mum, and I don't mind doing it.'

'I should be doing it,' she said. 'I'm your mother.'
But she wasn't doing it.

After school, I spent hours with Laurie and Sarah in the cold, empty front room whose lightbulb had finally been fixed by Uncle Duncan. I would rush to get my homework out of the way, then the three of us would sit in a circle on the mangy carpet, playing with Lego or drawing on the yellow paper rolls that Uncle Bill, who was a bus conductor, had smuggled out of his ticket machine for us. It was frustrating, because the ticket rolls were so narrow and the bright yellow paper spoiled the most sophisticated effects. But it didn't feel like doodling: I had started art lessons at school, and I knew what you could make a 2B pencil do, if your fingers were in tune with your brain. A crumpled Coke can, an old boot, a bowl of apples and oranges – I had made them all stick out, as if you could pick them up off the page, in my sketch book in class.

I plunged into the storybooks my sisters brought home from school, reading them aloud and putting on voices, never feeling embarrassed. Not like I did in class, where I squirmed when it was my turn to read out a poem or a passage from the English textbook – you could be sure everyone would mimic you afterwards if you sounded too la-de-dah, or if you seemed to enjoy rolling the posh, airy words around in your mouth. I envied Laurie and Sarah for being at primary school: you might get laughed at or bullied a bit, but it didn't seem to matter so much – nothing could singe your face with embarrassment or make you break out in a wet panic under your arms. Half of me was dying to grow up, but the other half kept looking backwards at my little sisters. It seemed so far away, being nine, like Laurie, who could get lost in the land of Narnia, or five, like Sarah, who was absorbed by *James and the*

Giant Peach. Every night, as soon as I got in from school, I would put my pride away, forgetting I was nearly twelve, to lie on my tummy with my sisters and make up stories. I knew it was babyish, but sometimes I couldn't resist.

It was so nice not to think.

The thing that had forced our mother to lie down all the time in Canada had followed us over the water and now had her in its grasp again. Massive headaches froze her face. Sometimes she couldn't speak, or even breathe properly. Often she would lie terribly still on her camp bed, the covers pulled up over her head, like a corpse. I wondered if other kids' mothers suffered from the same thing. Something told me they didn't, though I never dared to mention it at school. I had a secret fear that we were not normal. Mostly I made myself forget about it; if ever I stopped to dwell, I would feel it seething under my skin, frighteningly hot, as if it might burn holes.

Our mother's fingers now drooped like fish washed up on the bedspread. She let me run my fingertips along the veins that pulsed just under the skin, then lightly over the knuckles, from the bony wrist to the tips of her nails. Occasionally, scuffing in from school, Laurie, Sarah and I would find her playing Solitaire with a pack of cards Auntie Jackie had bought her. Already the cards were furred along the edges. Wrapped in her quilted pink housecoat, she gazed through dirty hair at spades and hearts and diamonds and clubs, while her cigarette burned between her fingers until the ash dropped off by itself.

At tea-time she would haul back up the stairs, staring at her slippers after each step, as if to check that her feet were still there. Instead of sitting at the kitchen table 'like little ladies', the way our mother preferred, my sisters and I were allowed to balance our plates on our knees. I felt guilty about trading in on her weariness, which kept her from objecting when we broke the rules, but was as tickled as Laurie and Sarah by the thrill of taking in telly with our chips and cheese-and-onion pies. After tea, my mother would let me sit with her in the attic to read out poems I'd written in the loos during the dinner break at school. I longed for her to look up from the cards, splayed out over the bedspread, wishing she would smile or say something nice. Usually, she leant back and shut her eyes, not stirring, not even noticing when the poetry had run out. Sometimes, she opened her eyes and let the cards jiggle and slide off her knees while she fiddled to strike a match. She would watch it burn down to her thumb, withering into a spindly, black question mark that she laid in her ashtray with all the others.

One night, when I bounded up after tea clutching my dinnertime rhymes, I heard a panicky plastic rattling on the other side of the door. My mother was leaning out of bed, shuddering, trying to shove a brown bottle into the bedside drawer – her sleeping pills. On the bedside table, a glass of water was shivering and spilling with the jerks. My mother grabbed me by the wrists.

'I was going to, Andy.' Her eyes sliced into mine. 'And I would have, if it wasn't for you.'

'Mum.' I slid my arms around her. 'Mum,' holding on to her hollow trunk. Her back was ridged along the ribs, and her body light, so that it was like hugging a wicker basket.

My mother had dried up in bed, too sick and tired to cry. But now I could feel her welling up inside. It would be like drinking something sweet, to see her eyes wake up and weep.

At last she began to answer the phone and see visitors. Auntie Pauline, her younger sister, dropped by with a bunch of grapes.

She came in a new saloon car that she seemed sorry to have to step out of at Auntie Jackie's dingy door. Our mother's shoulders failed to perk up. Auntie Pauline remembered a flea thingy that she had to pick up from the vet. She was gone before we could blink, leaving black grapes behind her that oozed bitter seeds across our tongues. When our favourite Auntie Livia arrived, we had to cling and cling to her jumper, getting the affection off our chests, before giving her up to our mother. My sisters and I knelt on the floor, lurking about her soft suede shoes, while she sat on the settee and laid her hand on our mother's knee to make it safe for her to cry.

Auntie Ethel, Great Auntie Agnes, even Nana Hawkins rolled up. Rallying round, they called it. They were all fat, the women on our stepfather's side of the family, and they sank into the settee while the foam bulged to escape along the splitting seams. Their powdered faces scowled when the tea ran out, until I brought them a fresh pot on a battered tin tray, balancing chocolate bourbons and pink wafers for dipping. I had to dash across the junction to the Spar shop with Laurie to squander our mother's hard-earned money on yet more fancy biscuits. Laurie and I christened them Elephauntie This, Elephauntie That, when we were ordered out of the warm living-room while Sarah was allowed to stay and play.

'We want a private word with your mam,' they mumbled through crumbs. 'Off you two go out for a bit, there's good kids.'

We left our mother to them, bony and frail in her cardigan, fingers quivering for a cigarette.

Their flowery bottoms finally squeezed into Auntie Ethel's car, which grumbled down the road in the dark. Our mother lit up precious fags: first one and then another and a third before she could speak.

'He wants us back, you know.'

'Who?' I stopped dead in the hunt for pink papery wafers and chocolatey oblong biscuits. 'Dad?'

'Your Auntie Agnes says he never stops talking about us.'

Not about me, I thought.

I said, 'Do you miss him?'

My mother pursed her lips and blew out, slowly. The last bit of smoke bubbled in a ring and burst. I wanted to laugh, to break the thoughts behind her slinky blue cloud.

'I don't know what I feel any more,' she murmured. 'I'm too tired to know what I feel.'

'I don't even know if I love him,' she spoke into the ashtray on her lap.

How can you? I swallowed.

'Anyhow,' she looked up from her dimps and shrivelled matches, 'I've said we'll go up on Saturday and do something nice with him and your grandad and Nana Hawkins.'

'Saturday.' I forced my face into the one my mother wanted, while Laurie and Sarah buzzed about her knees, wondering which cardigans they could wear and whether we would ride on the top deck of a bus or in the back of our stepfather's van.

I lingered around my mother, too, trying to pluck up the courage to open my mouth. I wanted to ask her: *Why have you agreed to see him, after what happened last time, in the park?* As if she could sense questions in the air, she got out her emery board and curled up alone on the settee. I watched her, rasping away, her face lost in a veil of dust, her nails coming out in perfect curves.

Laurie, Sarah and I were dumped in the launderette in Stockport where Nana Hawkins worked, while our mother went off with our stepfather to wander around the Saturday market. We stood against the wall, watching our stony-faced

Nana feeding men's trousers into the jaws of a huge steam press. Pair after pair: skinny and fat, black, brown and blue. She yanked the lever to let out screams of scalding steam, followed by deep moans as she lifted the lid. Our throats itched as we breathed in hot air laced with chemicals and squinted towards the door. Our mother and stepfather had promised to rush back as soon as they had finished shopping, to scoop us out of the hot clouds.

Seven o'clock saw us stuck on Nana Hawkins's settee, sulking behind Tupperware bowls filled with the same mush she used to make us swallow when we were smaller. Our mother had turned up with our stepfather as the lights were being switched off at the launderette. A necklace of gold leaves had sprouted across her chest. Now we watched the leaves twinkling while our stepfather unfolded his foolproof plans, to become a landlord in a pub in a posh district where we could all go and live together.

'In't it great?' He reaped smiles off the settee, before tearing our mother out into the dark.

'Why aren't Mummy and Daddy having any?' Sarah's face creased over her gravy and mash, threatening to screw up into one of her awesome, ear-splitting tantrums.

Nana Hawkins decided it was time for Wagon Wheels. Flat planets of chocolate and marshmallowy biscuit. 'Mummy and Daddy are having something of their own.' She gave us a smile so rare it seemed to be hurting her face.

After a squeaky night, smelling the rubber mattress cover under the sheets, Laurie, Sarah and I clambered out of the bed set up for Grandad Hawkins when his willy sponges were letting him down. As soon as we got downstairs, Sarah was grabbed on to Nana's lap, while Laurie and I were sent into the back garden with a packet of crisps for breakfast. It was cold outside, but when we came back into the kitchen to ask why birds landed on next-door's bird table, and not on theirs, she shooed Laurie and me out again – 'Shuddup and eat your Quavers! You can see I'm having a quiet word with your mam.'

Seeing us off with sour kisses, Nana Hawkins handed us triangles of Dairylea, intended to keep us quiet in the back of our stepfather's van, though none of us liked the squidgy cheese.

'Now, now.' She tucked a five-pound note into my mother's clenched fist. 'I can't let you go empty-handed. Get yourself summat nice and don't be foolish.'

We climbed through the back hatch of the van and squatted among the tools, anxious to save our Sunday dresses from oil stains. Laurie and Sarah gave me nervous looks that let me know my face must be on the slide, shifting into its old shade of carsick green. I thought I had outgrown my carsickness, but something was making me feel squiffy and sour inside. I took a deep breath, and tried not to think about my mother and stepfather getting back together.

'Stick yer 'ead out, why don't you?' My stepfather made me press my face close to his, to breathe in buckets of thundery air as we sped down the motorway to Auntie Jackie's.

We pulled up in the dark at the top of Denton Road. Our stepfather snuffed his headlights.

'Don't go back in, Lol.' His arms fastened around our mother, like a human seatbelt. 'You know we can make a go of it.'

Laurie, Sarah and I crouched among the tools, watching rain spit patterns across the window-screen behind their silhouettes.

'You belong with me.' Our stepfather fingered the gold leaves, then buried his face in our mother's hair to weep. 'I'm beggin' yer, Lol.'

Rain pummelled the roof of the van.

'I'll think about it,' our mother murmured. 'It's just too soon right now.'

He lifted his leaking face: 'It's that bitch, in't it? Poisoning you against me.'

'Jackie's been dead good to us.' Our mother buttoned her coat with fidgety fingers. 'She's helped us no end.'

'She's an interfering bitch is what she is.' He jerked the ignition and the van growled back to life. Our mother laid her hand on the steering wheel before he could do anything silly.

'I'll phone you to arrange something,' she whispered. 'From a phone box.'

We climbed out, aching, into the rain. The van melted into the lights at the junction, our mother unlocked the leafy chain from her neck and slipped it into her pocket. She shepherded us under her brolly, across the road to the Off-Licence. Nana Hawkins's fiver was unfurled to buy a twenty-pack of Silk Cut, intended to mellow Auntie Jackie, who would be rigid with resentment after a weekend of friggin' worry.

The Top Forty was long since over on the radio; our mother had retired to the attic for a smoke on her own in the dark, when Auntie Jackie's oil-painted kittens began to shudder in their fake-wood frames on the living-room wall. I raised my eyebrows at Laurie, who kept her eyes glued to the screen while I teased down the volume, bit by bit.

'I stood by you, Lorraine!' Doors slammed. Ructions shook

the hall. 'After all that's happened, you let that bastard go and badmouth me!'

'You're bloody well out on your ear now, you are,' Uncle Duncan chimed in.

I jerked the volume back up, to drown out shouting and swearing and crying. Our mother rushed into the back room with a blotchy face: 'Time to pack.'

We awoke among our stuffed bags and suitcase, to find a gap in the mattress where Laurie had been tossing and turning all night.

'Where on earth . . . ?'

It was Laurie who had squealed to Auntie Jackie, and now she had disappeared.

My mother dialled everyone she could think of, lighting a new Silk Cut after each call. She crowded the ashtray with dimps, tipping them in black clouds into the bin. Auntie Jackie stood by, chain-smoking to keep her company.

At last, the umpteenth call soothed the frown from my mother's face and she was able to breathe without the aid of a cigarette.

'Thank ber-luddy Christ!' She hung up the phone and slumped on to the settee with Auntie Jackie.

'You's don't have to go, you know,' Auntie Jackie said quietly.

I couldn't imagine life without the stereo blasting 'Bohemian Rhapsody' to make the walls shake. Our nerves screwed up into knots every time the man wailed for his Mamma, before untangling in a trickle of stroking words and sighs about how nothing really matters.

My mother shook her head. 'No, love.' She rubbed her face as if she were having a wash. 'It's time I took things in hand.'

*

The good news was that Laurie had turned up somewhere at last, clutching the pink pearly bag that used to be mine, in which she had stashed a Penguin biscuit out of Auntie Jackie's secret tin, an emergency hoard of tuppenny pieces and a wad of Monopoly money.

The bad news was that Laurie had run away to our bossy Great Auntie Agnes's house, down the old biddies' end of Thornton Road, the street we had been brought up on before Canada. That, my mother told Sarah and me, was where we were going to take our things and stay. From the way my little sister gripped my hand, I could tell that she, too, was thinking of the wart that sprouted hairs on the side of Auntie Agnes's nose; it took all of your willpower not to shrink back when her face zoomed in for a kiss. Worse still was the deep, wrinkly dip between her bosoms: when Auntie Agnes trapped you in one of her hugs, talcum powder puffed out of the depths in choking clouds that made your eyes water.

A taxi hurtled us through Rusholme. Sweet shops had transformed into alarm fitters, insurance brokers and show-rooms tumbling second-hand furniture across the pavement. Only chippies were still chippies, promising the same old Frying Times. We swerved, and I found myself speeding down Thornton Road, feeling queasy while old windows whizzed by, the same but not the same. Outside 104, the woman we were convinced had poisoned her husband was still standing on her doorstep, spooning Weetabix and water out of a mug, mouthing off about the end of the world.

At Auntie Agnes's, we found Laurie sitting in front of the telly, watching Emu attack Rod Hull. Squelching between her fingers, she held a crumpet, buttered but unbitten. It had been ruined by the slather of Marmite that Auntie Agnes swore was the key to eternal life. I helped my mother lug our bags upstairs, then came back down to face Marmite on toast. Sitting at a distance from my sister on the settee, I found myself feeling shy. I looked out of the corner of my eye at the person who had got up and marched across Manchester, through the fog that shrouded the streets while the rest of the world was asleep.

10

'Out of the frying pan' – our mother shook her head at the sight of our new bedroom, black bin-bags stapled across the window, walls scabbed with half-stripped paper – 'into the flamin' fire.'

In the corner of the room was a stash of paperbacks by a man called James Herbert. Slanting, red eyes pierced the bogeyman murk on one of the covers. Although they made my skin feel prickly and sort of dirty, I couldn't resist reading the books behind everyone's back. At night, Laurie, Sarah and I became sausage rolls, baked in musty sleeping bags on the bare floorboards. I nearly suffocated inside mine, toggling it up tight to shield the glow of a miniature torch whose batteries were losing their spirit. A penny of rusty light let me slurp words off the page, one by one, as if through a straw. I strained in my sweaty cocoon to work out why evil took root inside grown-ups, making them waste their lives in wicked ways.

I came back from school carrying a prize, a posh pen with a silver barrel and a fine felt nib, which I had won by writing an essay on the theme of 'my favourite place'. I thrilled at the feel of my new pen gliding on paper, but cringed when my essay went up on the wall at school for all to see.

'My favourite place is in my mind . . .' Kids read the first line out loud in gormless voices, crossing their eyes.

'In yer mind?' Lads tweaked the ends of my hair.

They looked at me as if there was something loose inside my skull, while I stared back, suspecting the same about them. Then they jostled me around, elbows jabbing my ribs, until I let every one of them have a go of my pen with its super-gliding nib.

Although my family was living out of bags again, and we were camping on a strange new floor, everything was going smoothly enough at school. I had plenty of friends, nobody bullied me too much, and my marks impressed even Auntie Agnes, who had a good nosy when I brought my reports home for my mother to sign.

But one day Mrs Chappell pulled me to one side and asked me to stay behind after class.

'Is something the matter, dear?' She wanted to know why my handwriting had suddenly gone awry, scrawling this way and that. 'It gives me a headache just to look at it.'

It gave me a headache too, trying to link something like sense out of the knots of ink.

'We're in the middle of moving at home, Miss.' I offered a version of the truth. 'I've been a bit distracted.'

Every evening after we finished our tea and slipped into our nighties, to save our daytime outfits from getting dirty, our stepfather would turn up and install himself on Auntie Agnes's settee. Like my sisters, I gave him smiles and kisses, but then disappeared to do my homework on the stairs where, I told my mother, it would be easier to think. I sat in the draught of the hall, shivering in my nightie, trying to concentrate. Forests and sea, we were asked to imagine, even the cheesy surface of the moon. My prize-pen dashed out descriptions, while my back tensed against the cold and my mind wandered through the glass door: our stepfather slouched with his hands behind his head, waiting for us to be swallowed into our sleeping bags so he could have our mother all to himself. I crouched on the stairs, scribbling at top speed, wondering when we would be bundled into the back of his van and driven off for another bash at the good life.

Dark closed in against the school windows before four o'clock. Even when the lessons were boring, I dreaded leaving the cosy classroom to face the rain and wind at the end of the day. A lad with blond curls and a killer conker used to skulk around the school gates, waiting to walk me to the bus stop. The weather grew icy; the conker cracked; my head had been turned by mathematics and merit marks. Now there was no one to watch for at the gate, wondering which way he would walk home after the bus door sighed open.

I leapt off at Princess Parkway, to wind my way through the cul-de-sacs and alleys of Ashton Estate, cutting every corner in the race to escape the bone-blasting cold.

I hustled down the last alley on the estate, in the shadow of gigantic hedges.

'Rrrrr!' A knife leapt out of the dark, glinting for a split second under a dim yellow light. Behind it, a horrible smile slithered over the face of a man with gappy teeth and long hair.

In spite of the freezing cold air, I felt tears of sweat dribbling under my arms. I wanted to scream, but the noise curled up in my throat while my breath fluttered out in frosty white feathers.

The man looked at me and laughed and tucked his knife back inside his denim jacket. He slid his fists into the outside pockets and took off down the alley, chuckling to himself.

When I got home, I rang and rang on Auntie Agnes's front door. My mother came out to give me what for, to send me round the back as usual so that I wouldn't muddy the carpet.

'Christ!' Her face whitened when she saw mine.

'It can't have been the Yorkshire Ripper.' I slurped three cups of tea, sludgey with sugar, one after another. 'Anyway, if it had've been him' – I made the most of the affection oozing from my mother and sisters – 'I wouldn't be here, would I?'

'In't that near where that poor lass got dragged down the entry and raped?' Auntie Agnes protested, when our mother insisted on moving us up the Moss Side end of Parkfield Street, into a two-bedroomed house, whose rent fell within her grasp because it was in a rough area and because the foundations happened to be collapsing.

'It's about to topple!' Auntie Agnes looked triumphant when she discovered the extent of the subsidence. She was keen for us to stay with her a bit longer, so that she could keep up the pressure she had been putting on our mother, to persuade her to stop playing silly buggers – to go back to our stepfather and make a nice, happy family.

'It'll do.' Our mother was determined to go it alone with her girls.

A sort of seasickness, we all three felt, when we walked through our new front door. The floor sloped, nearly a foot lower at one end than the other, the subsidence was so deeply set in.

'Don't worry, Mum.' Our spirits sagged at the prospect of no telly, but zinged back up when we were allowed to eat our tea in picnics, sitting cross-legged on a blanket in the middle of the floor, until we could afford more furniture. 'This is the biz!'

We had been making our home in other people's bedrooms for nearly a year, and we were happy just to have our own walls.

The only shadow over our paradise was cast by the outside loo. To reach it after dark, you had to tie your nightie in a knot over the knees, then shove your feet into the stinky, man-sized wellies waiting by the back door. The light was broken, which was just as well, if you didn't want to watch the spiders that would be watching you. We gave ourselves cramp, holding on indoors, to avoid the smack of wind or rain, followed by the icy spank of the toilet seat. Running out of toilet tissue, we resorted to tearing strips from the *Sun*. There would be no more loo roll, no margarine and no milk, until the fortnight was up and the new dole cheque had come through to be cashed.

Kwap! Our mother's purse clasped shut on coppers. Instead of coffee or tea or orange squash, we had to be content with tap water – corporation champagne, she nicknamed it, with a bitter laugh.

'God works in mysterious ways.' Gran counselled us to sit tight when money ran out.

'Mysterious ways, my arse!' Our mother was not inclined to put much stock in God after the punches that had been thrown while we were at his mercy in Canada.

Our stepfather's van pulled up, a three-piece cottage suite strapped to its roof. The frame was made of varnished pine, with brown velour seating pads. Buckled into the passenger seat was a portable telly.

'Ace!' We were willing to worship our stepfather, until the bashed box was plugged in. Black-and-white legs wavered across the top of the picture, walking on heads that had been cut off and left to gabble in the fizz at the bottom of the screen.

Our mother must have known he was coming: a hock of ham had been stewing in a vat of split peas all afternoon, giving off a snotty pong that made our stepfather rub his hands and grin, while my sisters and I felt our skins crawl. We sat at the laminated dinner bench that he had just assembled using a screwdriver and a few choice words. I kicked Laurie under the table, making sure that she laughed when our stepfather bothered to include us in his jokes. Jutting out of his breast pocket, three tubes of Smarties sat like keys, waiting to wheedle his way back in.

Our stepfather soon shattered our mother's cosy idea of a family by hurling the pepper pot against the wall while we were wading through the liver and onions he loved. Our mother jumped up and smashed the salt pot to match. He stormed out, without pulling anything sugary out of his breast pocket to make us think sweet things about him.

'She can't let him back in now!' Guilty gladness exploded in waves through Laurie and me as we snuggled down to sleep in our bunk beds.

'I will survive'. Our mother fell back on Gloria Gaynor, spinning the disc that never tired of telling the man to go, to walk out the door.

Bastard. BASTARD. BaStArD. Laurie and I clawed the word into the pink nylon strands of our bedroom carpet, letting it sit there for fantastic seconds, before furring it with our fingernails so that the letters remained only in our minds. Downstairs, our mother sank into a gloom of instant black coffee, with no telephone to reach out to friends, and no coins to conjure them up at the red box on the corner. She had already taken a slap or two from our stepfather. Little ones that hardly seemed to hurt: she had put her palm over her cheek, as if to cherish the tingle. So our shoulderblades stiffened when she lifted the needle off 'I Will Survive' and veered into 'Midnight Train to Georgia', about the lady who goes miles and miles away to be with her man because she'd rather live in his world than live without him in her own. Deadening circles rang through the house. Around and around and around: we watched our mother's heart swelling and shrinking in spirals, while the needle skated from the edge to the centre. Her eyes glistened, wet and silvery, the moment the grooves ran out. She blinked hard, then lifted the needle: there was nowhere left to go, except back to the whirling edge.

'Fuck!' My mother's hands shook as she hammered in hooks, to hang our stepfather's ship paintings up the stairway.

'Hmm.' She adjusted the frames to make them seem straight in spite of the subsidence, then turned to me for a second opinion. 'How do they look?'

Balancing on the steep stairs, I contemplated his ships, vast sails sealed behind green-tinted glass.

'They make me feel wobbly,' I had to admit.

'Me too.' She took a duster to the ship pictures, glaring at her reflection, caught in the polished glass.

As soon as our stepfather moved in, they started arguing, especially at night, after my sisters and I had fallen sleep. All three of us would wake up and lie there, not daring to speak, though Sarah might sob in the dark. Laurie and I would creep out of bed to comfort our little sister – often the three of us would crowd together in her bed, finally nodding off when the noise died down.

Our mother began to stay up all night, smoking. She

crawled into bed in the morning, the minute our stepfather slid out. A faint whiff, like digestive biscuits, worked its way into our after-school corduroys when they didn't get around to being washed. Caught up in their own affairs, our parents left my sisters and me to play in the street after dark, watching white lads stroll by to swig lager outside Pandit's corner shop, where they bullied the owner's son, tugging at his turban, until he let them have extra cans for free. After a lad off Heald Place Estate had loomed out of the entry – grinning over a sparrow in his fist, giving the neck a clicky twist – we rushed indoors, happy to put up with *Coronation Street*'s fizzing and floating heads.

Satsumas squirted a scent that meant Christmas. A tree went up, holding out baubles that shattered one after another, while a tangle of red and green lights sulked on and off and on. Our mother invested in a brick of marzipan, which she rolled out and moulded over a fruit cake baked for us by Gran. Icing would have spoiled it, my sisters and I assured her, when the big day dawned on the yellow mound.

'You shouldn't have wasted your money.' Our mother wept and went upstairs, after tearing at tissue paper to discover the huddle of brass animals that we had clubbed together to buy, using the money she pressed on us on Fridays, meant for sweet pink shrimps and white chocolate mice.

School cookery lessons made me glamorous at home. My mother grouched around in her purse for the fifteen pence that Mrs Bingham charged for ingredients. Bread-and-butter pudding, I brought home. Cheesy stuffed potatoes. I slipped in my sisters' esteem the night I turned up cradling a rhubarb crumble that looked like the real thing, but tasted of steel taps melted in sour pink goo.

'Make us a pilchard buttie.' My stepfather showed me how to chivvy off the lid with the lethally sharp hook of the tin-opener, before peeling the spine out of the split fish. I learnt how to whisk it out in one go, tinkling the vertebrae clear of the flesh. But sometimes I couldn't catch all the hair-like bones.

'You're bloody well out to choke me!' My stepfather winkled the pilchard ribs from between his teeth, and gave me a whack that left my cheeks and ears throbbing. 'Evil little swine!'

I treasured the afterglow of a slap. It made me feel closer to my mother, buried in bed with a migraine that she blamed on coffee, rather than our stepfather's fists or the fingers that scrunched her lips into a tight, red flower, to stop them from spurting swear words and pleas and tears.

'It's the middle of winter, Peter!' Our mother sometimes emerged from her days in bed feeling feisty. 'You can't seriously expect me to wear dark specs.'

The sight of her stepping into the street with a spoiled face drove our stepfather bonkers.

'Flauntin' it!' He dragged her back in, bolted the door and laid in some more.

Eventually even Auntie Agnes turned against him and decided to wade in. Like a gift from above, our stepfather had landed himself in deep water. During his nights out, he had been amusing himself by pretending to be a plainclothes inspector. He flagged down ladies in cars, took their names and telephone numbers, then let them go with a caution about their dodgy driving. After a word from Auntie Agnes, who was well in with the copper who caught him, he was let off with a caution too, if he promised to leave our mother and us alone.

He packed his shirts and the collection of leather belts that had been waiting, he was fond of warning, to teach us a thing or two. Coiled like snakes with sharp buckle tongues, he stuffed them into a black bin bag, along with his jeans and stiff-necked jumpers. The ship paintings left spaces on the stairway wall where the hooks still stuck out, brass tacks staring like one-eyed spies.

Our mother signed up to do shorthand and typing at the local community college.

'It's for our future,' she explained, when I was enlisted to help her to memorize the shorthand symbols.

Dear Sirs, Yours sincerely, close of business, contract, grateful, at your convenience, without delay. I stayed up long after bedtime had claimed Laurie and Sarah, whispering official-sounding words that my mother translated, like lightning, into dots, curls and swoops. I sensed something magical in the offing when midnight came and her cigarettes were still crowding the pack usually hollowed out by her flustery fingers, forever reaching to light up. Now she pressed a kiss into my forehead, flexed her knuckles, and folded a towel under the second-hand typewriter she had picked up for next to nothing because the 'e' and 'w' had died. Sinking into my pillow, I slipped off, lulled by the muffled chug of my mother's speed-typing, approaching sixty words a minute, like a distant express train.

Pain in the back side. My mother squiggled shapes in blue biro that only she and I could understand. It made my heart beat faster, seeing the daring signs on the spiralbound pad right under my stepfather's nose. He had moved back in at the end of spring, with a solid-gold pledge that he would go to see a head doctor and visit a marriage guidance counsellor with our mother. At first she had told him where he could shove his piddling promises. But our stepfather wouldn't take no for an answer. He knocked and knocked on our door at all times of the day and night, breaking down, on his knees, begging to be let back in. Our mother kept up a grim face and seemed to be sticking to her guns.

Once, in the middle of the night, she even woke me up and made me come downstairs. My stepfather was standing at the bottom of the stairway in the hall, looking up at me with wrinkled, cried-out eyes.

'Tell your dad we don't want him here.' My mother nudged me to speak when I just stood there, dumbstruck: 'He won't take my word for it, so you go on and tell him – we don't want him, do we?'

I looked at my fingers, a puzzle of knuckles, trying to work out what to say.

Is this a game? I wanted to ask my mother. My nightie felt flimsy and short. I would have given anything to be wearing my shoes.

'It's not that we don't want you, Dad . . .' I lifted my eyes to meet his. My chest swirled full of funny feelings, like love, when I looked into his pink, snuffly face. Yet, at the same time, the pinkness reminded me of everything my stepfather could do when his face was bubbling with rage.

Before I could gulp it back, the truth pinged off my tongue.

'We don't want you,' I said. I took what I thought was a last look at my stepfather, before my mother sent me back up to bed.

So my heart jumped, after that, when I spotted a packet of Superkings – his favourite fags – on my mother's bedside cabinet. I had to get used to the sight of the black-and-gold boxes again, lying around, here and there.

Our stepfather fell straight back into his old ways.

When kids called for us to play out, we urged them to cross

over the road where they would be less likely to hear the details of him letting off steam.

'Jee-zus!' Older lads shook their heads over cans of lager, when our windows fairly rattled. No other comments were ever made. Our stepfather strode out to fill the doorstep every night, arms akimbo, legs spread wide, giving off knuckly stares that kept the street in its place.

It was a relief when the Moss Side riots roared past our road. Things calmed down inside our house, as they heated up outside. Our stepfather was mesmerized by the fires and broken glass and the anger of the men in the streets. He let us climb out of bed to linger behind him in the doorway, goosebumps dancing along our arms at blokes whooping and smashing shop windows, lugging looted stereos and tellies, waving flaming torches that made their faces leap in the dark.

Outside school, on the walls: NF, NF, NF, NF. No one seemed to know what NF meant.

'National Front,' Miss Wykeham half enlightened us in our religious education lesson, after the letters turned up on her blackboard amid a shower of strange crosses. Some people had a stupid and narrow idea of Englishness, she stammered, before shifting attention to the crosses like square flowers.

'Swastikas.' Miss Wykeham stood in front of them, demanding that the culprit step forward and rub them off. When nobody moved, she stormed out, leaving the air electric. She huffed back into the room a few minutes later with a stack of paperbacks.

The Diary of Anne Frank.

Hitler, Nazis, Jews: a world of evil, including millions – absolutely millions – of dead bodies, lay behind the crosses that Miss Wykeham rubbed into a sinister swirl.

I devoured the book in a single night, kneeling against our bedroom window, stealing foul pink light from the streetlamp. Turning to the picture on the cover, I gazed into the brave girl's face, looking for bits of myself there. I went hot when I discovered that a boy had peeked at her through a mirror behind his desk; Dudley Barnes did that to me during Geography, using a wing mirror wrenched off a car. At the end, I crawled into bed feeling hollow, unable to stop thinking about Anne Frank, creeping about the annexe with her family.

Laurie and I made sheathes out of Sellotape and an empty packet of porridge oats to cover the four really sharp kitchen knives. Sarah insisted on colouring them all in with wax crayons. We slid the knives back into the cutlery drawer. Whereas nights used to be burst by bashing and shouts, now there was a razor-edged silence that made me press both shoulderblades against the wall in bed. I let my heart clang out through my back, so that it wouldn't scare Sarah, curled up against my chest where she insisted on snuggling in order to sleep. When morning dawned, I slipped the sheathed knives out of the drawer and took them outside to bury them in the bin in the back yard.

In spite of fights and sleepless nights, our mother had passed her first secretarial exam. Her second brought her home singing, flourishing a packet of custard creams and news of greater honours still. The night before her third and final test, which was to include an interview, she decided to iron her pleated caramel skirt after washing it with the rest of our clothes. We were in our nighties, stuffing everything else into the twin tub.

'Just the job,' Laurie and I assured our mother, when she tried on the green jacket that Auntie Livia had been good enough to lend. 'A real, live secretary, you look.'

She draped the clean laundry over the airing rack in front of the fire, then set to with the iron to tame the pleats of her posh skirt. Laurie and Sarah were busy persuading the Rubik's cube back into one piece after another dismantling. Inhaling the scent of drying vests and knickers, I hunched over *Flowers in the Attic*, growing hot and bothered, wishing the mother in the book would forget about the inheritance money and just pack up and get her kids out before it was too late.

My spine stiffened at the chug of our stepfather's van. Brakes grunted outside the door. He lurched in.

'Happy Families, is it?' He pictured the four of us having a party, every time he pulled off in his van. 'Can't wait to see the back of me, can you?'

Behind her iron and her caramel pleats, our mother stood her ground, instead of rushing to put the kettle on as usual, before helping him off with his shoes.

'Oi!' Our stepfather swayed in the doorway, his breath reeking as if he had been munching metal. 'Oi, you! Bitch!'

Sitting on the carpet, Sarah wound up the Fisher-Price toy telly that she sometimes cradled like a doll, although she was now six. *Row, row, row your boat, gently down the stream* – a boy floated along, snoozing under a straw hat – *Merrily, merrily, merrily, merrily, Life is but a dream.*

'Cunt!' Our stepfather smashed his boot into the screen.

Sarah's lips churned, wondering whether it was safe to cry.

Next he grabbed the iron out of our mother's hand. She gasped and wriggled out from behind the ironing board. Smiling to himself, he pressed the iron on to the skirt and held it down, waiting, watching it hiss and puff, before peeling it back.

'That's foiled yer, 'an't it?'

An iron-shaped hole gaped in the pleats that had been destined to make our mother a secretary.

'I'm taking that test, Peter.' Our mother straightened her shoulders, rising above the sight of the singed skirt. She had orange curlers in her hair, but she looked brave and beautiful, her dark eyes on fire.

'You can do what you like with your own future,' she spoke in a low, vibrating voice, 'but you are not about to foul ours up.'

'Oh, aye?' Our stepfather lunged into the kitchen, clanging among the cutlery. Unable to lay hands on a knife, he strode back into the living-room and went straight for our mother. Naked under her housecoat, her flesh flashed when he grabbed her and threw her against the wall. Sarah's head thudded against the dinner bench in the confusion.

I screamed 'Dad!' when my mother's feet left the ground. Above his fists, both clamped around her neck, my mother's eyes seemed to go out. Veins bulged in her forehead. My teeth sank into the skin between his forefinger and thumb. My mother slid down the wall.

'I'll kill you!' He thumped me across the side of the head, then picked me up by the hair and hurled me towards the fire, where I crashed into ceramic tiles.

I looked up into his face. Behind him, my mother grabbed the tomato-shaped pot, cream crackers leaping out of the lid as she brought it down on his head. There was a sound of banging and smashing in the hall: as if I had conjured them up, four police officers ran into the room.

Laurie had plunged into the street in bare feet and run through the dark in her nightie straight back to Auntie Agnes's. Two of the officers drove us there to pick her up, in a real police car.

'D'you think she'll need stitches?' Several heads, all in their bedtime curlers, bent to inspect Laurie's shredded feet. A steady stream of old ladies came for a nosy, drawn to Auntie Agnes's house by the sight of a police car. My mother eased shards of glass out of Laurie's soles, then doused the gashes with Dettol. I held my sister's hand while she winced.

'What the 'eck's that?' Auntie Flo pointed at the jumper shoved on over my nightie.

'Christ tonight!' My mother lifted a thick snake of hair off my shoulder. She stroked the throbbing bald patch on my head. 'He's ripped it right out.'

I looked at the hair, then at Laurie. We squirmed under the spotlight of Auntie Agnes's cronies, watching us watch her colour TV: cops scooted about, setting off sirens, clutching guns in their praying fists.

11

Helmets hovered about our front door. One of them seemed especially dedicated. We discovered Officer Parkes doing his duty indoors, whenever we got home from school. He cleared his throat and proceeded to take notes from our mother, whose fingers fussed about her neck, still ripe with yellow-green strangle-marks.

Standing to attention, he strapped his helmet back into position: 'All right?'

'Mm-hmm.' I nodded with Laurie and Sarah, then ushered them upstairs to our bedroom. There was something about the policeman's eyes, as if our stepfather was watching us through them.

After what our mother referred to as a misunderstanding, Officer Parkes withdrew his services. The blue rash around our door disappeared. More powerful than the police, our mother's friend Auntie Tamara moved into a house down the next street, complete with daily visits from her brother, who was big and black and broken-nosed: there was no way our stepfather would dare to come knocking now Uncle Clifford was hanging around. Half-black and half-white, Auntie Tamara's skin shone as if she had been dipped in treacle. She used to work with our mother, before I was born, behind the deep fryers at a local chippy. Now she was trying her luck at a more glamorous career, although we could never work out what it was. She came round on her way out, late at night, locked in bangles and slinky clothes. Lighting up with our mother, she crossed her gleaming legs to cuss this guy and that, saving nicer words for the ones who came up with funk and soul records, along with quarts of rum, to express their appreciation of her sensual side.

'I'm not badly off, am I?' She held up her arm to admire a gold link bracelet, before swigging Bacardi with a splash of Coke and stubbing her cigarette: 'Can't complain.'

Like a flower watered by Auntie Tamara, our mother grew glamorous. Laurie and I were amazed by the silkiness of dresses that could float off the back of a lorry.

'You look like midnight,' I told her, when she slipped into the black satiny one, speckled with stars and sickle-shaped moons.

Our faces danced every time someone tapped on our mended front door after dark. Swinging it open, our mother would hover on stiletto heels, casting a fabulous, lipsticked smile over instant aunties and uncles. All sorts of people were drawn to her – 'Bees to a honeypot,' Auntie Tamara smiled. Without our stepfather messing up her face and her moods, our mother could be herself. She fizzed full of life like she used to, widening her eyes as she laughed and joked, making people thirsty for a taste of her spirit.

Bones of fried chicken lay in ashtrays when my sisters and I got up in the morning and ventured into the living-room, which had throbbed with music and voices the night before. We collected drained bottles and glasses to save our mother the trouble when she woke up and padded about, holding her head as if it might break, like an egg. On Saturday mornings, we helped her to clean the house, top to bottom, before she set to work on her hair, fixing it in curls across her crown, ready to do the rounds with her catalogue. She had been made an agent for Great Universal, leaving her secretarial dreams buried in the typewriter under her bed. It made me sad to think that she would never turn into a secretary, but I was as quick as my sisters to pounce on the catalogue. Long, rainy afternoons would slip by while we knelt, dreaming, over the glossy pages – Laurie and Sarah stuck on the pictures of toys at the back, while I was growing fascinated and slightly frightened by the world of clothes.

'I Can See Clearly Now'. Our mother had a quiet smoke over her old Motown vinyls in the evening, before rushing out on the razz, leaving Laurie and Sarah in my hands, which was legal now that I was twelve. 'The Tracks of My Tears' . . . 'I Heard It Through the Grapevine' . . . 'You Keep Me Hangin' On' . . .

We boosted up the volume, then fetched the cards that our mother and her mates played with – laying them across the floor, gambling Revels and fruit pastilles, making up the rules. Midnight came and went without bringing our mother back. We took out our tiredness on one another, before sliding the records back into their sleeves and dragging ourselves to bed.

Our number finally came up on the waiting list at Moss-Care Housing Bureau. The house on Parkfield Street was scheduled to be demolished – our mother had tipped buckets of coins into the pay phone at the Bendix, calling the council to remind them – so it was about bloody time. A completely renovated, terraced house was now waiting for us.

'Not enough room to swing a cat, of course.' Our mother explained that my sisters and I would have to squash up in bunk beds, sharing a tiny bedroom. But the house came complete with fitted kitchen and indoor loo, which seemed too good to be true. It was just around the corner, on Chilworth Street, parallel to Auntie Tamara's house on the next street along. She and our mother carried the wardrobe, the beds and settee, while Laurie and I lugged mattresses, pots, plates and clothes and Sarah clutched her Etch-a-Sketch and wax crayons. We stepped through the shiny red front door. Our hearts ballooned, while our heads clanged with the tang of untrodden, rubber-backed carpet and still-drying magnolia paint.

Keen to keep the paintwork clean and the carpets fluffy, our mother dedicated herself to our new home with a passion. We relished the way she ordered us to take off our shoes the moment we clomped in from school. A wonderful wall of rules went up, about where you could and flaming well couldn't eat biscuits, on which surfaces you were and were not allowed to rest your glass, where towels were to be hung after a bath, where clothes went when they were dirty. We slid into bed, scolded and cosy. Our mother stayed up all night, blasting the Jackson Five, gunning away on the Singer sewing machine lent to us by Gran. 'A, B, C' . . . 'My Girl' . . . 'Can You Feel It' . . . 'Blame It on The Boogie' . . . We awoke to the rhythms we had fallen asleep by, to find our windows draped in a blue that made the sky seem drab.

Laurie, Sarah and I helped our mother tend her new jungle of ferns, wielding water pistols to spray tiny green teeth zipping along their fronds. When we got it wrong and her rubber plant drooped, its leaves choked by the furniture polish we had smeared on to encourage the shine, she ordered us to keep our flaming green fingers off the ivy and the yucca, the spider plants and the bony rose bushes planted in paint cans in the back yard.

*

'Flippin' freaks of nature!' Our mother glowed with Auntie Livia, debating the source of the brains that were helping Laurie and me to gather school merits. 'I bet they get their nous from my side of the family, after all.' She arranged the badges – blue ones, red ones, then gold upon gold – on a crocheted doily on top of the TV. 'I might have gone far, given half a chance.'

Because our new house had a proper aerial, the telly had finally stopped rippling. My sisters and I sat in a trance in front of *Bewitched* or *The Beverley Hillbillies*, then tore ourselves away from the box and gathered around the dinner bench to do our homework. Our mother bent over books with Sarah, helping her to catch up where she had fallen behind in our hairy moments.

'What's GIST?' Laurie wondered why I had to fill out pink forms for science, after blasting through maths and English and sharing the most luxurious French words with her.

'It stands for Girls in Science and Technology.' I recited what the lady had told me when she took me into the technician's lab for a special interview, away from the rest of the class. My mother listened at the sink, where she had got up to scrub vegetables, while I explained that I had been selected as part of an experiment to turn more girls into scientists.

'Why d'you want to be one of those?' Laurie found it hard to appreciate anything but gymnastics – which made rosettes bloom on her chest – and ballet, which she was teaching herself out of a book that Gran bought her for her eleventh birthday.

I was flattered by the extra attention at school, but I struggled to see the point of science myself. 'I might want to be a doctor, mightn't I, Mum?' I flustered. 'Or an astronaut.'

'What, like off *Star Trek*?' Laurie tweaked her ears to make them pointed like Mr Spock's.

I dived into the tables and diagrams on my pink sheets, while Sarah drew a space rocket on one of our mother's spare catalogue order forms.

'Don't forget me,' she crayoned her heart out, 'when you go to work on the moon.'

After tea, our mother stuffed our school socks into the special pan set aside for boiling them in bleachy water. They gurgled while she was busy with bleach of her own, dipping her fingertips in a bowl in her weekly war against nicotine stains. Once the nails were whiter-than-white, she was happy to take them out and play Scrabble.

'Fetch the dictionary!' Our mother was a stickler, making us check every one of our dubious concoctions. We had to know how to use words properly, she insisted, if we hoped to get anywhere in life. She kept no other books in the house, but our battered old dictionary followed us wherever we went – we even used it for swearing the truth on, after our illustrated children's bible got lost.

Bedtime took us by surprise. We kissed our mother good-night, and left her listening to the Pointer Sisters' new album, which Auntie Tamara had taped for her. 'I'm So Excited' . . . 'I Need You' . . . 'Should I Do It?' . . . 'Slow Hand' . . . Sexy harmonies sent us to sleep, shivery with pleasure and pinpricks of worry, wondering what would happen if the songs stirred up longings too strong for her to ignore.

'Absolutely brassic, we are.' Our mother composed the shopping list in perfect handwriting, on the back of an envelope from Norweb. It was like a poem, except that 'loaves' meant flimsy, thin-sliced white bread, 'margarine' meant watery, petrol-tasting stuff, and 'milk' came not in bottles or cartons but in boxes of powder that left lumps, no matter how long you whisked it in water with a fork. Fastening all the press studs on our anoraks, we braced ourselves against icy wind and rain. A mile-and-a-half's walk lay between us and Kwik Save on Dickenson Road. Four miles there and back, if you counted a detour to the freezer-food emporium, where pounds performed miracles for people even poorer than ourselves. Ladies with no stockings leaned into icy chests to pull out fish fingers and so-called beefburgers in bumper bags. Everybody knew that they shrivelled to a cardboardy pulp after the fat and water had melted under the grill, but at 69p a dozen nobody seemed to care.

'Tot it up for us, Andy.' My mother compared the amount in her purse with the figure I tugged out of the trolley, after adding the prices of packets and cans. We went through our cash-out routine, putting items back on the shelf to bring the total into line.

'Right, how much is it now?'

I subtracted a pot of jam, a jar of pickled onions and two packets of Rich Tea. My mother made a calculation in her own head, then put the jam next to the till to be checked out, bidding goodbye to the onions and biscuits, pursing her lips against our heartbroken looks.

Laurie, Sarah and I were equally expert at prising the lid off the biscuit tin, without letting the metal twang. Filched by the three of us, ginger snaps disappeared within days. Our mother held a ginger biscuit trial, but no one knew a thing.

'I don't even like them,' Laurie had the genius to announce.

'Own up!' Our mother primed the rubber sole of her slipper, ready to wallop the thief.

Three confessions leapt out. Nobody's backside saw the

slipper, but our mother smashed her fist against the table, shouting and swearing like a man.

'You just don't give a toss, do you?' Her screeches cracked and broke down into tears. 'You're going to drive me over the brink!'

Our mother would be nudged into a rage if we folded her underwear the wrong way in her drawer, or abandoned our muddy shoes in the hall, or left a scummy halo around the bath. Slaps left us sobbing, more dismayed than hurt, until she claimed we were trying to kill her with guilt, and we throttled our fruity tears.

'Yes, it's a cigarette!' She seethed in front of the telly, its screen seething back in her face. *Steer clear*, the wisps of smoke warned.

The person who brought our mother out of herself was Auntie Bridie, a friend from the old days, whose troubles were so much worse.

'Ma wee bairns.' Auntie Bridie groaned into the neck of the bottle of Bell's she carried under her coat when she walked all the way from Wythenshawe to cry on our mother's shoulder around midnight.

'You'll get them back.' Our mother pressed a glass into her hand, so that she wouldn't have to swig her whisky straight from the bottle.

It wasn't going to be easy for Auntie Bridie to convince the social workers that she was a sober and responsible parent.

'Why does she come round?' I couldn't help asking my mother, when she got out the disinfectant and sprayed air freshener as soon as Auntie Bridie staggered back into the dark.

She wafted the door back and forth, to shift a blend of

whisky, sweat and pee: 'We're all the same in the eyes of God, Andrea.'

'He must be a monster,' Laurie and I fretted, when our mother prepared herself for a date with a man she had met through Auntie Bridie and her husband, Humphrey. We shuddered to picture our mother on the arm of anyone remotely resembling Uncle Humph. Swelling fatter and fatter, his tattoos had ballooned and lost their colour, though blood had squirted out of the heart tattooed with another woman's name when Bridie's resentment had got the better of her and she stuck a fork into his podgy arm.

'It's a wonder he didn't burst!' Uncle Humph had been sent home from hospital with a tetanus jab and a recommendation not to talk while he was eating, since it had proven so hazardous to his health.

My mother instructed me to torture her with the spiky end of a fine-tooth comb, drawing lines across her scalp, yanking the hair in strands. Laurie sprayed the lengths with perm solution, then trapped them in tissue squares like Rizla papers.

'Okay, stand back.' My elbows needed all the room they could get; it was a tricky operation, rolling the hair around the curler, tight, at the perfect angle. My mother would get into a horrible fluster if I didn't fix each one just so.

'One down.' I trapped it in its plastic cage: 'Only fifty thousand to go.'

Eventually her head was loaded with purple plastic bullets.

We waited for an hour, poring over the catalogue, ready to rinse and release the curls as soon as our mother gave the word.

*

A fox fur jacket now nestled about her neck. An old, gold Jag had started coming to take her out at night.

'It's your knight in shining armour, Mum.' The car was back, purring to pick her up.

'Is he coming in, this time?' We were dying to see the man that our mother took so much trouble to please.

'Not this time.' She clasped her ankles in spiky heels, warned us not to open the door under any circumstances and vanished in a flurry of perfume and hair lacquer, sprayed like there was no tomorrow, leaving our nostrils and eyeballs stung.

A new night unfolded inside the night, another inside that one, then another and another. I lay on the bottom bunk, seeing things in the wire links supporting the mattress above me, imagining it smashing down to print its diamond pattern on my face. At dawn, I fell into a sort of sleep.

'Everything all right?' My mother tiptoed in at half-past seven, before Laurie and Sarah had woken up.

'Everything's fine.' I put the kettle on. She sighed out of her stilettos and hung up her fur, giving it a loving stroke.

We sat at the laminated table, sipping coffee with powdery milk.

'Did you have a nice time, Mum?'

'Mmm.' She yawned and gulped from her mug. 'It's the real thing, this time, Andy.' Cradling her chin in her hands: 'The real thing.'

Mr Yarrow made everyone lay their left hand on the desk, to sketch a picture of it with the right. It felt weird, staring at your own hand and trying to draw it – a spooky self-portrait.

'Are you really capturing it?' He floated around the room,

spying over shoulders to check that artistic spirit was being poured properly on to the paper.

'Beautiful.' I could smell coffee and Super Strong mints on his breath when he bent to inspect my drawing.

'Thanks, Sir.' I fiddled with my eraser.

'Absolutely beautiful.' I felt his breath on my neck as he leaned closer. 'And not just the drawing.'

His bald spot gleamed when he bowed over the next sketch.

In the old days, when she was struck by one of the awful turns that drained her and made her crawl into bed, I used to feel my mother slipping away from me. Her eyes would hollow out, so that I might feel lonely even while I was sitting with her and holding her hand. Now that she was happy, she was literally out of reach – always off with the new man. I couldn't talk to her about my uneasiness in the art room, the way the lab technician peered at me through the Bunsen burners during science, or what to do about lads who rubbed where they shouldn't when they shoved past in corridors. She smelt like a stranger when she popped home from the new man's flat.

'Spotless!' Her eyes widened at the gleam of dusted paint-work around windows, doors and skirting boards. Inside cupboards, pans gave you back your reflection. Sarah had even polished the ends of food cans after peeling off the price stickers in a ceremony our mother always insisted upon. Every evening after baked beans on toast, Laurie and I scrubbed and wiped and swept to the beat of 'Under the Boardwalk' and 'Up on the Roof', playing the Drifters to death.

'Wait till she comes home!' We egged each other on with rags and brushes. 'She's bound to bring him in when she sees how gorgeous everything is.'

We presented our mother with a sandwich of mashed banana, designed to make her melt, while keeping quiet about the vanilla slice that we had been so excited to buy for her out of our pocket money, before giving in and slicing it into three.

'Doesn't he have a phone?' We tried to hang on to her when she was ready to rush back out with a fresh set of clothes. We had washed everything in our twin tub, then lugged it down the road to do the drying at the Bendix – portholes swishing stockings, bras, secrets – before marching back home, where I ironed her blouses and trousers, concentrating to steam love into each crease.

'We wouldn't call if you left the number,' I promised. 'It'd just be nice to have it, in case of an emergency.'

'I've told you' – our mother refused to scribble any numbers – 'nip round your Auntie Tamara's if anything's the matter.'

We had nipped round to Auntie Tamara's one night, a three-headed bat in our anoraks, flying through the alley connecting our street with hers. 'What's up?' She let us in to sit on the floor in front of the fire, in a jungle of strange men's legs. 'Is that all?' she laughed, when Laurie admitted we were lonely. We belted back through the pitch-black alley, sloshing a half-empty bottle of Coca-Cola, magicked out of Auntie Tamara's fridge.

On school mornings, I would heat anoraks in front of the fire and zip Sarah into hers. I made a sandwich of two Rich Tea biscuits, with a glance of margarine and a sprinkle of sugar in between, and wrapped it in paper torn out of my English exercise book. Then I slipped it into Sarah's pocket and shut the door behind her and Laurie, before rushing to clear up the kitchen so that my mother would find it sparkling if she came home.

Once, after washing the breakfast things, I was struggling to fold the rusty-hinged ironing board, when something inside me collapsed too. My bones ached, hollow, with no sleep stored up. The radio announced the time as nearly nine. I could see the looks on my teachers' faces if I crawled in late again, swallowing yawns, homework only half done. The pink promise of my GIST forms had paled. I had actually been put into detention after shooting pellets of chewed-up paper through the empty barrel of a Bic pen, letting them splat on the blackboard, then refusing to cower under the glare of the new science teacher. I spent the dinner hour in a store room with no windows, testing a mountain of batteries and bulbs to see whether they were dead. It was like being locked in a box with a stranger.

Even books made me feel lonely now. At first, on days when something held me back from going to school, I would sit on my mother's rocking chair in the kitchen, creaking back and forth, devouring her Catherine Cookson romances or the slushy Danielle Steel stories Auntie Livia lent to her. But soon the pages began to shut me out: my eyes would skim over the words without connecting one to another, making me feel queasy, so that I gave up trying to lose myself in rocking and reading.

On this rainy morning, I slid off my tie and put on my jumper, covering the uniform beneath. If my mother happened to turn up and find me, I could tell her I had been sent home from school. I was always contracting tonsillitis; she no longer fingered my glands when they swelled into plums, or made me open my mouth to inspect the gunk flowering in the arch of my throat. Picking coins out of the rinsed margarine tub where she left money for me to buy food, I grabbed two plastic bags and headed for Dickenson Road. A new Kwik Save had been built only two blocks away, on Withington Road, but something made me trudge a mile and a half through drizzling rain to the old one, followed by a mile and a half lugging the bags back. I had an urge to go and linger down the same aisles that my mother used to mooch along with us, wheeling the trolley, pulling faces at prices, weighing our opinions as to the virtues of this brand of white bread over that.

Dawdling by the window of the dusty records-and-books shop, a title caught my eye. I sneaked five pence out of the shopping money.

Growing: Girl to Woman. I got home and scoured the yellowed pages. My cheese on toast grew excited, hissing and spluttering under the grill.

Clitoris. It looked and sounded like a flower. I peered at the diagram, read the instructions once more, then washed my hands in the kitchen sink.

So *that* was the place that Judy Blume was referring to, when Deenie touched herself in the bath to cheer herself up. All the hours I had spent caressing the insides of my elbows, massaging the hollows between my toes and tickling behind my ears, in search of 'the place' that made you feel creamy. I wondered why anyone ever went to school, when you could stay at home and do that.

'Mum.' I pulled her to one side the next time she turned up. 'I think I need a doctor.'

Treacly emanations had ruined my knickers. My guts were an accordion, stretching, clamping, excruciating pleats. Hours of sin in the afternoon, churning delicious waves across my middle, launching tingles like electricity down to my toes, must have wrecked my waterworks.

'But it was black,' I explained, when my mother suggested that the sticky stuff was blood. 'Thick and black; not like blood at all.'

She inspected my clammy, green face and the rinsed, still

rusty gusset of my knickers, then pulled a tampon out of her handbag: 'Welcome to the club.'

Hips began to bud inside my jeans. Breasts throbbed under my vest. Shop fronts, glass doors, car windows, even the shiny sides of vans: I spent my thirteenth summer on the trail of my own reflection.

'Watchit!' I bumped into the girl with the Human League haircut, whose fringe jagged over one eye so that, like me, she never saw where she was going. Wendy O'Malley. She lived in the house with a picture of the Pope in the window, on the corner of Chilworth Street.

'Sorry.' I looked her in the eye not hidden under the hairsprayed flap.

'S'all right.' The eye blinked. Like the lens of a camera, photographing my face and everything in it.

She tottered into the park on white winklepickers, pausing to light a cigarette inside the gates.

Why isn't she at school? I wondered. My curiosity boomeranged and hit me: *Why am I not at school?*

I had never stopped to work it out. It was easier to carry on walking, no matter how lost and confused I felt. Industrial action had started it off: the teachers were so often on strike, I got into the habit of missing classes, skipping them even when they hadn't been cancelled. But there was something else – inside me, nothing to do with strikes or school – that pushed me to prowl strange pavements, even in heavy rain. I would spend hours and hours, following my feet, trying to get away from the nasty feeling of sadness, a live thing with claws, always lurking behind my back. Sometimes an ambulance would flash past, howling, and I would think of my mother. Mostly I would just follow my feet until the rain came down too hard, soaking my head and driving me into some doorway to wait for it to finish smacking the pavements. I loitered to examine the rubble on Parkfield Street where our old house used to stand. The walls had crumpled under the swing of a bulldozer while neighbours clapped and cheered.

My mother collared me one Saturday evening, while she was getting ready to go out.

'Your Auntie Agnes says she spotted you down Kippax Street last week when you should've been at school.'

'Really?' I looked mystified, before clouds cleared: 'It must've been the day I went to the dental hospital.' (I did make trips to the dental hospital now and then. One of my teeth was growing sideways out of the gum.)

'You've not been wagging it, have you?'

If my mother had looked me in the eye, I might have said yes. She could spade out the truth when she wanted to.

'Interfering old cow, that Agnes.' My mother glanced at her watch, rushing to finish her hair. 'I knew she was just trying to stir it.'

I gagged the part of me aching to sort things out, and let her get on with what made her happy.

School holidays put a nice easy end to truanting. Our mother came home in the mornings and spent most of the day in the back yard, sprawled on a towel to catch the sun, listening to Piccadilly Radio. Her feet jiggled to Chaka Khan and Cameo, fell limp for Bananarama and Fun Boy Three – a bunch of tone-deaf pansies, as far as she was concerned. 'Wherever I Lay My Hat (That's My Home)'. She smiled and mouthed the words when throaty Paul Young oozed out. Smeared in margarine, she roasted herself like a chicken, the oven timer set for fifteen minutes. *Drring!* Shifting into a new, painful-looking position, she spread her legs and arms so that there would be no pale patches at the end of the day. Laurie and I wondered at all the work it took to be a woman. We lay beside her, rolling over at exactly the same time, turning browner and browner by the hour. Our mother laughed and called us fingers of fudge. Strangers in the street called us wogs.

Autumn came and made the streets blustery. I went to school more often, finishing homework on the bus and during breaks, scooping merit marks to balance out demerits for bad attendance. At night, Laurie and Sarah played Ping-Pong at the youth club I was too old for. Waiting for them to come home, I peeled potatoes for tea. One spud each, boiled and mashed with a dash of margarine and an avalanche of salt.

'Why can't we have chips, like Mum makes?' Sarah demanded. 'Why's it always toast or mashed potatoes?'

So the next night, I tried doing chips.

'This is the same as mashed potato,' Laurie moaned when I lifted the basket out of the deep fat fryer and dumped pale, soggy chips on to our plates: 'Only ten million times greasier.'

We scraped them into the bin and resorted to toast.

But on the third night, everything went like a dream. The lard eased into liquid gold, its temper building up over the blast of blue flames. Just as it was seething, I dunked the chopped potatoes, daring them to spit in my face. I eased down the flame and stood over them, resisting the urge to lift the basket until they had all grown crispy coats. They came out glowing, as if they were lit up from inside.

'Ten out of ten.' Laurie and Sarah set to with salt and vinegar, and stopped whining for our mother instead of me.

I broke the rule about keeping the door locked after dark, the night Wendy came to call.

'Thought you might feel like coming out.' The nose of one winklepicker twisted to nuzzle the other. 'Seeing's it's Saturday night.'

'Where to?'

'Platt Fields Park.'

'Can I bring my sisters?' It seemed cruel to abandon them to *3-2-1* and the soul-sinking dread of Dusty Bin.

'Forgerrit.' She took squeaking puffs at her cigarette, which seemed to have gone out.

'Okay,' I said. 'Wait there.'

To keep warm, I put on both of my vests under my school jumper: my ancient anorak and home-made cardigans were out of the question.

'Don't open the door to anyone.' I found myself using my mother's words on Laurie and Sarah: 'Not a soul. Promise?'

We hung on swings and trudged miles around and around the pond. When the rain threatened to make Wendy's spiky hair droop, we huddled beneath the burnt-out bandstand or in the huge concrete drains that tunnelled under the grass. The shadows were alive down there: young lads doing stuff with drugs; older men loitering alone; couples letting off gurgly moans and gasps. I could sense Wendy's excitement as we moved around in the murk, while I was trying not to get my socks splashed by the filthy gloop underfoot. I didn't tell her how frightened I felt: part of me was thrilled, but a much bigger part was terrified by the underground drains, whose darkness made you free to do anything – absolutely anything at all. I was glad when the rain cleared up and we took to the paths above ground, where there were more people about, and nobody seemed so strange.

Two girls alone: it was as if we were smeared in a kind of glue that made lads stick to us wherever we went.

'What's yer name?' the ugly ones leered.

The ones with decent faces didn't want to know when they saw that I was quite flat-chested, while Wendy had a horrid gap between her two front teeth. 'Giz a cig,' they pestered her, pinching her bum until she giggled and gave in. Then they scooted off into the shadows of the trees.

'At this rate,' she despaired over her empty fag packet, 'we'll get our pensions before we get our first snogs.'

I spotted the boathouse clock in the dark. 'I'd better be getting back,' I said.

I had a habit of making up rules and pretending (even to myself) that they had been imposed on me. I didn't like the idea that the night could go on and on, with nothing to make me go home.

'My mum'll kill me if I'm not back when she gets in at half ten,' I told Wendy. My heart turned over, in love with my own lie.

'Aw.' Wendy was itching to stay out until midnight, when her parents came home blinded by whisky, deafened by singing and bawling at the Irish Catholic club. 'But we were just about to cop off; I could feel it in my bones.'

It was a Wednesday night, after nine o'clock, when my teeth clashed with a lad's.

'What was yours like?' Wendy was eager to get out of the park afterwards to swap grisly details. We sauntered down

Withington Road, past Indian restaurants and shop windows piled high with glistening, sickly-sweet treats.

'I wish I'd stuck to snogging pillows.' I couldn't believe I had wasted my lips on someone shorter than me, and that our teeth had actually gone clunk. 'It was like trying to kiss a washing machine, tongues sloshing and everything.'

'It's supposed to be like that.' Wendy put another match to her cigarette, which was forever dying on her.

'*And* he stank like an ashtray.' I wondered how I was going to snog any more boys, since they would all have smoky breath. We came to the croft littered with bottles and cans, needles and condoms. No streetlights to show up faces: you were invisible, even to yourself.

'Here.' After weeks of saying no, I took a cigarette from Wendy's pack and propped it between my lips: 'Light us up, will you?'

I puckered to suck with all my might the moment the flame tickled the tobacco. Something smacked inside my forehead. The sky breathed in and out: a huge, dark purple lung.

'Wicked!' Wendy shook her head as I let smoke cruise out through my nose. 'You can really inhale.' She looked at her own cigarette, as if to blame it for her shallow puffs.

A party started in my heart, lungs and head.

After stopping off at Wendy's, stealing a squirt of her big brother's aftershave to douse the smell of smoke in my mouth, I hurried home to catch the last bit of *Dynasty*. Tonight, instead of glazing my face in front of the telly, watching the stations close down one by one, waiting, in case my mother should turn up, I went to bed at the same time as my sisters.

'Night, Andy.' Sarah was getting used to sleeping in her own bed, rather than cuddling in my bunk.

'Night.' In the dark, the air was alive with lips, tongues, teeth and smoke.

The boy's face wavered inside my eyelids. Narrow, no-colour eyes under brows knitting together in the middle, blackheads nestling in the hairs. I swayed into sleep, and dreamed of fish in the sea.

12

On Tuesday morning, Wendy and I met at the bus stop opposite the Manchester City training ground, where we treated ourselves to a good gander at the famous legs while we waited for the 47. Muscles bulged in unexpected places as the players squatted and jumped, thrusting hands and feet, making starfish in the air.

'Got your civvies?' Wendy wasn't shy about changing out of her school uniform in front of strangers on the top deck of the bus.

Instead of schoolbooks, my bag was stuffed with jeans and a green polo-neck from the Save the Children charity shop. The jeans had been flares when I bought them for 30p, but now they were do-it-yourself drainpipes, gnawing my skin when I walked. They forced me to sit down like an invalid, legs sticking out as if they were in plaster. Every night, while the late film droned, I attacked the denim with a needle, stitching over and over where my home-made seams had popped open after some unavoidable movement around the knee.

'Jesus, Mary and cunt-faced Joseph!' Wendy sweated into her own skintight cords, letting off words that had led to her suspension from Saint Mary's School, where her behaviour turned the nuns blue. 'Ah, fuck it.' She pulled down her jumper to cover the zip when it refused to fasten over her belly. Exploding at every swerve in the road, she glared at the grown-ups who turned round to frown at her language: 'Want a bleedin' picture?'

We got off in Piccadilly Square and passed through the doors of Lewis's, where Wendy's curses dissolved in the perfumed air. She told me to wait in the lingerie department while she wandered around the make-up counters. In five minutes she was back, ushering me out, back on to Piccadilly Square, where she shoved me to belt it for the bus.

'Is that it?' I had wagged it to come all the way into town, risking being spotted by someone who knew me, only to step in and out of Lewis's. And, in the run for the bus, the seams of my drainpipes had burst again.

'Shurrup, I've got you a prezzie.' Wendy grinned, fidgeting on the front seat of the top deck.

'Cop a load of that!' Three lipsticks, two eyeshadows and a tube of foundation appeared from up her sleeves and out of her knickers. 'Not bad, eh? Here, that one's for you.'

My fingers closed around a golden bullet. Lipstick; magenta.

'You should keep it.' I dropped it back into her palm. 'It's yours.'

'Look.' She held it up. 'D'you want it or don't you?'

My fingertips strayed to my lips. I saw my mother's face, twisted with disgust because I had done something dirty. But by the time we reached Rusholme, my cheeks and eyes were glowing to match my mouth. Lipstick wasn't just for lips, Wendy insisted. Instead of kicking around the park, I went straight home to make the most of my face before Laurie and Sarah came in from school. I buzzed between the bathroom, my mother's bedroom and the kitchen, examining myself in different mirrors and lights, before rubbing it all off and burying the lipstick in a sock in my drawer.

*

Our mother came home with a face that had been crying. She hung her fur jacket under plastic and spent the day knocking back coffee by the pint.

'What's up, Mum?' I fetched the ashtray, then boiled the kettle time and time again.

'Men.' My mother started on her cigarettes, stubbing them out with a passion: 'Men.'

'What about them?' I asked.

She hung her head in her hands: 'They're all the bloody same.'

That night, the Jag didn't come to pick her up. I thought I spotted a tiny mark under my mother's eyebrow, cherry-coloured and almost pretty, while I sat next to her in her bedroom, watching her put on her face to go round to Auntie Tamara's for a tipple. I gave her a meaningful look in the mirror.

'I walked into a door.' She dusted her eyelids with pearly grey shadow: 'I don't know how I could have been so stupid.'

Walked into a door. It was what she used to mutter, with a grim smile, to her closest friends when things were going wrong in the old days.

Walked into a door? I felt sure she would tell me more if I pushed it; I even imagined she wanted me to ask, so she could let it all out. But I felt sick at the thought that someone other than our stepfather could hit my mother. It made the batterings seem more scary, as if they were not confined to one horrible man, but had – in some way I didn't want to delve into – more to do with her. I looked away from the mirror while she concentrated on her make-up, putting the finishing touches to her face.

*

Christmas was coming and our mother's purse was getting fat: in the run-up to the festive season, her catalogue commissions had rocketed. She let my sisters and me comb through the catalogue to compile wish-lists.

'I'm not promising anything, don't forget!' She tried to stick a stern face over her playful one, alive with secrets and plans. 'I don't want you kids ending up spoiled.'

A pair of purple suede winklepickers, a 32A bra, blue legwarmers and a palette of pastel eyeshadows glowed among the tangerines and chocolates scattered across the carpet on Christmas morning. I finally had what it took to be a teenager.

'Aw, Mum.' The splurge of presents left Laurie and me stuck for words. Sarah was torn between plastering everyone's cheeks in kisses, and tucking into her selection box.

'Just some little daft nonsenses.' Our mother tried to hide her pride at having got everything right. She mixed pink wine with lemonade and handed us a glass each, while she sipped her own, stronger version at the stove. Standing by with dishcloths and towels, Laurie and I cleaned pans, spatulas and spoons so that there would be hardly any left to worry about when we sat down to our roast potatoes and chicken. On the record player, Val Doonican's Christmas album was whirling, with spurts of Johnny Matthis and Diana Ross to clear the air in between.

Our mother wore a red tissue crown, unfolded from the crackers we pulled before clinking glasses: 'All for one, and one for all!'

My hand shook when I lifted my glass to my mouth. Life was so good, it made me nervous. Elastic dug in around my rib cage; cotton wool nestled inside my first bra. Toes throbbing, my feet were in winklepickers at last. We were going to spend Boxing Day with Gran, whose gallstones had been removed with no complications. To top it all, our mother was floating on air again.

The gold Jag had finally appeared again one night, and she had agreed to go out for a quick spin, sloping back in the next morning with a big, clumsily wrapped box. Inside was a face-steamer that she plugged in and bowed over for ages, coming up looking dreamy. After that, the man in the car had picked her up for a few more dates, always dropping her back before midnight. She would tiptoe in humming to herself, before settling in to her bed, where I woke her with coffee and toast in the morning.

'Oh, bloody Nora!' Our mother lifted a lid to find that the Christmas pudding had shrivelled and burnt because the saucepan had boiled dry. For a moment, it looked like she might cry. My sisters and I glanced at each other, afraid of the day being wrecked by one of her mood storms. But then she clanged the top off our tin of fancy biscuits. We had won them in the door-to-door raffle for the blind, she reminded herself aloud, so they had to be a good omen.

'This is more like it!' We swirled shortbread in the white sauce meant for the pudding, feeling guilty, as if we were cheating.

On New Year's Eve we had the same chicken dinner, only without the crackers, and with sherry trifle for afters. Val Doonican had been shoved back in the loft for another year; Frank Sinatra was having his turn.

'1983' – our mother spent the afternoon sipping tea with a whisper of whisky, which made her remember us as babes in arms. She kept sighing the same happy-sad sigh: 'Where have all the years gone, eh?'

She lay on the settee, stoking herself up for the evening. A few friends had promised to come round with bottles of bubbly to see the new year in with a bang.

'You'll be meeting someone special tonight,' she murmured

while she was tickling her lashes with mascara: 'His name's Terry.'

Our mother carried on with her face while Laurie, Sarah and I nursed mince pies, crammed with questions we didn't dare ask.

We knew it was him, as soon as he walked through the door, looking more alive than anyone else. Except our mother, whose dimples deepened the moment his hands landed on her waist. Rainie, he called her. She put up her hand to touch one of his strawberry-blond curls. Black nylon flares swished over Cuban heels that made him a shade taller than her. A ruffle of white rippled down his shirt, smelling of Old Spice. On the little finger of his left hand, a lump of gold nestled behind the knuckle.

Our mother nudged us to say hello.

'Are you Terry?' I felt myself drowning in waves of shyness.

Above a too-big nose, his eyes twinkled, blue kaleidoscopes.

'Aye. But why don't you kids call me Tez?'

'Tez.' We tried it out between ourselves in the kitchen, passing it over our tongues until we could say it without giggling.

By midnight, watching him swivel his hips to James Brown, dancing brilliantly for a man, we were ready to say it to his face. Someone turned up the telly while Big Ben chimed and everyone cheered. Our mother had tears in her eyes. We clustered to kiss her before the bells stopped clanging, but she turned to kiss Terry first. A real, film-style kiss, that took up their whole faces.

'Happy New Year, girls,' Terry said, after the bells rang out.

Our mother stole a moment from smooching to hug us and send us to bed: 'Time to let the grown-ups get on with the show.'

We sank into our pillows, knocked out by the scent of Old Spice mingling with Chanel No.5.

When Terry turned up for breakfast in his ruffly shirt, nobody batted an eyelid. His face looked puffy, but we liked him as much as the night before. More, because he fried French toast to start off the new year. Our mother wanted to help out in the kitchen, but Terry was having none of it.

'Sit tight, Rainie.' He flourished elbows and fingers over the frying pan, like a chef off the telly.

'Can you fix our tape recorder?' Sarah asked him after breakfast.

'Shh!' Our mother gave the back of her hand a light slap. 'Don't be mithering Terry now.' But he insisted on looking at the tape recorder, unscrewing the case to peer at the chaos inside.

'Scalpel.' He stuck out his hand for a screwdriver, then fastened the box back together. Opening the plug, he winked at our mother, then fiddled with the wires.

'I think you'll find the patient's fully recovered.'

Sarah pressed PLAY and our home-recorded songs crackled back to life. She beamed, while Laurie and I blushed. *A little loving, a little giving* – the three of us had wailed to make a tape for our mother, Laurie strumming on a guitar borrowed from school – *to build a dream for the world we live in.*

Our mother tried to switch it off, but Terry persuaded her to let the song play to the end while he stroked her hands. When it had finished, Sarah smacked his face with a wet kiss. He looked at his watch, gave his gold ring a quick twizzle, then reached for his double-breasted jacket. Our mother went out for a goodbye hug in his car.

'He's not very tall, is he?' Laurie voiced my own misgiving.

Our mother caught us discussing him when she came back in to wash the plates.

'Diamonds don't come as big as bricks.' She smiled to herself over the sink.

We were actually inside the gold Jag, stroking the leather seats, sticking our fingers down foamy holes where they were falling apart. The engine sputtered and cut out.

'Only the umpteenth time,' our mother muttered. We hadn't moved from outside our house. She wound down the window to shout to Terry, whose head was under the bonnet: 'We can always go another time, love.'

He emerged, a warstripe of oil smeared across his nose: 'We're off!'

'Okay, darling.' Terry carressed the steering wheel, sliding the key into the ignition: 'Do it for me, Sugar.'

The engine sputtered again, then purred.

'Yes!' He kissed the middle of the steering wheel, then grabbed our mother's hand to kiss that too, springing her smile back into place.

The seats finally vibrated beneath us. Our street melted away.

The Jag chugged and coughed more than we had expected from its golden outsides. It broke down on the motorway, where we were happy to sit in the layby, nibbling salmon paste butties, making moo-noises at the cows on the grassy slope, while Terry got out to sweet-talk the engine.

It was pitch black by the time we hit the main road of Blackpool, strung with necklaces of light. Terry made us pelt along the beach, where the waves heaved like beasts in the dark. Tasting the sea on our faces, we came back to the promenade. Lights pummelled, arcades buzzed, hooted and rang.

'Here.' Terry changed fifteen pounds into tuppennies and pennies: 'Go mad, why don't you?'

Loaded with coppers, we forgot about our mother and him and the rest of the world. Laurie, Sarah and I stationed ourselves around a penny cascade, where we slid in coin after coin and pressed our foreheads against glass, willing the copper shelf to collapse and crash out a fortune. No more than five or six pennies ever clattered into the silver jaw.

'I think some of them are glued down.' Laurie gave up and started on the one-armed bandits, which spat coins back at her although she didn't understand the spinning symbols. She yanked down the knob, waited for oranges, cherries and horseshoes to whirl into line, then stooped to scrape up her winnings. Clutching her last handful of coins, Sarah took off to the shooting gallery, to watch Terry teaching our mother how to hit moving targets. He spent the night hugging her from behind, training the barrel and pressing her finger against the trigger, blasting holes through a cardboard heart.

I stuck to my place on the cascades, besotted. My coins clanged down the metal chutes along the side. Five whole pounds, frittered into pennies, washed down the drain. I looked at my empty money bag, which had been bulging to start with. My mother would be shocked. But it had been worth it for the rollercoaster in my chest.

After Blackpool, Terry stayed at our house more and more often. Breakfast became a party. When he wasn't there, our mother looked at the world through grey glasses, seeing only things to gripe about. We had to wait for him to roll up in the evenings before her softer side would come out. He sometimes stayed for no time at all, rushing away in the dark, leaving her with a twitchy face. Other times, he came round loaded with groceries to show off his cooking skills, calling himself Gordon Blur. Amazing things simmered in our pans. We lifted the lid on pork curry, spaghetti bolognaise à la Tez, or his own special concoction called pepper pot, then came away wearing the flavoured steam on our faces. Tea-time came later and lasted longer on Terry nights. He wrenched the cork out of a bottle of purply wine, while our mother played his favourite album, by Barry White. We enjoyed songs stuffed with sexy groans, women dribbling harmonies over the man's meaty voice.

Later, approaching midnight, he would often rush off after a shot of whisky and a round of kisses from us all. He never mentioned where he was going, but our mother crinkled her forehead, hugging him as if it might be the last time. Other nights, he told her there was nothing doing, eased off his Cuban boots and cracked open a can of lager to play cards. Gambling matchsticks, he instructed Laurie, Sarah and me to keep our mugs straight if we wanted to be poker sharks.

'There's someone cheating in this here game, and it don't do to name the guy,' Terry drawled through loose lips, swigging lager in loud glugs. *'But if I catch him cheatin' just one more time'* – cocking the trigger of an imaginary gun – *'I'll close his other eye.'*

Real milk crept into our tea. Ketchup and jam turned up in the cupboard, along with Salad Cream and Branston pickle. Our mother was no longer afraid to treat herself to half a pound of White Cheshire cheese when she had the urge. Along the window ledge in her bedroom, bottles bloomed: Chanel No. 5, Chanel No. 19, Fenjal bath oil, almond body lotion, a rainbow of nail varnishes.

But, better than all the perfume in the world, Laurie, Sarah and I were blessed with a colour TV.

'I don't like it.' Our mother tried to stop Terry from hauling it out of his Jag. 'It doesn't feel right.'

'It's for the kids.' He plugged it in, then rubbed the small of her back. 'Where's the harm, eh?'

'I just don't like it.' She gnawed the pad of her thumb.

'What does Tez actually do?' I asked, when my mother and I were cruising, alone, in the gold Jag. It was my honour to help her with the shopping while he was having a lie-in and Laurie and Sarah were at Auntie Tamara's.

'You could say he's in the oil business.' She kept her gaze on the traffic.

'What, as in *Dallas* and J.R.?'

My mother gave a bitter chuckle. 'As in filling motors at a gas station, more like.'

I pictured Terry pulling petrol in one of his wing-collared or ruffly shirts. 'He makes all that money as a petrol pump attendant?'

'Not quite.' My mother's face tightened into a sneer as she wrestled with the gear stick. 'He's got a few' – the gears crunched – 'private sidelines.'

Backing into a space, she parked like a dream, although she trembled to twist the wheel.

'All those years not driving,' she muttered, and flexed her fingers to stop them from shaking.

I sensed something was up when I saw that it wasn't Kwik Save. Breath snagged in my windpipe: my first step inside Asda.

'Even the air smells posh,' I found myself whispering to my mother in the aisles. Kwik Save smelled of the weather, tramped in off the streets by tired and sweaty human beings.

'Shh.' She didn't want to be distracted. I watched her lifting boxes, packets and tins, contemplating the picture on the package, not bothering to look for the price.

Do I want this? her face seemed to be asking itself, instead of the usual: *Can we afford it?*

It was as if we were shopping for another family. Tins of tuna, frozen steak and kidney pies, Jaffa Cakes, Colgate toothpaste, grainy brown bread, Weetabix, Country Life butter, ice-cream. Even yoghurt, which my sisters and I had never tried. What looked like a lifetime's supply of Tampax and Kleenex toilet rolls piled up on top of the food. By the time we wheeled the trolley to the check-out, my fingers were trembling as much as my mother's. I tucked them in fists under my jumper and put on the poker face Terry had taught me, determined to look like someone born to trundle out with a mountain of luxuries.

My mother bent to write in a green cheque book. Beneath her clear lacquered nails, a signature swirled. Whatever name it was, it wasn't hers.

We filled the boot and the back seat with Asda bags. The sight of them, brimming with food that would last for ages, set off laughter in my belly. My mother slammed into the front seat, blinking back tears as she looked into the rearview mirror. For a moment I thought she was going to say something. I crossed my fingers. *Don't tell me.* I wanted to enjoy the stuff in the bags.

My mother breathed out, got a grip on the steering wheel, and turned to look me in the eye: 'Don't ask.'

*

Blaupunkt. I inspected the logo on our wide-screened, colour TV, while *Coronation Street* washed over us all.

'It's German' – Terry lay along the settee, our mother wrapped in his arms – 'for blue spot.' This made me feel much happier about our new television. If, just if, there was something dodgy about how it found its way into our front room, there was no need to feel guilty. The Germans had done horrendous things in the past; history was evening itself out.

History was cast aside when Terry turned up with a video machine and buckets of Butterkist popcorn to go with *Raiders of the Lost Ark, E.T., Police Academy* or *Airplane.* Films and tasty food made us feel like a real family. So what, if it involved cutting a few corners behind the world's back? All the ladies who dropped round for tea or coffee, whisky or rum seemed to believe the same: it was downright daft, they assured our mother when she expressed her qualms about the good life, to worry too much. Everyone was on the fiddle, one way or another, weren't they? Adjusting the mileage, spraying used cars to sell them; fibbing about tax; buying clothes, tellies and stereos off the back of a lorry; signing on the dole and working at the same time.

'Mug's game, fretting is.' Auntie Livia, hardened by years of Uncle Max's wheeling and dealing, seemed to have it all worked out: 'You've got to rob Peter to pay Paul, these days. And why not fly by the seat of your pants, eh? At least you'll get somewhere that way.'

On Friday nights, I slathered on lipstick and eyeshadow to fetch our tea from the chippy, next to the bus stop where lads lurked in padded anoraks that swallowed them up but seemed to make them feel big. I teetered in my winklepickers through a tunnel of whistles and stares, suffering the odd pinch. Often, Wendy was there, lapping up filthy compliments, even letting lads fondle the curves under her own Michelin Man anorak.

'It's only the lips that mean owt,' she informed me, when I wondered why she let them touch her up: 'The other bits don't count.'

'So why d'you kiss the real dogfaces, then, like Martin or that scuzzy one, Darren?'

'I do it, missy prissy' – Wendy thought I was too squeamish for my own good – 'for the snog, not the lad. I'm getting in practice, like, for Mr Right, and you should do the same, if you don't want to be left on the shelf.'

I had chosen not to go beyond my first toothy collision. The lad I had snogged was fresh out of Borstal, as I discovered when he landed himself back inside by trying to steal yet another car. Now I was determined to wait until I found a mouth attached to somebody nice.

Wendy rolled her eyes. 'Coming out after?' she asked, when we emerged from the chippy.

'Not sure.' I looked at her, surrounded by lads with haircuts like accidents, smoking under the bus shelter to protect gelled fringes from drizzle. Battered cod, scampi and chips steamed through newspaper in my hands. 'I will if I can, like.'

I hurried home, before too much of the vinegary heat could escape.

Boys were fine to read about in magazines like *Just Seventeen*. Sometimes, in the bath or in bed at night, the thought of them would give me a terrific ache in my middle, prickling up to my chest and oozing down towards my legs. Face to face, however, they were never worth the sweat. Not the ones I had bumped into in the park, at school, or on the back of the bus with Wendy. Besides – the *Rocky* theme tune was revving up as I stepped through our front door – you didn't need boys if you had a video.

Evenings melted into weeks and months: I soaked up movies, sitcoms and soap operas; played rummy and Scrabble with my sisters; and devoured the dirtiest, most shocking bits out of well-thumbed and stained paperbacks. The spotty male assistant let me take them from the crime-and-thriller rack at Fallowfield library, although I was well under the required age of sixteen. I picked out books with more and more outrageous covers – women's legs in lacy garters and high heels; rope in the shape of a hangman's noose; blood trickling between a pair of breasts, a hunting knife gleaming in the background; finally axes and chainsaws – always bracing myself for some alarm to go off. But the lad would just smile at me, glance down to stamp the books, then look up and smile again, lips quivering slightly while his eyes gunned straight into mine.

Homework was the only blot on the horizon. I would get the urge to do it while I was crashed out on my stomach in front of the telly – when it was impossible to peel myself up and do something about it, no matter how boring the programme. In the middle of *The A Team*, for example, or when *Miami Vice* was crawling with greasy-haired guys instead of gorgeous girls. Cars zoomed and exploded, trucks toppled over cliffs, men hurtled from skyscraper windows, while sticky maths problems or bits of biology floated behind my eyes. Chlorophyll, stomata, sunlight: I anticipated the smiles I would win from my biology teacher if only I could drag myself away from the telly to draw the diagrams properly, upstairs on my bed, instead of rushing them over breakfast and on the top deck of the bus. And yet I could see no reason to pull up my socks, since answers seemed to come out sharper at the last minute, while my scruffy pages kept me cool in the eyes of kids who ruled the roost from the back rows.

Terry moved in with his Spanish guitar, which loitered about like another person: dressed up with pearly tuning keys, carved wooden flourishes across its belly, it leaned against the wall, just waiting for the right moment to strut its stuff. He spent hours playing Latiny love music for our mother, his fingers plucking and stroking a wordless serenade.

Life was one long smiling honeymoon. The two of them radiated a happiness that felt hot. A disagreement might bubble up, a squirt of jealousy could sour the air, but then the phone or doorbell would ring and they would dissolve their differences in other people. Ladies caked in glittery make-up or drooping sad eyes under stale perms, men with fantastic tattoos beneath overalls or pinstriped suits: the whole world seemed drawn to our door, turning up with dramatic news, heartbreaking problems or some sale-of-the-century deal. It was hard to remember the nights when my sisters and I had been left alone until dawn, sometimes missing our mother for days on end. Now our house was brimming with drink and smoky, loud-mouthed opinions that clashed with common sense when you stopped to think, but sounded colourful and brilliant while they were being spurted over a lager by one or another of Tez's mates.

I was sprawled on my bed, steaming through my fourth Stephen King book, *Carrie*, lapping up all the gore and shuddery, headbending stuff, when my mother and Terry came in from a ride in the car and stormed upstairs to their bedroom. Instead of the usual honeybee buzzing behind the door, their voices were waspy and stinging.

'Relax,' I heard Terry muttering, before resorting to the phrase he had picked up from a posh bloke he met in prison, where – he let spill while he was boozing with Uncle Lenny – he had made a brief visit years ago, for breaking and entering.

'*Carpy diem.*'

Laurie and I squeezed it into any sentence that would take it. It was Latin for 'seize the day', Terry told us.

'*Carpy diem*,' my mother lectured him as if he were one of us kids, 'is not the same as *carpy* other people's gear.'

There was a tight moment of quiet, before Terry carried on:

'Look, Jimmy and me, we never do anyone who's got nowt. These geezers are insured up to their eyeballs.' You could hear nerves twanging in the flow: 'Nobody loses out, that's the beauty of it. What do you take me for, Rainie?'

'I just don't want to lose you.' My mother's words turned soggy, sliding into a kiss: 'I don't want to lose you, yer daft bugger.'

We thought he was teasing when he talked about selling his car. Tez wouldn't be Tez without his gold Jag to go with the ring on his little finger and the gold filling in his broken tooth. We hung our heads and climbed in for one last cruise around the block, before the new owner came to take it away.

'She sounded dead posh on the phone,' I told Laurie and Sarah. Our jaws sagged when she turned up: a tiny old lady, shaky patches of rouge, lipstick that hadn't stayed within the lines of her lips.

'Are you sure you'll be able to manage the gears, love?' Terry had to crank the seat forward, until it was practically touching the steering wheel.

She clicked the press studs on black leather gloves. The bonnet of gold glided away, not a sputter or clank.

'That *cannot* be our new motor.' Laurie and I stood on the doorstep, staring darkly at a blue Mazda pick-up truck. Our mother had put her finger on it in the *Exchange and Mart.*

'Start of a new era,' she declared. Terry was going to make use of his building skills, from bricklaying to carpentry and window glazing; she would be his mate on the bigger jobs. There wasn't a tool he could ask for, without our mother plucking it straight out of his oily crate.

We peered into the cabin, big enough for only one extra person, two at a push, beside the driver.

'Where are us kids supposed to sit?' Laurie asked Terry, when he came out to look at the truck, as if he were trying to get used to it too.

'Right here.' He pointed to the open-air back. 'I'm going to stick up a metal frame and strap on a hood of tarpaulin, like. Bit of foam wrapped in placky to keep your bums dry, stop your bones from rattling: Bob's your uncle.'

Terry chose the night of our first trip to make an announcement: 'Your mam thought you might want to start calling me Dad.' A blush, the colour of raspberry jam, spread over his face. 'It's all right with me, like, either way. What d'you reckon?'

Any sulks about the new travel arrangements were washed away in a tide of *Dad*s.

Our mother buckled up in the cabin, while we clung to the frame at the back. Rain lashed the tarpaulin; not a drop got in. We could see our mother through the glass, smoking with Terry. Our Dad. Occasionally, she would twiddle the knob of the radio on the dashboard, then turn round to give us a grin.

The two of them raised their eyebrows and pointed, acting surprised to find us still there, while we made faces as if we were hanging on for dear life.

It was ten o'clock at night. Sale Water Park. The gates had been locked at nine, according to the sign.

'Where's your blummin' imaginations?' Terry wanted to know, when the four of us groaned and got ready to pile back into the truck.

He hoisted us over the railings.

'Mum?' Sarah's voice wobbled in the dark.

A croak came from something not human, followed by a magnificent plop. Laurie and I strangled giggles. Creeping along the edge of the lake, we followed our new dad, who kept scurrying ahead, disappearing in the shadow of reeds.

'Terry?' Our mother's voice turned as shaky as Sarah's: 'Terry, love, where are you?'

I squealed when my shoe squelched off in the mud, sparking a chorus of yelps as the others panicked and ran away. My purple winklepicker was left behind in the rush to get to the gates, where Terry was flashing the truck's headlights and making the engine growl.

'What kept you?' He laughed over our furious faces: 'I was just about to take off.'

The summer holidays zipped by, propelled by midnight jaunts that brought us home muddy and breathless and no longer afraid of the world, the way we used to feel when it was just our mother and us.

'Who's for a spot of pointing?' During the day, Terry sometimes took us on one of his jobs. We swelled with pride, watching him mend walls and put up fences.

He rolled the song 'Chain Gang' – around in his chest, while Laurie, Sarah and I made clinking-clanking noises under our tongues.

On the way home, he would drive slowly past certain houses, to let us admire a porch he had helped to build or a wall he had pointed.

Dad. I looked at the bricks, held together with mortar scraped in painstaking lines, and thought, *Dad.*

It was always cash in hand. Our dad's nails were dirty now that he had turned to his spanners, hammer and trowel, but the money seemed fresher when he pulled it out of his back pocket. Once, he forgot to empty his jeans before shoving them into the wash, giving Laurie and me the thrill of our lives. We stood over our twin tub, plucking clothes out of the bubbles to shove them in for a rinse and spin. Tens and twenties mingled with socks.

'Dad!' We hollered when the Queen's face rippled in the suds.

'Laundered money!' Tickled by his own joke, he called our mother to come and see.

She offered to iron the notes dry, but our dad had a better idea. Our mother shook her head when he pegged the notes along the washing line in the back yard. 'You're not all there, yer daft ignoramus!'

We told him that things were often nabbed off the line, even knickers and bras.

'San Fairy Anne,' he shrugged.

Laurie and Sarah were awestruck; they stood next to the kitchen window, eyes pinned on the money, waiting for robbers in balaclavas to leap over our back wall. For a while, my tummy fluttered too, watching the notes on the breeze. Eventually, I had to go outside, to be ready in case any blew loose. I saw a twitch in the bedroom curtains, where our dad was keeping his own eye out.

'Dad's a cheat!'

The notes were unpegged and laid on top of the gas fire, leaving us giggling, trying to hide our disappointment. Our dad might act like a daredevil, but he was only human after all.

'It's A Man's World'. Dad was wiggling at the stove, steak sizzling in the pan. 'Papa's Got A Brand New Bag'.

Word of mouth had won him some red-hot contracts. When people wanted a porch or a new front door, they knew that our dad was the man for the job. The sky – he looked up each time he said it – was the limit.

'Get On the Good Foot'. He did a fancy shuffle in his new cowboy boots, grabbing our mother to spin her under his arm. 'I Got You (I Feel Good)'.

The doorbell rang. My mother passed me a five-pound note and the slip full of crosses for the man who came to collect the money for the Football Pools.

'Your dad in?' Four blokes stood outside the door. Leather jackets, donkey coats, jeans.

'I couldn't stop them,' I told my dad, when they strolled into the kitchen, showing off badges, waving a warrant. The needle scratched to shut up James Brown. My mother snuffed the gas under the frying pan.

'All right, Terry?' The most handsome of the men laid his walkie-talkie on the table and sat down. 'Time to talk.'

When they had searched our bedroom, Laurie, Sarah and I were sent upstairs. We locked ourselves in the bathroom, where we fastened our ears to the floor to keep up with what was going on in the kitchen. The man's voice droned. Dates, names of blokes that we recognized, lists of expensive, plug-in things. *Spare the bullshit* – words leapt through the floorboards here and there, as if he were speaking to us – *you know the score.*

Our mother knocked on the bathroom door.

'Come and say goodbye to your dad.'

Sweat had mushroomed under his arms. The silver threads on his shirt looked grey.

'See you later.' He ruffled each of our crowns. Someone read him his rights.

'You don't need those.' He looked ready to cry when handcuffs came out. 'You can't do this to me. Not in front of me kids.'

'Should've thought of them before,' one of the officers sneered.

The handcuffs meant that he couldn't wave. We tried to catch his eye through the window of the red Volvo, but his face had fallen off.

The car skimmed down the street.

His neck shrank to a pink dot.

Our mother let out a shriek like a firework, bursting sobs that exploded sobs, finally quietening into tears.

13

*I*m' *not a bluddy animmal,* he wrote in his first letter from
Strangeways Prison. Our mother read bits out to Auntie
Livia, chuckling on the verge of tears at his Technicolor
spelling, which made him sound too innocent to be in jail.
*There were too other fellers squoshed in his sell. One coud'nt stop
hiting the other. He got a black eye him self, becos it was hard not
to get in the way, like. They strech saifty nets, to catch any bloak
throne over the rales. Rainie* . . . The rest she kept to herself.

We were supposed to be looked after by our dad's mates. Eddie
dropped round with a frozen chicken; Jack brought a bottle of
wine that he drained himself; they sometimes slipped a note,
tightly rolled, into our mother's hands. Too polite to inspect
it under their noses, she kept it clenched in her fist until she
had closed the door behind them, securing the chain, sliding
every bolt across.

'Five quid!' Our mother let off steam on the phone to
Auntie Livia: 'Five flamin' quid, after everything he risked, and
not grassing them up!'

Our mother resolved not to tell our dad that his so-called
pals were taking us for a ride; it would only rattle him, and
there was precious little he could do while he was behind bars.
We were back on baked beans, went without jam and ketchup,
and got used to powdered milk again. Our mother scraped
together every spare penny to buy pouches of Old Holborn

tobacco for Dad. She loaded her head with heated rollers each morning, rehearsing her hairdo for her first prison visit, then sat down to write her daily letter to him, borrowing Sarah's felt tips to make the most of the margins, where she swirled love stuff in yellow and purple and pink. By the time we got home from school in the evenings, the letter had been posted and the curls had sagged with her mood.

Sarah, who had only just turned eight, was too young to visit prison, but Laurie and I, being twelve and fourteen, were allowed to bunk off school to join our mother in the cab of the truck. Dad had been transferred from Strangeways to Kirkham, near Preston, where there was something called an open prison. It was a long drive, but the dashboard radio and the spring day made the miles breeze by. Our mother frowned at the petrol gauge, watching the engine guzzle our food money.

'It's gorgeous!' Laurie and I could not believe the greenery unfurling in front of our eyes. We wound down the windows and breathed as if we were gulping water. Chugging through the village of Kirkham, our mother cooed over tiny shops clustered around an old square.

Only two minutes' drive from this quaintness, the prison belonged to another world. Our mother made us comb our hair while she livened up her own in the rear-view mirror. We had to line up in a concrete yard with women clutching kids, slapping them across the head, giving them an earful in flat accents. Some of the younger ones had done themselves up: hairspray and high heels. Stares made me look down at my chest, covered in lemon lambswool. My tank top, like Laurie's jumper, was from the Save the Children charity shop, but nobody would have guessed. These people thought we were posh.

A buzzer went off. We dribbled out of the sunshine into the waiting room, tight and airless as an armpit.

'Hawkins, Lorraine.' The warden left his scowl on his clipboard and came up with a greasy smile when he looked over and saw the face that went with the name. Laurie and I were 'plus two'.

We didn't need to be told that it was table 23; our dad's eyes were blue beacons. Wading into a sea of fellas and their families or lady friends, we took care not to brush the backs of chairs where kisses or arguments were in full swing. Some of the tables let off sparks: nasty electricity crackling between stormy-faced women and caged-looking men.

'Hiya, Dad.' He was wearing a shirt and workpants, made of dull and duller blues rather than jailhouse grey. No stripes or arrows. Our eyes raked his: if he had been to hell and back, they were not about to tell the tale. He fiddled in his trouser pockets to unloose a trickle of copper, then grinned at the odd flash of silver. Although it was only enough to buy toothpaste and a few cigs, he was paid a sort of wage for his labour as a carpenter, sanding new front doors all day. He laughed at the joke of his job: 'It'll teach me to enter people's houses the proper way, eh?'

Our mother wrestled the clasp of her purse and came up with a fifty pence piece. 'Why don't you fetch us all a brew?' She sent Laurie and me across the room to the boiler. We took our time filling the cups – knowing she was really thirsty not for tea, but for a few moments alone with our dad – then balanced the tray back across the dim hall. Light broke in dribs and drabs through bars across the windows.

'I've signed up to take the trumpet,' I told him when he asked what was new at school.

In the truck on the way, my head had rattled full of things I was dying to say to my dad. Now I was finding it hard to talk at all; my thoughts kept sliding back to the hole he had left behind him at home.

'And our Laurie's won yet another trophy for gymnastics.' Our mother chattered to keep things cheery. 'Haven't you, Laurie, love?'

The two of us sat behind cups of stewed tea, turning slimy on the surface, stale coconut biscuits abandoned in the saucers. We tried drinking, but it tasted of prison.

'You've not drank your tea.' Dad looked hurt.

So we sipped again, swallowing cold tea, and spent the rest of the hour peering over the rims of our cups at other kids. As soon as the bell rang, I wished I'd spent more time memorizing our dad's face.

'Don't be giving your mam grief, now, will yer?'

We promised to behave. Then we watched the wardens, who snatched away their eyes while our mum and dad had a long, chewy kiss. Our mother had folded a ten-pound note as small as it would go, and wrapped it in cling-film, so that she could have a little cough, pass it into her mouth, then smuggle it on to our dad's tongue.

'Bye!' She made sure to smile at all the guards.

Behind the prison lay fields where inmates tended vegetables and flowers to be sold in the village market. Our mother pulled up and made me jump out of the truck to toss three packets of tobacco over the fence. A lad in blue overalls threw down his hoe and rushed, hopping over cabbages, to pluck the pouches out of the soil.

'I hope they get to him.' She put her foot down: 'That's my catalogue money gone up in smoke.'

'Don't worry, Mum.' I watched men waving, gazing after us out of faces buttered by the sun. 'They'll get to him.'

The prisoners stood rooted in the soil, while we sped away.

My mother made up sick notes so that I could keep her company on the long haul to and from prison every other Thursday. Laurie preferred to go to school. My chest hammered every time I chucked baccy over the fence and met the green eyes of the lad who caught it.

Once, when Dad opened his palm to reveal a present, my mother burst into tears. 'Oh, love.'

Filing and filing at a ten pence piece, he had finally come up with a heart-shaped pendant. The sight of it made me feel lonely and in the way. My mother hung it on the gold chain around her neck, while Dad stroked her face with his work-chapped fingers. Then, thinking his hands were too rough, he leaned over to dry up her tears with his kisses.

My mother put on a brave face for her fortnightly visits, but it would usually crumple on the motorway, heading back to Manchester. Sometimes, to keep our spirits up, we would take the Stretford exit on the way home and drop in on Gran. It was lovely to sit with my grandmother in a haze of Woodbines, lapping up her words of wisdom, washed down with Tetley's tea and sterilized milk. Waking at dawn every day, with no television, and only Radio Two to distract her, she had time to work the world out.

If you love something, set it free. A poster above her pillow helped her to sleep in peace: *If it comes back, it's yours. If it doesn't, it never was.*

I recited it to my mother, who turned her eyes to her tea, so that I couldn't tell whether it made her feel better or worse.

'You shouldn't miss school.' Gran squeezed my hand fiercely as we were leaving her flat. 'You've a chance to make something decent of yourself – break the mould.' An awesome frown took over her cheeks, blotting out her usual mild smile.

My skin felt like a kebab, roasting on the rack. I imagined my grandmother somehow knew about all the hours lost on buses, down strange streets, even wandering around Manchester airport, watching planes take off.

'It's only one day a fortnight' – my mother came to my rescue, assuming it was our prison Thursdays that were the issue.

'Days add up,' Gran said, while we were waiting for the lift. The doors opened. 'It's your future.'

The future, as far as I could see, was not so much about school as about having the right clothes, being able to keep up with fashion and to actually enjoy it, instead of panicking at how fast it moved. Ra-ra skirts, minis, long pencil skirts that made you shuffle, short, flared ones with braces, horrid puffball things; ski pants, drainpipes, jumbo cords, pedalpushers, baggy jeans that wrinkled like elephant skin around the ankles. I spent hours at jumble sales, rummaging for things that could be altered to fit the bill. My fingers were full of scratches where I had slipped and jabbed with the needle, setting off glistening baubles of blood. But no matter how furiously I stitched, I was always a step behind.

Records made me hot under the collar, too. We had loads of albums and singles at home, but they were mostly from the Sixties and Seventies. You had to know all the latest hits and where they were in the charts, if you didn't want to be shown up at school or down the end of the street where the hard kids loitered. It helped to have Wendy as a mate, because her front room was always twanging with songs by whining white boys like Depeche Mode, Tears for Fears, Japan and Ultravox. The records were bought by her big sister, Gail, who had a job selling insurance, which she got with only three grade D CSEs. Gail had to spend all day on the phone, saying the same thing over and over and over. But then she could go home wearing fluffy jumpers and tight skirts, with real leather boots that zipped up to her thighs. On weekends she went to Yates's Wine Lodge, then to Friday's, a disco, where men bought her Malibu cocktails faster than she could glug them down. At least three blokes were in love with her at one time. She could get married as soon as she made up her mind.

That was the future.

Whenever I was tempted to truant, Gran's face steered me to school.

I had a strange crush, mingled with a lazy sort of hatred, on the snooty girls Susannah Maxwell and Charlotte Cox, whose parents had sent them to our school because, although they were well-off, they were socialists and wanted to show that they believed in comprehensive education. Tamsyn Lee seemed just as posh, though her mother was a dinner lady and would rather have sent her daughter to a grammar school or a private one if she had been able to afford it. All three girls knew about politics and history, and were never afraid to speak their minds. Mrs Arnold staged debates in the English class: everyone else fell silent while they thrashed it out. Their voices started off haughty and smooth, as sure as the politicians you might hear on the news, but ended up grating like nails on a blackboard. Charlotte believed in communism, revolution and something she called The People; Tamsyn swore by Margaret Thatcher and had her sights set on gathering enough O levels to make her middle-class; Susannah called herself a Liberal and poured energy into disagreeing with the others, at the same time hammering on about how much she valued their points of view.

Miners. Taxes. The IRA. Butter mountains. Brezhnev. Strikes. Arthur Scargill. Nuclear disarmament. Colonel Gadhaffi. The Falklands.

It wasn't the subjects that were so fascinating. It was the way long words spurted out, while their cheeks throbbed red, each one throwing herself into the argument heart and soul.

The only paper we always bought was the *News of the World* on a Sunday; sometimes our dad got the *Sun*. If the news happened to come on the telly at home, someone would switch like lightning to another channel, afraid of being bored to death. So it was hard to scrape together enough facts and figures to transform my gut instincts about the world into hard-edged opinions for school. I shuddered at the prospect of a nuclear holocaust; I wondered how I would ever get a job if the recession was still so deep when I turned sixteen; but most of my energy went into worrying about the hairs on my face, arms and legs.

'Immac,' lads called me, plucking at my shins. 'Your name Andrew?' they shouted, when light caught me at an angle, giving me a moustache.

'Don't put yourself in line for misery.' My mother exposed her own prickly legs to warn me against shaving. 'It's a never-ending battle.'

'You're a bloody fool!' she flared once, after I braved the razor behind her back. 'Now you've started you'll never be able to stop.'

I tried to explain that I couldn't go on living with hairy legs. My mother shook her head at the bits of tissue stuck to my ankles, where I had taken off slivers of skin in the rush to be feminine.

'It's your life,' she sighed.

'Zoom!' My heart went boom along with Fat Larry's Band.

Within a week of acquiring smooth legs, I fell head over heels.

Neil Kirby hung around the chippy, but he wasn't like the other lads. For one thing, he didn't swear, he didn't thrust out his tongue to wiggle it, and he had never tried to pinch my bum. For another, his face was delicious, with honey-coloured eyes and lips that broke into a smile of straight white teeth whenever I walked by. I had explored every bit of his mouth in my imagination. It didn't matter that he smoked. It did matter that Wendy fancied him.

'Hands off,' she warned, noticing that he had kept me chatting under the bus stop three nights in a row: 'He's mine.'

I made a real effort to steer clear. Somehow, that made it harder to resist.

Neil Kirby invited me to his house to watch a film with his friends. The movie turned out to be full of bouncing, sweaty breasts. I was the only girl in the room; my nipples burned as if they were blushing.

'Fancy coming up to my room for a bit?' Neil's fingers hovered near mine.

I forced down a sip of Skol lager. 'Don't you want to watch the rest of the film?' I stalled.

When he took my hand to pull me upstairs, our palms were oozing the same sticky heat.

*

'I hope you're being sensible, young lady!' My mother was torn between nagging me to be careful and congratulating me on finding a boyfriend. Such a nice lad, too, she boasted to Auntie Livia and Auntie Pauline and Gran. Seventeen, he was, working at the butcher's on Yew Tree Road, until his papers came through for the army. In raptures over his neat hair and clipped fingernails, which showed that he came from a good family, my mother was already dressing me in white in her mind, ready to scoot me down the aisle as soon as the time was right.

When Neil bought me a ring, I slipped it on to my right hand, well away from the marriage finger.

'He's a soppy git!' Wendy saw fit to forgive, when he turned out to be so gooey. 'I like my blokes to be hard,' she declared, keeping her eye on the ring.

Fourteen-carat gold, in the shape of a lucky horsehoe, it held the shyest diamond in the world.

I let my mother believe I was in love with Neil Kirby. I let Neil Kirby believe the same. What I was really in love with – apart from the ring and boxes of chocolates – was the world beneath his Manchester City quilt. My skin woke up when it touched his. The taste of his breath, the smell of his chest, emptied my head. Belly on fire, my muscles throbbed in time with my heart.

'No.' My fingers caught his when they tugged at my knickers. There was a line I had no intention of crossing, though it was thrilling to hover along it.

'You're killing me.' He nuzzled my neck. 'Don't you love me?'
The knot of our legs tightened.

No. I was devoted to my own creamy explosions. *No.*

'Will you have any babies, miss?' Our chemistry teacher, Miss Gilman, was going to be married on Saturday. We took the opportunity to avoid volumetric analysis by bombarding her with questions.

'Don't do it, miss.' Joyce Harding spoke up: 'It kills.'

Joyce was fourteen; her baby was more than a year old. Before now, none of us had known it existed. She had missed a lot of school, but, because Joyce was ugly and not funny, not one of us had stopped to wonder why. Our chemistry lesson was devoted to the bloody story of her labour.

'It's the head that hurts the most.' Lads clowned around at the back of the lab, sniggering, while girls sat in a hush with Miss Gilman behind the glass apparatus. 'It can rip you right open, like. You – you have to – scream.'

I blasted away on a trumpet with the boys in the brass section every Wednesday afternoon. The school orchestra was still booming in my chest when I got home for tea.

'There's no way on God's good green earth' – my mother planted fists on hips when I lifted the school trumpet out of its purple velvet case – 'that you are going to play THAT THING under this roof.'

I went and sat on my bed, watching my fingers cancan through notes in silence, trusting that things would be different as soon as Dad came home.

After the confinement of inmate blue, our dad went through a rainbow of his brightest shirts in his first week on the outside. Friends came round every night, popping corks, buzzing with news, dangling their latest schemes under his nose.

Our mother made ominous noises, rasping her cigarette.

'Nah, mate.' Dad put his arm around her, shaking his head at the lads: 'I'm touching nothing bent, me.'

He knew his priorities. And his limitations. They had been drummed into him at Her Majesty's pleasure.

'Rock the Boat'. Our dad struggled to keep everything above board. He had to sign on while he got his act together, and that made it illegal for him to work. But there were never enough jobs to allow him to come off the dole and go self-employed. The recession had bitten in; people hadn't the heart, let alone the readies, to improve their houses.

'It's like me hands are still in cuffs.' He shook his wrists. Nervous about invoices, he was forced to turn down hefty contracts when they did crop up.

'It's the bloody Higher-Ups,' our mother ranted, while Laurie and Sarah wondered who she meant. 'Just there to stop the little people from making summat of themselves, they are.'

Instead of oiling his tools and sawing planks in the back yard, our dad spent more and more time in front of the telly. We often came in from school to find him concentrating hard on cartoons. *I coulda been a contender.* He tried to joke, but we watched the light go out in his eyes when another fella's promise failed to blossom into a job. *I coulda been somebody.*

A flurry of Rizla papers passed across our dad's lips. He rolled cigarette after cigarette, balancing them in log piles, before he smoked them one by one.

'What's got into you?' our mother shrieked when his hands exploded in her face.

The first slap seemed to hurt him as much as her. He winced and locked her in his arms, crooning *ChristChristChrist* until her elbows stopped chugging to escape.

'That's not the answer,' our mother sobbed. Her nose dribbled on to his jumper. 'Don't you know I'm on your side?'

The next time he hit her, it sparked an air of dismay rather than surprise. We froze after the whack, watching the fight that went on inside our dad, between the half of him that was sorry and wanted to drench our mother in kisses, and the half that made him stand his ground.

'Slut!' He sometimes sneered, snatching for reasons to hit her again. 'You dirty whore! What were you doing, eh, all them nights when I was inside?'

Our mother shook her head, unable to believe her ears. 'Ask the kids what I was doing. Go on, ask them how much fun it was waiting, with no money and no nothing. We put our lives on hold for you, you worthless shite.'

Dad wavered, then stiffened: 'You make me sick.'

Our mother let him get the rest of the slaps out of his system. She held her stinging cheeks.

'You make yourself sick.'

Trees let go of their leaves in the park behind school. I spent the dinner hour kicking through red and gold with Tamsyn Lee. Thrown together by the choir (since I had traded in the trumpet for something less troublesome), we were turning out to be soul mates. We hit the airy notes in harmony, collapsing under heavy ones meant for bigger chests.

'So, then he gets sent to room 101.' Tamsyn was talking me through a story she thought I should read. 'It's all about Big Brother, you see.'

She planned to work her way through what she called the classics, books that would help to make you middle-class. Being middle-class was something I could never dream of, especially since my dad had been sent to prison. I hadn't told

Tamsyn about that. She was lovely, but she was so well turned out it made me nervous: her voice was clipped (she never dropped her aitches, her 't's practically stood to attention); she always looked nice and neat, with shiny, perfect hair that she had cut and styled at a hairdresser's; and she lived in a semi-detached house in Didsbury with her mother and father, who had stayed married to one another all this time. I was afraid that she might not want to talk to me if she knew what my life was like at home. I thought it was best to keep quiet, too, about my mate Wendy and the whisky we used to swig from her dad's silver flask on Saturday nights, wincing at its metallic whack down our throats, before wobbling around the streets in pointed shoes, on the look-out for lads.

Because this year was 1984, Tamsyn was reading a novel called *1984*, by George Orwell. She told me so many details, I felt like I'd read it myself. The story made me think about my dad and the way he and my mother felt spied on by the government, even behind closed doors at home. A great urge came over me to get hold of the book, to read it from cover to cover and understand everything in between. But I didn't dare touch it. It seemed to come from another world, a posh one, that I wasn't part of. Instead I peered at the library book in Tamsyn's hands.

If you want an image of the future – someone had pencilled stars in the margins – *imagine a boot stamping on a human face for ever.*

After swapping secrets about our bodies and the way we felt about boys, I began to hint to Tamsyn about what went on inside our house. Only the fists. I never mentioned the filthy words or the cowboy boots, kicking my mother in her back while she crouched like a mushroom on the floor.

'It's because he loves us.' I resorted to my mother's logic

when Tamsyn's eyebrows locked against my dad: 'It makes him feel helpless not to be able to make money. That's when he blows up.'

Tamsyn looked disgusted. 'Why does your mum stay with him?'

'She loves him' – I scrabbled for words – 'as much as she hates him.'

'What do you feel?' Tamsyn asked.

My eyes wandered through bare branches to the sky.

I saw his fists flying before they faded in the blue of his eyes.

'He's my dad.'

14

After itching for weeks, Dad finally took his drill to the electricity meter: he made a hole and slid a needle through it, to stop the wheel from whizzing. Shame broke out in the form of sweat, creeping along my hairline, making my face clammy, whenever I thought of the tiny, pin-sized hole. Mum and Dad were united against the man from Norweb. There were gallons of hot water for laundry and for bubbly baths that came up to your neck. But it left you feeling dirty, under the skin, where no soap or scrubbing could reach.

After tea, based on bread, chips and baked beans, Mum and Dad would plant themselves in front of the TV with their new roll-up machine and a pouch of tobacco. They veered between Old Holborn and Golden Virginia, as if one or the other might change their luck, embarking on liquorice-flavoured Rizla papers when life seemed specially dull.

'Ugh!' Dad grunted when *Wish You Were Here* flaunted white beaches, crystal water and cloudless skies. Our mother fumed at life's unfairness. Dad switched over for quiz shows. He bristled on the settee when the buzzer beat him to the answer he swore was on the tip of his tongue.

Now that Neil Kirby had gone into the army and Wendy had a full-time boyfriend of her own, I had no reason to leave the house. Because Tamsyn lived miles away in Didsbury, and her parents wouldn't let her come to rough areas like Rusholme, I couldn't see her after school. I huddled with Laurie and Sarah, knees tucked under chins, eyes on our mum and dad. Some nights they joked and kissed. Never a finger raised. They rolled and lit up, rolled and lit up, while we choked on the edge of it.

> *Do not go gentle into that good night . . .*
> *Grave men, near death, who see with blinding sight*
> *Blind eyes could blaze like meteors and be gay,*
> *Rage, rage against the dying of the light.*

A wave of grieving anger rushed through me and crashed inside my forehead, when I dived into the Dylan Thomas poem I had to analyse for class. *Because their words had forked no lightning . . . Their frail deeds might have danced in a green bay . . . Old age should burn and rage at close of day.* Age, death and grief were the 'salient themes of the poem', it said in the back of the textbook anthology. But for me, the dying of the light had to do with being buried alive in your own smoky front room with your family, stuck together for ever and ever, in front of the TV.

'Clear up that crap!' Dad hounded Laurie and me away from the kitchen table when we spread out our schoolbooks. The sight of them made his nostrils flare: 'Spoiled brats.'

'It pains him to see you kids getting what he never had,' our mother reminded us, as though that ought to take the sting out of his slaps: 'Christ knows, he's had a hard life.'

One night, when Terry had stormed out after a fight and our mother refused to let him back in, his older brother Trev had come round to soften her with the tale of their childhood in Hulme. Their mam, he told us, used to dump plates of gravy and mash on their da's head, smack bang on his noggin, when he came home legless. Their da would sit there, saying nowt, gravy dribbling down his face. Next night, like, he'd be sure to beat the shit out of their mam. When their da finally buggered off, their mam turned on Terry, insisting he'd driven their da away. She'd clang his skull against the taps when she was washing his hair in the sink. Gave up cleaning and cooking, she did – always out sniffing after another fella, leaving the brothers to fend for themselves. Little Terry found a tapeworm in his undies when he was ten years old.

'Why do we have to pay for what his mum and dad did all that time ago?' Laurie and I protested. The clanging against the taps made us want to cry, the thought of the tapeworm made us squirm, but the story didn't stop our ears from ringing after Dad's past had burst out in his hands.

The buzz saw snarled and rattled . . . snarled and rattled, snarled and rattled, . . . And nothing happened.

My heart snarled and rattled too, sawing inside my chest, as I read the poem Mrs Chappell pointed to in the English textbook. 'Out, Out—', by Robert Frost.

Then the saw leaped out at the boy's hand – *the hand!* – and he held it up with *a rueful laugh.* He lay down and someone listened at his heart. *Little – less – nothing! – and that ended it.*

I read the poem over and over, willing the boy to watch out, feeling shocked every time the saw caught his hand and the words left him dead at the end.

'Now, then: RUE.' Mrs Arnold chalked the word up on the board: 'What do we think that means?'

Rue. I copied it into my exercise book and stared. Such a puny word, considering everything it sucked in.

'Andrea?' Mrs Arnold picked on me when my frown of concentration gave me away.

'Is it the ache you feel,' I mumbled, while my face burned, 'when you wish things could be rewound, even though you *know* it's too late, to make it all turn out differently?'

My marks shot up in every subject, soaring through the seventies and eighties to tickle the nineties. Tamsyn wavered between admiration and resentment: 'How d'you do it?'

After tea and doing the dishes, then any ironing or dusting Dad demanded, something beckoned me to lie on my tummy in front of the telly, with a book opened under my nose. I pored over one book at a time, so that he couldn't attack me for messing things up. Whatever the subject, I found I was fascinated: every page was an adventure, knowing I might, at any moment, cop a right load of flak from my dad.

'In our house,' I told Tamsyn, 'homework makes you a rebel.'

'Why can't you act like a proper family?' Our mother's blood pressure rose when one of us forgot to put on the right face for tea. 'Stop pushing your food round your plate!'

'Misery guts,' Dad called Laurie, who let feelings seep into her eyes.

My sister disappeared into our bedroom after tea, as soon as the dishes were finished. *Pliés, pirouettes, arabesques.* Her body brought mysterious words to life while the rest of us slouched in front of the TV, floorboards squeaking above our heads.

'Shut that racket up!' Dad bellowed.

The ceiling sulked, silent for a few seconds.

Then it groaned again.

Dad stormed upstairs: 'I'm trying to watch the fuckin' *Krypton Factor!*'

An almighty slap and a thud. Sarah gulped and glanced at me.

I looked at my mother, wrapped in her cigarette.

'She brings it on herself, that one.' Our mother sided with Dad when he gave Laurie a hiding.

After a modern dance competition at the Royal Northern Ballet, my sister had come home half an hour late, failing to look sorry. A streak of electricity in her silvery-blue leotard, she had amazed the judges. They could hardly believe that she had no formal training, apart from the odd lunch hour with her PE teacher, and had taught herself most of the moves out of an old picture book. A sense of excitement buzzed through me, too, when I stroked my sister's star-shaped medal and thought of the prize she had won: she was one of only six 12-year-olds in England who had been chosen to spend a week, all expenses paid, at a dance school in London.

'You can forget that!' Dad decided that Laurie was getting above her station: 'Swanning in and out all hours, obsessed with this dancing malarky, treating our 'ouse like an 'otel.'

When she opened her mouth to object, he hit her in the face and sent her to bed. This he repeated, as soon as she got in from school, every night for a week: 'You're going nowhere, Twinkletoes.'

If Mum thought Dad's punishments were too harsh, she would sometimes try murmuring to wheedle him round. His face turned to stone; she backed off. Jiggling her eyebrows when he wasn't looking, she searched for ways to let us know she was on our side, really. Laurie and Sarah felt betrayed, but I thought I understood: when Dad was on the warpath against us kids, I told them, it was downright dangerous for our mother to step in. What I suspected, but never said, was that the battle with us kids gave them precious time off from the war with each other.

'Why does it have to be Them against Us,' Laurie asked, 'whenever it's not Him against Her?'

'It's not like that, Laurie.' I often said things I didn't believe, in an effort to keep the peace.

Fair. Unfair. Right. Wrong. Nothing mattered as much as keeping everyone's voices from rising or breaking out. Shouts led to fists, which could leap to knives in a flash.

I kept my head down, reading or doing homework or losing myself in the sketchbook I brought home from school. Learning to make all the right noises, I tutted and sighed to agree with Mum and Dad, at the same time straining to cast Laurie's, Sarah's or my own behaviour in a better light. We were rarely able to do anything right. Selfish gobshites, we were, forever giving them grief.

'Yes, but...' I became fluent at agreeing, before wheeling in the other side of the story to save the day.

I drew a bristling crouch of fur, fangs and eyes glinting: using a black biro on white cardboard, scratching away whenever the house was calm, I brought a black-and-white leopard to life.

'Flamin' marvellous!' Dad clicked his tongue between his teeth and did a little whistle.

He was happy to see me engrossed this way. 'Better than them poncy books you waste so much time on,' he muttered. 'Full of codswallop.' He never used to object when I dived into Stephen King and James Herbert and all the dirty horrors and thrillers I was once obsessed by. Now I had outgrown them, they gave me the wrong kind of shudders: they seemed cheap and flat and not terrifying at all. Instead I found myself drawn to musty old books that I came across at school, or fancy-cover classics that I discovered through Tamsyn. *Far From the Madding Crowd*, *Selected Modern Verse*, *Great Expectations*. They touched on deep, disturbing things too, but they lifted you up, towards a sort of light, instead of dragging you down into darkness. And the excitement stayed with you, even carried on growing, after you closed the book.

Since the sight of the posh books made Dad sneer, I took to sticking them under my jumper and smuggling them out into the back yard: it was worth braving the cold and drizzling rain so that I could lose myself in the stories without being harassed by shadows over my shoulder. The books that really got my dad's goat were the red leatherbound ones that Tamsyn had given me for my fifteenth birthday, their titles standing out in gold letters: *Jane Eyre* and *Wuthering Heights*. He had no idea what was inside them; he just hated the sight of my face after I pulled it out of the pages and went about feeling crammed with passion and a murky sense of something brewing. Some brilliant storm.

A letter came for Laurie from the Royal Northern Ballet Company. Dad tore it to shreds.

'Dad . . .' Speaking up gave me goosebumps of terror.

His eyes glittered: 'Cruising for a bruising?'

I thought of Laurie, jailed in bed, and pushed the point.

'Insurrection in the ranks! Mutiny on the Bounty!' He had a range of battleship sayings to keep the house in order, eyes turning flinty – 'Noted and logged' – if anyone threatened to step out of line.

Sometimes he skipped his jokes and went straight to the thwack across the back of the neck.

My mother advised me to do myself and everyone else a favour: 'Keep it zipped.'

But tears stung our mother's eyes when Dad turned on Sarah.

'She's got to learn, Lorraine.' He put my eight-year-old sister over his knee and made her scream. 'There's to be no thieving in this house.'

Sarah had pilfered thirty pence from the jar filled to meet the gas bill. Instead of buying chocolate and eating the evidence, like Laurie and I had sometimes been tempted to do, she had turned the money into a packet of balloons which she had blown up, before trying to hide them under her bed.

'It's the half-term holidays,' our mother pleaded when Sarah was sent to bed for a week. 'The poor little bugger'll go barmy.'

Dad exploded the balloons with a fork, pulled the curtains tight and stripped the bedroom of every last book and game. Clutching his drill like a gun, he fixed a padlock on the outside of the door, to keep Sarah in and Laurie and me out.

We went to bed early, to comfort our sister, although we were forbidden from speaking to her. Sometimes she was asleep when we crept in. More often, she was awake, eyes glistening in the dark.

'What's this?' I whispered, when I discovered a hard-backed book under her pillow while I was stroking her hair.

Old Testament Psalms. The only thing not caught in the tornado that ripped through our room, taking the rest of our books and things with it.

'I don't read it.' My little sister spoke under her breath: 'I just like the feel of it under my head.'

*

Stuff at home made my chest feel heavy and clogged, but running reminded me I was alive.

Knees, heels, lungs. Knees, heels, lungs.

Air razored my throat; my lungs felt as if they were bleeding. The only girl on the long-distance-running team, I escaped netball practice to push myself along the dirt track behind school. I was finally free of the terror of missing the net, of the whistle shrilling against me for eyeing the hoop too long.

Mud under my feet, birds scattering into the sky, I ran for miles and miles – muscles burning as if my legs were on fire – to match the distances I covered in dreams.

15

We woke up in Auntie Pauline's caravan, parked outside
her back door.

'Why can't we stay here?' Sarah spoke for the three of us,
when we had swallowed our hot Ribena and it was time for
Uncle Bill to drive us back to our house, where he had come
to rescue us the night before. I had managed to call him and
Auntie Pauline, grabbing the phone and dialling with desperate
fingers.

After smashing all the ornaments, Dad had grabbed the
remains of a cut-glass decanter and waved the jagged edge like
a dagger.

'You think you're so hard!' our mother had taunted him,
thrusting her face in line for a slash, while Sarah cried and
Laurie and I begged them to stop. Our dad had seemed as
relieved as everyone else when Uncle Bill's car screeched up
outside.

'We've got to go back and face the music, girls.' Our mother
drained her coffee and fastened her cardigan.

I stiffened my lips and blinked to keep my eyes nice and
dry. I had to set an example for Laurie and be strong enough
to comfort Sarah, who whimpered: 'Why?'

A frightening sweetness filled the air when they kissed and
made up.

'Sexual Healing' . . . 'Ain't Nothing Like The Real Thing' . . . 'The First, The Last, My Everything' . . . It was all Marvin Gaye and Barry White and dancing with their hips glued together, like in the beginning.

The fresh starts usually lasted a week and ended in smithereens. With no ornaments left, Dad would go straight for our mother's ribs and face. Laurie, Sarah and I caught the odd fistful of anger, when we dared to hang on to his arms to keep them from flailing at her. He was like a windmill in a hurricane, the night Uncle Al and his mates came to drag him away.

'Rainie . . .' He waited until the middle of the night, when everyone had gone home and our lights had been turned out, before creeping back to tap on the letterbox.

'Rainie, baby,' he moaned under the flap. 'You know I love you.

'Let's not be silly, doll.' His whispers seeped through the door, while our mother sat on the stairs, smoking in the dark.

'Go away.' Her voice eventually cracked into a shriek: 'Why don't you just go away and leave us in peace?'

As soon as tears gurgled in our mother's throat, we knew she would let him back in.

When my mother was sent to the hospital for a head X-ray, I went with her to hold her hand.

I wanted to giggle: heart-shaped earrings dangled from her skull on the screen.

'Thank Christ,' my mother sighed, when the doctor assured her there were no cracks. The deafness in her left ear would cure itself over time.

I looked at the negative. All the bones were lit up.

My mother was still staring, trying to see inside her own head, when the doctor flicked off the screen.

'I had a sore throat,' I told Tamsyn, who wondered why I had missed school.

She shot me a look: 'Again? Why are you keeping stuff from me?' She stopped to face me in the park after dinner: 'Don't you trust me any more?'

'Don't be crazy.' I met her eyes. 'I'd tell you everything,' I assured my best friend, 'if there was anything to tell.'

16

On Sundays, Dad slept off the worst of the week before, then slithered out of bed and reached for his fishing rod. Laurie had friends to meet, our mother had an appointment with herself in the bath, but Sarah and I were keen to keep him company at Sale Water Park, knowing his mood would be fantastically calm once he was close to the water, making him more like his old self.

The three of us sat, cross-legged, on plastic bags laid against the damp grass.

Hours of amazing silence on the edge of the lake, reflecting a lilac sky.

'When will you catch one, Dad?' Sarah whispered, as the sun began to slide. We squinted to spot the orange nipple floating in the gloom.

'Soon.' He kept his chin tucked in the collar of his leather bomber jacket, eyes cast over the lake, as if he could see everything underneath. 'Have no fear.'

When a slick of silver turned up, writhing, on the end of his line, Dad held it in his hands like a baby. Gills fanned and collapsed, flapping for life. A terrified eye stared.

'Gently does it.' His scarred fingertips and knuckles worked to pull the hook loose from the fish's gasping lips.

'Till next time,' he murmured, and slipped it back in, with a flurry of silent, dark ripples.

*

'Will you never learn?' Our mother fretted when Dad decided to go into business with Uncle Max.

Uncle Max was going to buy delapidated houses, Dad would renovate them, they'd split the profits as soon as they were sold.

'What could be more simple?' He was already racking up his tools, ready to sweat his way to a fortune.

'Only your brain' – our mother was wise to Uncle Max's scams – 'if you believe any of that castles in the clouds shit.'

Auntie Livia and Uncle Max had bought a huge house in Sale, after opening a dingy second-hand-furniture shop behind the warehouses off Piccadilly Square. Making money out of scratched sideboards, wobbly tables and exhausted settees, they proceeded to fill their own house with beautiful, solid furniture and antiques.

'We'll have gear as smart as theirs, when I get going,' Dad assured himself as well as us: 'Just you wait and see.'

Dad's promises heightened our awe of Auntie Livia and Uncle Max's house. My sisters and I went quiet at the sight of their leather Chesterfield, their four-poster bed, the mahogany dinner table that shone, untouched, while they ate off their knees in front of the telly. Bronze horses reared their hooves on either side of the marble fireplace. Above it hung a vast, gold-framed mirror, an oval pool that let you float in your own reflection when no one was looking.

I was chuffed when Uncle Max offered to pay me ten pounds every Saturday for helping to pick up old cookers and fridges from smashed-up houses on bleak estates before scrubbing them to get rid of the filth. I rolled up my sleeves and worked through the smell, dreaming about the universe of clothes and shoes I would be able to move about in if I saved a few weeks' wages. Once they were clean, Uncle Max sold the fridges and cookers to tired-looking people who brought in government vouchers and scraps of cash, after which we delivered them to different houses on the same estates. At the end of the day, we locked up the delivery van and sighed into Uncle Max's Mercedes to cruise back to their house, where Mum and Dad would turn up with Laurie and Sarah for the evening.

'Nice piece of metal, mate!' Dad whistled at Uncle Max's latest discovery, a bronze lampstand in the shape of a lady, nearly life-size, robes clinging to her breasts.

'Aye.' Uncle Max stroked the curves. 'She's a beauty, all right.'

'Aw, Liv!' Our mother clucked at the sight of the lampshade: a crown of pearly peach and pink shells. Auntie Livia let Sarah click the lamp off, to repeat the wonder of switching it on: 'Better than Blackpool 'luminations!'

Uncle Max and Dad checked the football scores, then slid into double-breasted jackets with wide ties and disappeared in the Mercedes.

My mother splashed more Bacardi into her Coke: 'What's up, Liv?'

'Same as ever.' Auntie Livia chomped through the Lean Cuisine cauliflower cheese that was supposed to shrink her thighs: 'Gambling. Drink. Dodgy deals. Other women's fucking perfume.'

She forced down the last of her cauliflower, got out her whisk and fluffed up a bowl of butterscotch Angel Delight, which she shoved into the fridge. Then she started on a Mars Bar, swallowing back tears: 'I found an earring, hooked in his jumper.'

Auntie Livia was gorgeous, but Uncle Max didn't know it, so neither did she. While he was out chasing skirts, she spent hours cooped in the spare room, smothering her face under creams in front of a mirror framed by baby bulbs, torturing herself with hot wax to strip hairs off her legs, grilling herself on the sunbed. All the wives of Uncle Max's mates did the same: at night, the street was caressed by eerie white-blue lights, seeping out of upstairs windows, as if spaceships had landed inside. Itching to bitch about their husbands who were off playing with dice at the casino, they came round for Malibu nights at Auntie Livia's, glowing as if they had run away together on a ladies-only holiday. Our mother felt pale and dowdy next to them.

'They look like their own handbags,' Laurie and I insisted: 'Fancy, but leathery.' Our mother was beautiful on the inside as well, we sweated to assure her, and that was something no money could buy.

She was much happier with herself the next day, when she was on her knees in her threadbare housecoat, digging her handbrush into the stairs. Cleaning made her feel spiritual, especially on Sunday mornings.

'Money,' she muttered into the carpet, 'is not the be-all and bloody end-all.'

It was easy for our mother to look down her nose at money, now that Dad was bringing in enough to put meat on the table. We hesitated before tucking in, not knowing how long the juicy phase would last.

'Ask no questions.' My mother's eyes flashed when I wondered where the cash came from for real mincemeat instead of the tasteless soya stuff.

'How Sweet It Is To Be Loved By You'. Dad was bellowing his old favourites in the bath, sprucing himself up for a bevvy with the boys. 'Too Busy Thinking About My Baby'.

Our mother was ready now to overlook the odd dodgy deal. Our dad might be up to his old fandangos, but – unlike Uncle Max and the rest of them sharks – he wasn't messing around with other women. He hadn't smacked her in weeks. These days, when our dad raised his voice, it was to laugh at one of his own jokes.

'Don't go getting too big for your boots,' our mother would say when Dad rubbed his hands over what he called funny money.

Uncle Max had something up his sleeve. A deal to end all deals.

Before they could hit the jackpot, the deal crashed. Auntie Livia's front window was shattered by a brick, Tipp-Exed to tell them to WOTCHIT.

'Back to the drawing-board, mate.' Uncle Max was sorry to let our dad down, after he'd invested his precious dosh: 'Some toes you don't step on.'

Dad's Spanish guitar was a barometer, forecasting our future and measuring the pressure inside our house: his baccy-tanned fingertips squeaked, plucked and pinged when things were on the up and up; strings moaned under his hammering thumbs when Fate had screwed him over yet again. He slumped on the settee, pumping smoke into the air, along with curses against God, the government and Uncle Fucking-Flaming Max. Occasionally, he let his bad luck get the better of him, and lashed out at our mother.

He always cried afterwards. 'Rainie, me love. I'll make it up to you. Give me a chance.'

As soon as his pockets were bulging again, he bombarded her with Chinese take-aways, sparkling wine and the Fenjal bath oil she adored. Our mother would accept his presents with shaky fingers, smiling hard.

'Open it, open it!' We gathered around the box embossed *H. Samuels the Jewellers*, after things had gone beyond a slap. Our mother looked at the rose-shaped gold earrings in her palm, mulling over the promise in their petals. After a while, she slid them into her earlobes, blinking back tears while Dad nuzzled her face and hair, tracing a necklace of kisses from ear to ear.

What Dad wanted, from the pit of his soul, was to build a house for us.

'Using me own 'ands.' His eyes were always shining when he said it, with excitement or tears of frustration.

Sometimes, instead of riffling through the *Sun*, trying to work out who was to blame, he would sit on the settee with his spirit level in his hands: an aluminium strip, painted yellow, with a glass bubble winking at its heart. Stains showed under our dad's arms when he lifted it in front of his eyes. Tilting, ever so slightly tilting, he willed the bubble to rest in the right place, while the rest of us held our breath.

For those couple of months, my own dream was to escape my anorak. If I could save enough from my Saturday job to buy a second-hand sheepskin jacket, then my life would begin. I would find the right boy; he would see that I was the right girl. One Saturday in March, Auntie Livia gave me a bonus for scrubbing extra cookers. I stepped into Affleck's Palace with twenty pounds, braving the stares of supercool kids with rings through their noses, and came out with the future on my back. Lads gawped at me on buses, men gaped through windscreens, leery ones slowing their cars to try their luck, while I smiled to myself and walked on by. Once, on the way to school, a bloke fell off his bike for staring.

Still, I had bumped into only two boys since Neil Kirby, and both were dead ends. One was Neil's best friend, Steve: guilt made the first kiss delicious, but soured any after that. The other was a lad with fantastic cheekbones but dead eyes. I never knew his name. He had been watching me, night after night in the park, where I went after school to hang around the swings with Laurie while Sarah, who was nearly nine, chatted to other primary school kids on the roundabouts. When *The Addams Family* fastened my sisters in front of the telly at home, I went to Platt Fields by myself to gaze at couples clunking about in rowboats on the pond.

The boy came up and fell in with my pace on the path: 'Gorgeous, you are.'

We wandered on to the grass. I wobbled in the slingbacks I had inherited from my mother, heels sinking into the earth. He steered me to a tree.

A weeping willow.

His palm cupped my cheek. My heart fluttered and fell to my knickers.

Then it clanged back up to my throat. His tongue was like steel.

'Fuck!' He was pressing against me. Eyes glassy: 'Fuck!'

He fumbled with his jeans. The rip of a zip. Something hard and wet against my thigh.

I tore away from the tree trunk, my hair snagging on bark. 'You don't even know who I am!'

Not angry or sorry or suprised, he yanked up his zip: 'So what?'

My mother unpicked the seams of her old moon-and-stars dress, and laid the parts on newspaper. She traced round them to make a pattern, which she pinned to stretches of white curtain lining. Chugging on the Singer sewing machine, she came up with my new dress, then stitched her own back into one piece.

'It's for the theatre,' she told Dad, who wanted to know what all the fuss was about.

'They should be teaching you proper bloody English,' he grumbled, when I informed him that the school were charging two pounds each for tickets to see *Romeo and Juliet*, by William Shakespeare, 'not all that ancient gobbledygook. That's not going to get you a job, is it?'

'Wherefore are yer, Romeo?' he teased, when I tried on my frothy white dress. A jackpot scoop on the one-armed bandits with Uncle Max had put him in a swaggering mood.

'Here.' He uncrumpled a five-pound note from his pocket, and ruffled my hair: 'You can keep the change for popcorn!'

The steepness of the upper gallery made me dizzy. I had to cling to red velvet, inching along the rows, trying not to look down at all the heads. As soon as I was in my seat, my neck hinged back to contemplate the white and gold ceiling.

'Yawn, yawn!' Matthew Chappell was the son of the first-year English teacher. He was very short: moaning about all the plays he had been forced to sit through at the theeyatah seemed to make him feel taller. Susannah and Charlotte, the posh girls whose parents were teachers and doctors, clustered either side of him in dark blue, cardboardy denims, stroking the creases ironed down their shins. The rest of the class, seething in their Sunday best, was a riot of swear words, crinkling sweet wrappers and giggles that crescendoed and clashed with hysterical shushes as the lights began to die.

'Shakespeare. Stayawakespeare,' I whispered, when elbows nudged to point out the Deputy Head, dozing into his beard.

The curtain stirred and slowly rose.

A pool of light.

My white dress shimmered in the dark.

It was a tragedy: I knew it would have to end badly, no matter how beautiful the lovers and their lines. But it was fascinating to follow the downfall – *These violent delights have violent ends* – to feel the rhythm of something wonderful going so horribly wrong.

'Kiwi fruit,' Tamsyn's mother announced. I was trying not to stare at the cheesecake resting on a silver stand in the middle of the table. Fleshy green coins glistened around its edge.

'It's delicious, Mrs Lee.' Wielding a spoon and fork, I acted as if I had eaten cheesecake plenty of times, never mind kiwi fruit.

Tamsyn's mother and father had invited me to their house in Didsbury for tea, which they called dinner. It had been a torment to get through my lamb chop and peas without spilling. The tablecloth was white lace. Every crunch and gulp resounded in my head; no chatter cluttered the table. Tamsyn's parents spoke one at a time, in low, luxuriously slow voices. In a corner of the room lurked the television, its screen a black hole. In our house, *Coronation Street* would be booming out while knives and forks scraped and everyone chunnered a-mile-a-minute.

'So, Andrea, what does your father do for a living?' Mr Lee leaned forward over the coffee, brewed in a glass pot after a screech of beans in the kitchen.

Mrs Lee darted a look at Tamsyn, then cleared her throat: 'Milk or cream?'

I glanced at Mrs Lee, wondering what Tamsyn had told her. It was a good job I hadn't blabbed more about my family. I looked down into my coffee cup as she poured in real cream.

'My dad' – I watched it swirling under the silver spoon in my cup – 'is a builder.'

Before Mr Lee could say anything else, Mrs Lee asked him in a tight voice: 'Are you playing golf this weekend, dear?'

The talk swerved to caddies and tee-times and damned awkward holes.

Upstairs, in her room, Tamsyn had a desk of her own, facing a huge bay window. She let me swivel in her fancy chair while she lay on her bed, sighing about boys, wondering which one on her list would turn out to be the better investment. Timothy had bought her a stuffed hippo, which she hugged under her chin while she talked.

'But then, Martin lets me read my poetry to him.' She fingered the ear of the hippo.

'You mean, you actually read your poems to other people?' The idea made me shudder: I wrote poems and stories, but I kept them pressed under a flap of carpet beneath my bed.

'Course I do.' Tamsyn sat up and fiddled with her hair, admiring herself in the mirror on the door of her built-in wardrobes. 'What's the point of writing them, otherwise?'

A poem was a box for your soul. That was the point. It was the place where you could save bits of your self, and shake out your darkest feelings, without worrying that people would think you were strange. While I was writing, I would forget myself and everyone else; poetry made me feel part of something noble and beautiful and bigger than me. But my poems were all about drowning, worlds inside mirrors, flesh, bone and blood, the gloopiness of time – things that other people might not understand. So I slid them under the carpet as soon as they were done, all the images and rhymes wrestled into place. By the time I had copied them out, I found I had memorized every line. Then they would surprise me by surging through me, like songs I knew by heart.

'It's romantic, reading poems to a boy,' Tamsyn mused. 'You should try it.'

'Well, I've got no one to inflict my poems on if I wanted to.' I grinned to flash the brace fastened across my teeth. 'Not while this is in the way.'

Every other Tuesday, at ten o'clock in the morning, I was tipped back in a black chair while Mr Fitzgerald the orthodontist peered into my mouth. He reached in with stainless-steel pincers to tighten the wire running through silver boxes cemented to my teeth. My head throbbed on the bus back to school, but the pain made me feel secure, forcing my teeth into line for the future while things remained crooked at home. One damp morning, after my appointment, a restless itch came over me, and I got on the bus into town instead of going back to school. I wandered through the underground market beneath the Arndale centre, gazing at calf-length leather boots with laces criss-crossed up the back. I wanted to remind myself that my feet would be in such things after a few more Saturdays scrubbing fridges and cookers for Auntie Livia and Uncle Max.

'All right, doll?' Most of the stallkeepers were men. Holding up the boots I had my heart set on, they looked my legs up and down, winking, in the underground glow: 'Do you a deal?'

I rushed back up to the pavement. Glad to be freshened by the drizzle, I clambered on to the bus, willing it to speed through the streets to school.

In spite of my brace, which made me keep my lips sealed, teachers nicknamed me Smiler. Because my marks were famously high and my behaviour generally good, but for a bit of cheek, they did no more than tut or shake their heads in mock despair when I turned up at school wearing earrings in the shape of zips, my skirt rolled well above the knees, my fingernails painted black. I was at the top of the boys' list of girls with good legs and nice faces; I was seen as wacky, a bit wild, and was hardly ever bullied; I was in line for nine O levels. At school, I couldn't help but grin.

At home, something ripped under my skin when I smiled, trying to pretend that everything was fine. Deadly moods lurked in a purple-white haze, smoke clinging to the curtains, turning stale overnight. Laurie and I threw the windows as wide as they would go each morning. We dumped hills of dimps and ash into the bin, and scoured cups whose insides had been tanned by coffee and tea. No matter how vigorously we shook the nets and beat the cushions, the air sagged, sick and tired. Days piled up in deafening silence as Mum and Dad refused to talk to one another. Things grew more and more suffocating. Something was going to lift the roof.

Although she was now nine, Sarah took to crawling into my bed again.

'It's the only place that lets me sleep, Andy.' She snuggled into my pillow.

I stroked her white-blonde hair, focusing on the silky feel of it under my fingers.

'Someone to Watch Over Me' – my sister liked me to croon her to sleep – 'Beautiful Dreamer' . . . 'Swinging on a Star' . . .

Our mother used to sing to us: 'Spread a Little Happiness' and 'Que Sera Sera'.

Protecting Sarah and Laurie made me feel stronger, but also more lonely. I tried floating on my own reassurance, hypnotized by the chant that it would all be all right. It will all be all right. It'll all be all right. It cut me off not only from Laurie and Sarah – still young enough to fall for the lullaby – but from myself – stuck behind a brave face while things were crumbling inside.

*

247

'Jee-zus! Not again!' Dad clipped me around the ear the second time I fell down our steep stairs.

'But there's nothing to hold on to if you slip,' I reminded him. The banister rail had come off in his and our mother's hands when they were struggling on the stairs one night. One minute they had been shouting, the next they were shocked into hysterical laughter. Both noises echoed like planks of wood, clacking.

The third time I slipped, I landed on my tailbone and could hardly sit down for days.

I never cried. Only before my periods, when my womb churned and I felt something monstrous in me. Once, I shut up the pain by sliding a needle through my earlobe, feeling the point pierce the flesh at the front, popping, sighing out the back. I slipped a small, silver hoop earring into the new hole. Whenever aches swelled in my guts or twisted my chest, I twiddled the silver ring.

Another month, shivering and clutched by cramps, I became obsessed by my fingernails. The sight of the black varnish made me feel sick. I had no money for remover and cotton wool; I usually lacquered over the old layers when they started to chip.

'What the hell are you doing?' My mother grabbed the potato peeler out of my hand when she found me sheering layers of black varnish off my nails.

'I had to get rid of it,' I sobbed, when she sat me down at the kitchen table to find out what on earth had possessed me. 'I just wanted to slice it all off. Don't you ever feel like that?'

'It's your hormones, Andrea.' My mother's eyes frosted over when I let myself melt in hot floods of tears. 'Why are you going on as if it's the end of the world?'

*

While we were forced to act as if everything was normal, Laurie and I both dreamt that our teachers would guess what was happening in our house and find a way to pull us out of it, even if it involved the police. Our mother had forbidden us from saying anything to anyone in authority.

'I couldn't put him back behind bars,' she insisted to Auntie Livia, Auntie Pauline and anyone else who suggested the law was the answer. She was terrified of being lonely. Even when her face was pulpy with tender spots, our mother remained adamant: 'I couldn't live with that.'

When it came to Parents' Evening, I was glad I had said nothing to make my teachers look down on Mum and Dad. Shame simmered in my veins, mingling with fiery pride, when I walked into the hall between them. Dad's neck was locked in a tie. My mother had applied a home perm; the curls were still coiled tight. She looked pretty but petrified.

'You both look fantastic,' I insisted. But there was no way they were going to step across the hall to meet Tamsyn's mother and father or any of the teachers. It was as if I was the parent and they were naughty children, hiding from the grown-ups.

'We weren't going to light up,' Dad whispered when I caught him and my mother rolling cigarettes behind a pillar in the hall: 'It's for when we get out of here.'

Miss Craig strode up and thrust out her hand to shake Dad's.

'Ahowd'yerdo?' He nearly choked over the aitch. The roll-up machine disappeared.

Miss Craig held my mother's hand for longer, looking her in the eye.

'I hope you realize what talent you've got on your hands.'

She made it sound the opposite of a compliment. 'Andrea's a very gifted girl.'

Miss Craig urged them to send me to a good sixth-form college, to see that I read the papers – the broadsheets, she explained in a condescending voice, such as the *Guardian*, the *Independent*, *The Times*, not the tabloids, like the *Sun* and the *Mirror*. Not even the *Daily Express*, she made clear, when my mother wondered. Above all, they must ensure that I did my homework in quiet and peaceful surroundings.

'Your daughter is university material,' she said, before moving off to shake more hands: 'It would be criminal to let her abilities go to waste.'

'Snooty bitch!' Dad ground the gear stick into reverse, screeching out of the school car park. 'What've you been telling her, eh?'

'Nothing, Dad,' I swore.

'Miss Craig's always a bit high and mighty,' I tried to reassure my mother, who was still smarting from the snide tone and innuendoes. 'Everyone says so.'

I sat between my parents in the cab of our truck, my heart jiggling along, secretly memorizing everything Miss Craig had said. I had a chance – we jolted over bumps in the road – I had a chance. To get somewhere.

Though he had left school at fourteen, with not one qualification to his name, Dad made a point of exercising his grey matter every day by arguing with the headlines and editorial comments in the *Sun*, before moving on to the crossword, which, he was proud to admit, he always completed in record time. I would make him a cuppa, while he sweated over the puzzle. 'E-summat-A-F-summat-N-summat.' He would ponder a few seconds, caressing the barrel of his biro, before shoving all clues aside to squeeze in his own wild words. I watched him wipe his brow, fill the boxes with a flourish, then sit back, satisfied – 'There we go: ELAFENT!'

When Dad had enjoyed his daily wrestle with the crossword and fallen into a snooze, I crept upstairs and spread the posh papers over my bedroom floor, where I set to with the scissors, to cut out items that I would paste into a scrapbook, the way Miss Craig had suggested. The miners were on strike. Precisely why the dispute could not be resolved, I was still not sure. Somehow Libya slipped into the equation: Arthur Scargill visited Colonel Gadhaffi for tea, which involved armaments, money, promises. Trying to untangle Ireland and the IRA was even more exasperating. I kept cutting and gluing, cutting and gluing, patching the world together.

On days when our house felt frighteningly brittle, it was consoling to go upstairs and turn the stuffed pages. Massacres and mangled bodies, explosions and mass drownings, gave me a terrible glow. It made me feel less alone, almost cosy, to see suffering splattered across the globe.

'After *Footloose*, he took me to the Chicago Diner for ice-cream,' Tamsyn murmured.

She and her new boyfriend, Timothy, had got a table right next to the window, where they shared a Knickerbocker Glory, complete with sparklers, she told me – lifting long spoons to each other's lips.

'You don't need sparklers,' was my expert opinion, 'if it's The One.'

After the initial burst of gladness that she had found someone who made her feel fuzzy, I began to be bashed by Tamsyn's happiness. *TimothyTimothyTimothyTimothyTimothy.* Ice-skating, bowling, the cinema. The Chicago Diner, where all the kids from Didsbury went, after they trailed out of the cinema, laughing and holding hands.

'You should come with us.' Tamsyn encouraged me to join her and Timothy and Philip, his best friend, when they went to the pictures on Friday night. 'We can make a foursome.'

'Don't be dense,' she laughed, when I told her I couldn't afford it: 'They'll pay for the tickets. That's what boys are for!'

Although I walked past it every morning and afternoon, on the way to and from school, I had never actually been to the cinema. I stepped into the blue velvet foyer on Friday night with Tamsyn and the two boys, and breathed in a blast of sweaty, popcorn air. At last, I was someone who went to the pictures.

Nightmare on Elm Street. Gripping the arms of my seat, I watched the girl on the screen spooning coffee granules into her mouth, glugging them down with Coke, clawing to stay awake. For me, nightmares were not frightening: they sorted out stuff in your head, flushing away grisly things that got in while you were awake. What I found terrifying was the idea of not being able to close your eyes and escape, by sinking into sleep, when something deadly was breathing down your neck. That, and Freddy Krueger's fingers: a screech and a flash of blades.

'What did you think?' Philip asked when we came out.

He had laid his hand over mine each time blood threatened to spurt.

'Exhausting,' I laughed.

'I didn't mean the film,' he murmured. He put on a low, serious voice that made me want to giggle, even as it filled me with dread.

Tamsyn and Timothy were shuffling along in front, trying to kiss and walk at the same time.

'Didn't you?' was all I could say. I was afraid that if I

opened my mouth one more time, something mean would blurt out, about his chin and the way it jutted, or his round moony eyes, which struck me as stupid although he strained to make them seem deep. He looked trapped in his own face: stuck with an idea (which his features couldn't live up to) that he was terribly handsome.

I kept my mind on the film. It had been thrilling to be packed in the cinema with other people, all sweating and sharing the same fear. It made me feel normal, just like everyone else, for an hour and a half: terror was something you put yourself through for fun, rather than something dangerous and dirty that you swept under the carpet at home.

Now I knew why people paid so much money to get into the pictures. But I wished that I hadn't had to rely on Philip for my ticket. My pride was starting to throb, setting off pangs that hurt my chest. Tamsyn had told me to think nothing of it, but something about the situation made me wince.

'Thanks a lot,' I said to him – repeating myself when that didn't seem to be enough: 'Thanks.'

I gasped when Philip's hands landed on my shoulders. His chin loomed: his mouth was coming down to mix with mine.

'But . . .' He looked confused when I pushed him away, my lips clamped shut. 'You let me pay for you at the pictures!'

Unsticking Tamsyn's face from Timothy's, I urged her to lend me some money until I got paid for cleaning cookers the next day.

'There!' I shoved three fifty-pence pieces into the boy's palm, before storming home: 'You can't buy a kiss off *me* for one-pound-fifty.'

The floppy collar of a green raincoat. A black jumper, worn through at the elbows. Brown curls, the odd one sticking out.

Polished shoes. A shy smile. I caught glimpses of The One wherever I went: dawdling past men and boys in the street, eyeing them across the pond in the park, blushing to sit next to them on the bus. The only things missing were the eyes, which I was never able to picture.

'What you hankering after, you?' Dad wondered why I wasted so much time lying on my bed, soggy teabags on my eyelids.

'I'm not hankering,' I murmured. 'I'm waiting.'

He didn't stop to ask what for. The teabags frightened him off.

I thought I had discovered how to transform the painful ache of wanting into the more pleasurable one of waiting. Taking tips from Auntie Livia's glossy magazines like *Vogue* and *Elle* and *Cosmopolitan*, I used refrigerated teabags to make my eyes sparkle; I was forever filing and lacquering my nails; locked in the bathroom, I cracked eggs on to my hair or rinsed it with vinegar, while Dad pounded to be let in for a pee. Hours were absorbed by photos of women curled up against satin, or running along beaches with steel-chested men: I calculated that I would be fatal to the opposite sex if only a mane of glorious hair were to cascade over my shoulders. I resolved to give up my habit of hacking at my hair with the kitchen scissors. To stimulate the follicles, I did headstands against the wall, balancing on my skull until I saw stars.

A pearly smile always went with the hair. I invested in a packet of baking soda toothpowder and spent ages brushing my teeth, scrubbing the silver boxes of my brace, while listening to the BBC World Service. Uncle Max had fobbed our dad off with a shortwave radio when the bottom fell out of another deal.

'It's just the thing' – my English teacher Mrs Arnold told

me how to find the right frequency – 'if you want to hear long words in action.'

Sollydarnosh, lessay-fair, dayus-x-mackinna, coo-day-tar, Devoorjack: I discovered how to get my tongue around the words I stumbled on in the newspaper. It was like tuning in to the future, learning the language they spoke there. I smuggled headphones under the covers, which helped to tame the panic that snaked through me whenever I woke in the middle of the night.

After school and on weekends, I used to lie on my bed for ages, letting pictures unroll inside my eyelids like a film. My Future. A big house, full of light, books lining the walls, swishy clothes, holidays in hot places, a lovely man, smiling . . .

The reel would snag and run out when Mum and Dad burst into screams or started banging around downstairs – slapping each other, knocking furniture over, threatening vile stuff. When they had had enough, the house would calm down to a murmur, the pair of them nursing their wounds over a pot of tea, talking about what was on telly, acting like nothing had happened. I would lie back on my bed, but my eyes would refuse to close. At times I could calm down by curling up, tucking my fists inside the cuffs of my jumper, pulling into myself.

Sometimes I got sick of waiting for my own life to start. The walls of our house felt as if they were closing in. It was hard to breathe. I was desperate to chisel the brace off my teeth, to let my mouth mingle with someone else's. Yet I knew that, even if my teeth were already straight, nothing romantic could happen to me while I lived at home. It was often sweetness and light: Mum lolling on Dad's lap, the two of them laughing and kissing, deep tongue kissing, while us kids tried to watch telly. But fights broke out so suddenly –

spurting insults and fists, ashtrays flying – it wasn't safe to bring anyone in.

Laurie, Sarah and I had a crush on Jehovah's Witnesses, who eased through the front door with their nice, soothing voices and put our dad on his best behaviour. We regarded them as if they had been dropped from heaven to ring on our doorbell. I rushed to brew a pot of tea, Laurie scrabbled for biscuits to arrange on a plate. We wanted to keep them there, nodding at Dad's theories about the buggerin' government, flapping leaflets under our mother's nose, droning on about God.

Where's God? – the earth would have opened if I ever spoke up – *When we close the door behind you?*

Dad railed against the miniature bibles that the Jehovah's Witnesses had pressed on us – propaganda, he called them, chock-a-block with secret messages injected by the government. Laurie and I pretended to agree with him (that was always the best plan), and kept our bibles out of sight. But at bedtime, before we turned out the light, we would spend ages devouring the tiny print, chapter and verse. It was as if we were doing homework for God. A different prayer for each day of the week, we had lined up, with special adjustments to add emphasis when things were really grim, or to show gratitude if we thought we saw a glimmer at the end of the tunnel.

Since God never seemed to come up with the goods, we eventually found ourselves concentrating less on prayers and more on high marks at school. Laurie was in love with languages, especially German and French, and a bit of Spanish. She loaded her tongue with foreign words, which no one else in our house could understand. Science struck me as reassuring: so many equations to rely on; always a right and wrong answer.

The Periodic table was imprinted under my eyelids. My spirit soared when I assembled molecules in Chemistry – I felt I had my hands on the universe, juggling red and green styrofoam spheres, connecting them with white straws to reveal the patterns that lay behind everything.

When I tuned in to God from my pillow, I recited the results of tests I had passed in sciences and maths, the dates of historical treaties, battles, births and deaths, tricky constructions in French, the lines of war poems I had learnt by heart:

Everyone suddenly burst out singing;
And I was filled with such delight
As prisoned birds must find in freedom,
Winging wildly across the white
Orchards and dark green fields; on – on   and out of sight.

17

My feet were in a plastic bucket, my hair was standing on end. As the newly elected head girl, it was my privilege to demonstrate the Van der Graaf generator at our school's summer open evening. Kids in the lower years held their breath when I stroked the silver globe. A current of electricity passed through me. Older lads shoved to have their own hair shocked into the air.

'Stick your feet in the bucket before you touch it.' I stepped out to let Godfrey, the head boy, take over, although his hair couldn't spring up since his Afro was shaved so short. 'You have to earth yourself.'

Mr Galsworthy, our headmaster, had asked me to split my time between the labs, chatting to convince fathers in nice jumpers to send their sons to study science at Whitbrook, and the English room, where my poem about war, skin colour and nuclear meltdown was spread across the wall on six sheets of paper. 'It's not too long,' my English teacher Mrs Arnold had assured me, when I got into a flap with Sellotape: 'It deals with big questions about human nature; it's what we call epic.'

Although I would have to leave our school because the sixth form had closed down, I had tried to keep all of my favourite teachers happy by promising to do A levels in Biology and Chemistry, as well as English Literature and General Studies. One moment I was determined to become a lawyer, defending desperate women like my mother, the next I knew I was destined to save lives as a doctor. Whatever career I chose to pursue, Mrs Arnold insisted, it would be sacrilege to give up reading and writing poems.

'It's your element, Andrea.' She talked about Literature, capital L, as if it were a company I could work for, or a country I might live in.

'Lit-ter-atch-yoor.' Tamsyn and I sighed over the same vague dream, built on the feelings we got – velvety, spiky, watery, like fire – just from words.

Whereas I used to hide the fact that I smoked cigarettes or swigged whisky or wagged days off school, the things I now kept secret at home were words. Long, complicated ones I discovered in stories by Jane Austen and Thomas Hardy and the Brontë sisters, whose books I was given by Tamsyn or Mrs Arnold. Short, simple ones that would sparkle unexpectedly in the middle of poems. *Long lion days. Life with a Hole in it. That vast moth-eaten musical brocade. The Importance of Elsewhere.*

I worshipped Philip Larkin, who got stuck into the dullest corners of life and picked up ordinary, everyday stuff to smack you with art. *In the hollows of afternoons / Young mothers assemble . . . Behind them . . . An estateful of washing, / And the albums, lettered / Our Wedding, lying / Near the television.* It was as if he could step inside people's skin, to take photographs of them from the inside out:

> *Their beauty has thickened.*
> *Something is pushing them*
> *To the side of their own lives.*

I would pore over the poetry anthology from school, feeling words gathering and buzzing inside me, like the mob of bees inside the box in Sylvia Plath's poem: *Small, taken one by one, but my god, together!* When Dad was having a go at me, poking his finger against the bony bit of my chest and ranting, assuring me I was good for nothing, I imagined letting them loose like swear words, only carrying a more beautiful sting.

'A fine combination of passion and practicality.' The admissions tutor congratulated me on my unconventional mixture of proposed A levels, when I went to be interviewed for a place at Xaverian Sixth-Form College. 'Now then, what are your ambitions for the future?'

It was like being on one of the game shows my dad loved to watch, sweating to come up with the answer that would win me a ticket into the college. The very phrase 'the future' made me want to rush to the loo, out of excitement. My head crowded full of all the things I had ever dreamed of becoming: a firefighter, an air hostess, a farmer, a pilot, a lawyer, a doctor, a writer. I was tempted to mention my fantasies about being a writer, pouring stuff out of my head on to paper, so that people could read it and let it seep into their own heads. But I was afraid that the man in the suit would laugh.

I imagined trying to squeeze my hopes out in nice, round sentences. In the end, I stuck to the subject of my A levels and talked about going on to study law at university. It was hard to concentrate, to speak without trembling. I could hardly think beyond the school's glorious old-brick buildings, like castles, each set on an island of grass, gravel walkways lacing them into one green, brainy world. Christian Brothers floated along the paths, black gowns in full sail. The school was tucked between the posh Victorian houses behind Withington Road – a rush of Indian restaurants and sari shops, furious traffic and exhaust fumes. I would never have guessed it existed, if it hadn't been for Tamsyn and her mother, who knew about these things. After visiting Shena Simon, the shabby Institute for Further Education where you could combine English with

History and Hairdressing, Tamsyn had insisted that we both apply to Xaverian.

'If they're Christians,' she had it all worked out, 'it won't matter that we're not Catholic.'

My secret fear was that I was not posh enough, as well as not Catholic enough, to go to such a fancy college. I was terrified that they would see Tamsyn's Marks and Spencer clothes and let her in, that they would know mine were secondhand, and I would be left out in the cold. But on the day of the interview, I looked as smart as everyone else, in a long and clinging greeny-blue skirt which made me feel like a mermaid, from the Dress for Less reject shop, topped with an ivory blouse that my mother let me have on credit from her catalogue. Instead of turning up their noses because we were from Whitbrook Comprehensive, the teachers at Xaverian seemed all the more impressed by the promise shown by Tamsyn and me, since we had managed to do so well in spite of going to such a rough inner-city school. The question of being Catholic never came up, after they had read our school reports. We might be heathens, but we were both predicted to get eight or nine O levels, the majority of which promised to be As.

'Gluttons for punishment, or what?' Mark Harris, like a lot of the kids at school, saw no cause for congratulations when he heard that Tamsyn and I had been accepted to study for A levels. Most of the fifth year were in awe of our stupidity, not our brains. No one could understand why we were so keen to carry on, especially not all the way to university, where we would be stuck until we were twenty-one.

'I'd be bored shitless, meself.' Robbie Carter was already making money as a trainee mechanic, fixing cars at the garage where his dad was in charge.

Some kids had dropped out before the exams to take up jobs in shops or on building sites, although it was against the law because they were under sixteen. A few girls were busy having babies; Borstal had nibbled away at the number of boys. Getting O levels, everyone agreed, was a bit poncy but fair enough if you had it in you; plodding on after that was a sheer waste of time. Angie was starting out as a shampooist in the hairdressers on Princess Parkway, Jayne had a job at her local chemist's, Nicky's mother had signed her up to work at the cashout as soon as the new Gateway supermarket was unveiled in Withington.

'Aren't you dying to get out, like?' They seemed sorry for me when I let myself in for two more years of school: 'Don't you want to make loads of dosh?'

'You're sixteen.' Dad was always pushing me to get out and make loads of dosh: 'When I was bloody well sixteen, I was grafting to keep me mam as well as meself.'

He reckoned I should at least be putting a few pounds towards the family food money; but I wasn't even making my ten pounds a week any more, since Auntie Livia and Uncle Max's shop had gone bust. So as soon as the exams were over, I put on my long greeny-blue skirt and shuffled up and down Withington Road in search of a job.

'As luck would have it' – the greasy bloke who ran the cinema stared at my hips as if he could see through my skirt – 'our matinée usherette just walked out.'

Instead of stopping to wonder why, I stepped straight into her shoes. I couldn't think of anything more glamorous. I would get to see all the films for free.

After sitting through seven showings of *My Little Pony*, having sugared popcorn chucked at me along with words like Fuck and Cunt (which sounded worse out of the mouths of kids), not to mention the manager's leery looks, I was practically blind.

'It must have been all them hours in pitch black,' my mother mused. She and Dad suspended their usual sniping when they noticed me squinting, nose pressed up close to the telly.

'Don't worry,' I urged: 'I've booked an appointment at the optician's.'

What I didn't tell them was that Thomas Hardy was to blame. All week, pink and blue ponies had talked and sung and done little dances across the cinema screen. The only way to stay sane had been to sit at the back, my usherette's torch trained on the pages of *Tess of the D'Urbervilles*, one of the cracked-spine paperbacks that Mrs Arnold had passed on to me after clearing out her loft at home. Straining to read in the dark-yellow glow of my torch, I imagined myself in the place of Tess: a poor milkmaid transformed into a goddess by the secret, mystical light of the morning. My eyes began to ache. Eventually, stinging made them water. I read on, obsessed by the idea that I was tainted, like Tess. The chance of a lovely life ruined by shameful things in the past. My heart clobbered and rose when blood seeped through the ceiling after Tess killed Alec, the one who had spoiled her. Maybe she could slash her way to a happy ending with Angel by cutting the other man out? But even in a story, it wouldn't work out that way: my heart sank as Stonehenge loomed and Tess faced her dead end.

For years, I had lived with a sticky sense of being spoiled. I could almost feel it clogging my veins, making me feel mucky inside.

'Your face will take you places, luvvie.' Auntie Livia used to stroke my cheek when I worried that I would never get anywhere.

Tess's face hadn't saved her: it had been her downfall as well as her way out. And once you were ruined, it seemed, that was that. But – I reasoned with myself – if I never spoke about it to anyone, perhaps I wouldn't end up spoiled by my past.

I clutched at the thought of my O levels, haunted by the clang of fate: *Too late, too late, too late.*

Tamsyn and I went to pick up our results, and wandered back down the echoing school corridors with a straggle of other kids, grades flapping on white strips of paper like bandages or white flags of surrender. All the deadly boredom and bullying that had crowded the place; it felt like the end of a five-year war.

'Six As, two Bs, and a C,' I told Tamsyn, whose results turned out to be slightly heavier on the Bs and Cs, though both of our grades were more than enough to let us into Xaverian College come September.

'Wow.' She looked at my fist, clenched around the scrap of paper, as if it might blow away. 'You must be ecstatic.'

'Yeah.' My insides would have done somersaults at the sight of my grades, if they hadn't been weighed down by things at home.

I opened the spiralbound sketchbook that the school let me take home to keep after finishing my O level in art. A secret diary. I had never dared to keep a real one, using words, but here I could pore over ink strokes, chalk dustings and coloured pencil shades, remembering the feelings – invisible to the rest of the world – moving through me when I made them. A dark, bare-chested man facing the sun in a desert, his skin a blend of pencil crayons and spittle rubbed in with my fingertips; a girl borne on wings full of veins and tiny eyes; a lamp-post, seeping eerie streams of light.

At the back there were blank pages.

Sometimes, if Dad had hit one of us or Mum had blown her top, telling us all to go to hell before locking herself in the bathroom, I would lie on my bed, sharpen my pencil, and hold it over the clear white sheet. The lead point hovered. I imagined it stabbing through the paper as if it were skin, leaving gashes like bullet holes. But something kept me from lashing out to wreak havoc. It would be a terrible waste. And there were things I didn't want to show up on paper. The idea of damaging something made me feel afraid, as if I might be sucked into the dark stuff in our house.

Instead – hovering, hovering – I let go of the rage in my head while my hands lost themselves in light, airy strokes, unravelling lines to make a map of some other world.

'Off your arse!' Dad chivvied Laurie and me to empty, wash and polish the ashtrays so that he and our mother could fill them back up. 'Hop to, jump to!' We had to keep up a steaming supply of coffee and tea, replenishing the mugs at their feet while they sat on the settee, soaking up telly.

'In our day . . .' They moaned about the flaming amazing opportunities thrust under the noses of the next generation. Mum sparked with pride when one of us passed a test or won a prize, but Dad would soon make sure it tipped into bitterness.

'Oi! I thought I told you to brush the stairs!' They always found some cleaning task to shove on to our shoulders if they caught us reading a book, sketching, getting ready to go out to meet friends. It was easier not to go out at all, to avoid the anger it would stir up, ready to burst in your face when you stepped back through the door.

'What's this?' Dad would be waiting, fuming and holding up a plate or a cup, some fatal trace of scum on its edge where Laurie or I had rushed to wash it before going out. We had to roll up our sleeves and scrub every single dish, plate, cup, fork, knife, spoon and pan again. Silence reigned, broken only by the clink and glug of pots in the sink. The slightest sigh, the merest murmur about unfairness, won you a whack on the back of the head.

Dad sometimes consoled himself for his rotten past and unlucky present by splurging on treats from the chippy for himself and our mother, while Laurie, Sarah and I made do with toast.

'Steak-and-kidney pud, with mushy peas, chips and gravy for Yours Truly.' He sent Laurie and me on expeditions all the way down Claremont Road to Charlie's Chippy, where they knew how to do good, old-fashioned gravy, which he claimed made it worth our long trudge. Counting out coins, he worked out the precise price in advance, so there would be no way for us sly buggers to pocket any change: 'Grab us some scampi and a nice piece of cod for your mam.'

Sometimes, my sisters and I would be sent upstairs, where it was cold, while our mum and dad tucked into their take-away in the warm living-room. Other times, especially when Dad had gone off in a huff and come back, triumphant, with an Indian meal, he seemed keen for us to stay in the room full of exotic smells, watching him pull tin-foil treasures out of a brown paper bag. Laurie, Sarah and I would sit nearby, taking care not to stare while our mother tore into the Peshwari Naan that was her favourite. She looked guilty, breaking open the bread, her fingernails seeking out clusters of mashed almonds, pouncing on scalding sultanas. But not that guilty.

While Mum and Dad were engrossed by each other and this or that treat, I slipped away to read more and more poems, huddled on my bed against the cold. It was like holding my breath underwater, immersing myself for as long as possible, until some yell or bang or even a burst of laughter broke in and ripped my eyes off the lines.

We have lingered in the chambers of the sea
By sea-girls wreathed with seaweed red and brown
Till human voices wake us, and we drown.

Mum and Dad would screech to summon my sisters and me down to the living-room on nights when they were in the mood for a movie. They liked us to gather together, like a proper flaming family, after they had splashed out to rent a video from the corner shop. Tonight it was *Poltergeist*, which I had watched to death, years ago, when it was first released.

'Is it okay if I read while it's on?' I whispered to my mother, who nodded. I was half a centimetre into *Sons and Lovers*, which Mrs Arnold had urged me to read, and suffered a kind of lovesickness if I had to put it down, even for a second. Life seemed harsh but glinting with promise for Paul Morel. I would give anything for coalmines or countryside or something romantic, to make my life as picturesque as his. Curled up on the living-room floor, I turned the pages as quietly as possible. I kept my head down after the film began to roll, looking up only now and again, to catch the best flesh-crawling bits.

'Oi, you!' Dad disturbed me for the third time in a row, though we both knew it should have been Laurie's turn: 'Stick on a brew.'

Usually, when Dad had it in for me, I consoled myself by hugging my breasts under my jumper, where I stashed most of my dark or angry thoughts as well as my hopes and plans about getting out. It was a trick I learned when I was small, after I realized I could keep secrets – a whole other life – under my vest. I knew how to keep my mouth shut, and was forever nagging Laurie and Sarah to do the same, to protect their own ears from clouts, and to avoid trouble for Mum, who had to deal with split loyalties and mop everything up. But now something in me was bursting to get out. College was just around the corner, yet in the belly of summer, it seemed a world away. A tut sneaked off my tongue.

'Cheeky sod!' Dad fumed, though he couldn't bring himself to get up off the settee to give me what for. 'I'll make you wish you'd never been born,' he growled, settling back into his cushions.

'Don't worry,' I muttered under a sigh, 'I already do.'

The sigh was sharp enough to catch his attention; not loud enough to disguise the words.

'Terry!' My mother tried to pull him back as he bounded off the settee.

A fantastic crack sounded when my head hit the wall.

'Ungrateful sod!' Dad quivered, while my mother grabbed me and rubbed my crown.

'Put on a cuppa,' she told Laurie. Fingers feeling for lumps: 'She's in a daze.'

The wall had knocked my face into a smile that put her and Dad on edge.

I disappeared upstairs to nurse my bruises. Lying on my bed, I sank back into *Sons and Lovers*, my fingers straying to the lump at the back of my head. All these years he had got away with beating our mother and lashing out at us. I was sixteen, he was quick to remind me when he bullied me to get out and bring home some dosh. I was sixteen; I could go to the police.

One more – my smile surfaced through the tears when I touched the tender spot – *just one more.*

An unusual kind of hush – happy and excited – came over the house when our mother put down the phone to the man from the Moss-Care Housing Association. After years on the waiting list, we had been offered a three-storey town house in Withington, not far from Didsbury, where there were no junkies or prostitutes, no street gangs with knives and guns.

'Four bedrooms! Right next to the posh shops and all.' Mum and Dad gripped hands, their fingers laced into one bristling fist. They were almost afraid to laugh, as if it might shatter our luck.

'Brand-new neighbours!' Laurie and I thrilled in private at the prospect of living next to people who would think we were normal. A brand-new, sparkling reputation, our parents would have to live up to.

The women down our street acted sad to see us go. They were caught between liking my mother because she was warm and funny, hating her since her face and figure had been made in heaven, and pitying her for what I had heard them refer to as living hell. They prickled between the three when they spoke to me, too.

'Ta ra!' Our mother bid them quick goodbyes, then stood in the stripped living-room, staring at the carpet she and Auntie Tamara had once laid with the aid of Stanley knives and a sense of humour, oiled by Bacardi and Coke. 'Moons ago,' she sighed. Cigarette burns, coffee stains, streaks of grease, petrol and stubborn specks of blood. I looked at the trodden green too, feeling sorry for everything it had gone through.

Our new house seemed to stand by itself, big bay windows facing on to a main road. Laurie and I grinned at its grand front, then exchanged grim looks with one another: no neighbours on either side. Mum and Dad were proud to call it detached, since it jutted out alone on the corner, but its back wall was, we were secretly relieved to discover, actually attached to another house on the end of a terraced block running down a side street.

'A man's home is his castle.' Dad rubbed his hands, surveying the gloriously wide windows and the door with five steps leading up to it, shrouded by a bushy hedge. As soon as we had unloaded our furniture, plugged in the television and put the kettle on for a brew, he unearthed a rusty pair of shears from the cellar and went out to tame the hedge.

'My hedge.'

Kerschwunk, kerschwunk, kerschwunk: he snipped the privet into battlements, then came inside to gloat. Strangers passed outside the windows, unable to see in through the hedge, while he squeezed the trigger of an imaginary rifle, firing chuckles at their heads.

We stayed up long past midnight, arranging furniture, hanging those pictures whose frames had survived the years. We sipped through one last pot of tea in silence, putting off the moment of going to bed.

'Might wake up tomorrow,' our mother rested her cheek against Dad's shoulder, 'and find it's all a dream.'

She jumped at a small crunch in the back wall – someone pulling their plugs for the night.

Laurie and I breathed: 'Next door.'

*

It snowed fifty-pound notes in our house when Dad wangled not one, not two, but *three* contracts to put up porches and extend kitchens, securing some of his payment up front. 'Two thousand smackeroos!' He kissed the lips of the stern faces on the notes, before letting them float over our heads.

'Come on,' he decided to blow a bit for good luck, 'get your posh togs on – we're off to paint the town, we are!'

My sisters and I huddled under the tarpaulin in the back of his truck, keen to escape the rain and the stares of people in other cars. We used to love scrambling among Dad's tools, singing 'Ten Green Bottles' and waving at strangers. But now I was sixteen and Laurie fourteen: only our ten-year-old sister Sarah still enjoyed the ride.

After a splurge on the video machines in the arcade off Piccadilly, Dad decided it was time to eat. The karate-choppers on the screen put him in the mood for Chinese.

The five of us sat on high-backed gold chairs like thrones, around a table sizzling with bloody sauces, glistening meat and snaky noodles. We gazed at our dad over piles of pearly rice.

'Best nosh-house in Chinatown,' he was assuring the manager, a tiny man in a black suit who – drawn by our flushed cheeks and wide eyes – had come over to find out whose birthday it was.

'Everyone's!' Dad grinned and held up his glass to clink ours one more time.

The manager clicked his fingers for another bottle of red wine: 'Compliments of the establishment.'

'Man of substance, me.' Dad explained why the manager kept hovering around our table: 'He thinks I'll leave him a fat tip.' Putting his hand over his heart, he brushed the wallet stashed in the breast pocket of his pinstriped jacket: 'I will, an' all.' He raised his eyebrows: a waiter scurried to top up his glass, stiff face cracking into a smile, a dragon roaring across his waistcoat.

'Two K up front, Rainie, babe,' he kept repeating in a squiffy voice. The wine had puffed up his plans, then fuddled them, so that they slurred through purple-streaked teeth.

Edible eyeballs called lychees, sticky nut diamonds and tortured-looking bananas were wheeled out and stuck under our noses.

'Better get used to the high life, kids,' he declared, when we groaned that we were stuffed: 'Might be the first time you've been in a restaurant, but – mark my words – it'll not be the last.'

'Classy joint, that.' Dad was impressed when I clinched a job collecting glasses and serving meals at Ye Olde House at Home pub down Burton Road. 'Classy grub, too.'

I smiled to myself at the thought of the dishes, rummaged out of the deep chest freezer, shoved into the microwave, given a last-minute tan under the grill. Dressed up with a sprig of parsley like a bow tie, ye olde lasagne or moussaka was then carted out on a tray by me, shimmying in a tight skirt and heels. Though he paid me less than £1.50 an hour, the landlord relied on me to melt customers out of their tempers when they discovered the still-frozen bit at the heart of their meals: 'Use your charm, lass!'

'Aw, Andy, love.' My mother brimmed pride when I put on my uniform, a white paper cap propped over the bun of my hair: 'You look like an air hostess.'

She cast her eyes down at the awful orange check overall she had to wear in her new job as a home help – shopping, cleaning and taking care of old or disabled people.

'Well, I can't be putting on the Ritz, can I?' She made an effort to laugh at her own reflection: 'Just to be pooed and peed over all day long.'

By the end of her first week, our mother had gathered a whole slew of friends. 'Partners in grime,' the home helps called themselves, making comedy out of the dirtier side of their days. Although he had allowed few outsiders through the door of our old house, Dad was now happy to let our mother invite her new workmates round for tea. They praised his handiwork after the tea sent them upstairs to the loo, where he had stippled the walls and glossed them peach, our mother's favourite colour. Zooming out for late-night trips to Do-It-All and B&Q, then staying up plastering and painting until dawn, Dad had turned our bathroom into a palace: gleaming mirrors with a matching toothbrush rack and toilet-roll holder; a real mahogany loo seat. The women went away chattering about our mother's right posh house, her daughters – brainy, pretty, polite – and her fantastic, blue-eyed fella, dead brilliant, like, with his hands.

I felt tipsy when September finally came: Tamsyn and I wandered around Xaverian College, meeting people with nice skin, nice voices, nice clothes, and nice parents behind every-thing. Masses of glowing faces came up, keen to work out whether I was worth knowing, not for where I came from, but for what I might have to say – and how wittily I could say it – about *A Clockwork Orange, Brighton Rock, A Portrait of the Artist as a Young Man,* the genius of Morrissey and the Smiths. I had never thought of books, poems and plays as ways to get closer to boys. You could go on about stanzas, alexandrines, surreal symbols, while all the time your mind was on someone's mouth, analysing the myriad possible meanings behind a pair of slightly parted lips.

My brace was still cemented across my teeth, a fence between me and romance. I joked and flirted with clever boys – rich accents and grins – but saved my serious swoons for James Joyce, Graham Greene and Thomas Stearns Eliot. Happy to hold hands with J. Alfred Prufrock, I listened to mermaids singing, each to each. I had a feeling they would sing to me, eventually.

Before my seventeenth birthday, I came home from the dental hospital ecstatic but shy about smiling, for fear of dazzling everyone with my flawless white smile. My mouth felt borrowed, or newly bought: I had to practise grinning, resisting the urge to fasten my lips where the brace used to be. The words that came out, Dad teased me, sounded new too. 'La-de-dah!' he mimicked me whenever I opened my mouth. Whereas I had slapped my accent around to fit in at Whitbrook Comprehensive and to avoid catching any flak on the bus, college inspired me to sharpen consonants and to project words from the depths of my chest, coming up with voluptuous vowels where flat ones used to be good enough.

While my voice dressed itself up, my clothes learnt a chic sort of skulk. After making the terrible mistake of turning up for my first day at college in a shimmery white jacket that I had blown my pub wages on, I slid into threadbare jeans and clompy ankle boots, an old man's shirt knotted at the waist, alternating with a black polo-neck or secondhand Aran sweater when the weather turned foul. Occasionally I would put on something fancy but not too flashy, like the satiny sky-blue waistcoat or pink mohair jumper that I bought in secret using the tips that were slipped me at the pub.

At first I felt bad because Laurie had no money of her own. There she was, still stuck at secondary school, wearing the same old clothes, while I was going to college, meeting interesting people, discovering all sorts of new stuff and wearing what I liked. Comparing our lives made me feel so lucky it ached. Guilt prompted me to lend my sister gear that would make her look cool; it even drove me to give her the odd thing now and then. But it was a relief when she took on a job and could buy nice clothes of her own. She sacrificed her Saturdays to be a part-time shampoo girl at the local salon called Curl Up and Dye, where the old ladies adored the way she massaged their scalps, and queued up especially to put their balding heads in her hands.

Now that I had found a second skin, wearing things that allowed me to blend in, I could relax and enjoy the fact that my face stuck out. At last, I was beginning to grow out of that awful squashed sense of myself. Looking around the common room, my gaze bumped into others', fixed on me. With no brace to hold me back, I fell in love a thousand times – hundreds of times a day – with boys, girls, teachers, books, words. Quintessential. *Quidditas.* Seraphim. *Ignotae artes.* Even the colour of the sky knocked me sideways as I crossed the grass to my English class, wondering whether a minus or a plus would be dangling from the A that was known to bloom at the end of my essays.

Endless Andreas crowded in front of me when I stared into the three-way mirror on Gran's dressing table. Adjusting the wings so that they caught and threw back, caught and threw back the reflection, my face went on for ever, shrinking but not giving up.

All those Andreas, and no Gran.

Pride had made her eyes water when I presented her with my flap of O levels and announced that I had got into such a good college. 'Just think of everything you're capable of, Andy, love!' She had smiled and rubbed my hands between hers. Now she would never know what else I might have in me.

Her fingers had brushed the butterfly brooch over her heart, while her face scrunched up one side. A lady had seen it all from her window on the second floor. Gran had sat down on the bench outside the flats. When the milk bottle had slipped from her fist and smashed, the lady rushed to dial 999.

'Personal effects of Mildred Chadfield.' At the hospital where the ambulance had deposited the body, the nurse handed my mother and Auntie Pauline a clear plastic bag, stuffed with the bobbly skirt we used to pluck; Gran's cardigan with the butterfly brooch; her outdoor slippers; her bra – two horribly hollow bowls; wrinkled tights; vast knickers made of something stiff the colour of flesh; and her dentures, fixed in an eternal grin. I wanted to wrap my coat around the bag, to protect Gran from people's eyes.

'Do we have to?' Laurie and I appealed to our mother when she pulled out of the oven the cheese-and-onion pie that she'd brought home from Gran's kitchen.

'It's the last thing she ever did.' Our mother was determined to keep Gran's memory alive as long as she could. 'It was milk to brush the pastry, she'd gone out for, when it came on.'

Dad tried a mouthful of the pie. He couldn't bring himself to swallow. Laurie, Sarah and I watched him leave the table and go down to the workshop he had set up in the cellar, where we heard him hammering around. We churned through cheese and onion, weeping.

'It's how she would have wanted us to remember her.' Our mother braced herself for another trembling forkful: 'She was your gran.'

*

Gazing into the gas fire, our mother clutched a toilet roll and did nothing but sniffle for hours on end. The shrieks of a heartbroken elephant trumpeted through the house each time she blew her nose. Laurie, Sarah and I sat at her feet in the blaze of the fire, letting our faces burn alongside hers. Dad actually brewed pots of tea, served with Jaffa Cakes to help us through our sorrow. Our mother stayed deaf, dumb and blind to everything but the fire.

While we were glued together by grief, Dad was at a loss. He had admired our grandmother's quiet strength and always turned on his best blue twinkle, hoping to grow close enough to call her Milly and give her one of his roll-yer-own smokes, the way Uncle Bill always did. But he suspected she guessed the truth – concerning his other side – and they had never seen eye to eye. Now he tinkered about in the cellar, waiting for our mother to get over her grief. In spite of the cold down there, I sometimes left my mother in front of the fire and went to help him plane or sand a plank of wood while he attacked fresh timber with his crocodile saw.

'Get this!' Dad had discovered a way to blow glass, breathing into clear, thin tubes that he found on the rubbish dump, while blasting them with his bunsen burner. He and I took turns, twisting melted glass like runny toffee, blowing bubbles that set when you pulled them out of the flame into the frosty underground air.

'Go give it your mam,' Dad urged, when my glass monsters grew into swans or came out as snowflakes and stars. 'It'll cheer her up.'

'Mum . . .' No matter how carefully I cradled the things, they shattered at the shock of cold air, before I could get to the top of the cellar stairs.

*

Dad came home with a budgie for Mum. She bought seeds, a small bell and a mirror, then made curtains for its cage. Her old laugh broke out of her chest when she unhooked its door: drunk on so much space, the bird whizzed in mad spirals, divebombing Dad's head, before landing on his shoulder and pecking like fury to make a meal of his ear.

'Little fu— blighter!' Dad's sense of humour outshone the pain when the budgie drew blood. Without ruffling its feathers, he made a basket of his fist and put the bird back behind bars. Attaching a label to its cage, he created a prison cell: KiLLeR 401.

When Mum and Dad burst out shouting, Killer hopped from one end of his perch to the other, headbutting his bell to pit its tinkle against their chaos. Once they had forgotten their differences and were back in love with the world and each other, neither of them could understand why that bloody idiot of a bird was always squawking and shuddering and pecking feathers off his own breast.

Then one day Killer plopped off his perch and Dad flushed him down the loo. 'Maybe it was the paint fumes,' he murmured. Out of work again, Dad had gone on the prowl for things to fix, putting up shelves, changing fuses in all the plugs, finally plastering more fresh white paint over the walls. But before he could finish, the paint ran out. There was no money to buy even one more can.

'It's that or food,' was the bottom line.

Our mother was aggravated by the ceilings looking so much dingier than the whitewashed walls. Laurie, Sarah and I were more concerned about the state of the kitchen cupboards: after a honeymoon of Heinz, McVities, Crosse & Blackwell, Nescafé and Knorr, our shelves were swamped once more by stark white labels from Kwik Save.

'At least it's Marvel,' our mother sighed, pulling powdered milk out of the shopping bags.

'Yeah.' I stirred it into instant, no-name coffee, admiring the way it dissolved: 'No globs.'

We needn't have worried about what visitors would think if they found powdery clouds in their cups. Our mother's mates dropped off one by one as they got wise to the goings-on behind our closed doors. My dreams of bringing home friends from college, maybe even a boyfriend, had evaporated. Our mother spent the evenings weeping on the stairs, where she went to sit by herself in the cold and dark, while the rest of us watched telly in front of the fire. She was convinced that Gran's ghost was just waiting for the right, quiet moment before stepping forth in all its glory. Having treated our mother this long with kid gloves, Dad had run out of patient ways to pull her up when she found herself sinking back into her misery. Instead of stroking her hair to ease her sobs, he ended up yanking it and slapping her face: 'Snap out of it, Rainie! Snap out of it!'

'Just a silly ding-dong,' I heard my mother protesting, when her workmates Sally and Josie came straight out and asked her about the rusty shadow in the socket of her eye. They might have believed her if the rest of her face wasn't sunk under wrinkles.

'You look like you've the weight of the world on your shoulders, love.' Her friend Karen stuck by her. Wide-hipped and big-mouthed, she wore loud-coloured jumpers that showed she was afraid of no one and nowt. Her own husband had been God-forgive-the-bugger vicious. She had put him behind bars where he belonged. For his own good.

'Taste of their own medicine.' She prescribed the same treatment for our dad: 'Lets 'em know how it feels, being locked up all day, treated like shit, wondering what the bloody hell they've done to deserve it.'

There was a police station tantalizingly near to our house; Laurie and I could see its blue sign glowing when we looked out from my room in the attic. But our mother refused to let us go over and grab an officer when things got out of hand.

'They won't do any good.' She was sceptical about their willingness as well as their ability to help: 'They think a woman dun't get a slapping for nothing.'

The police had come round a couple of times, called by someone across the road, and had given our dad a mild ticking off, which only prompted him to hit our mother harder the minute the door shut behind them. Once, a young man from the next street came round and rat-tatted with authority on our door, to ask us to keep the noise down and to find out what was going on. My sisters and I peered through the window nets, spying him as he adjusted his trousers and straightened his spine to look taller. But he turned tail in a flash when Dad went to the door and told him to fuck off and mind his own cunting business.

We felt even more abandoned by the outside world when Karen eventually lost patience and stopped calling for her usual smoking sessions with our mother, the two of them nattering, putting the world to rights, over a pot of tea.

'I can't keep coming round, Lorraine, watching you dwindle into nothing more than a punchbag.' Her eyes blurred under tears that were rare for her. 'Why're you letting him beat the living daylights out of you?'

'It's me own fault,' our mother insisted. 'I bring it on meself, being so morose.'

She no longer bothered to protect her own head when it was rained on by Dad's rage.

'At least in the old days,' I said to Laurie, who had also detected a turn for the worse, 'she used to land him one on the jaw when she got the chance.'

I pleaded with my mother to get some kind of help, now that she had lost her old elastic. If she wouldn't go to the police, surely she could speak to the doctor?

'Don't be nagging me, Andy.' She came home with a bottle of tranquillizers guaranteed to take even more wind out of her sails. 'I know what's best.'

The barge she sat in, like a burnish'd throne,
Burnt on the water. The poop was beaten gold,
Purple the sails, and so perfumed that
The winds were love-sick with them ...

I would go to bed as early as possible and sink into my pillow with a book and a miniature bottle of Bailey's cream, my tongue skating the silky rim of the neck, while I sipped words off the page. When Mum and Dad started shouting and screeching, I resisted the urge to run downstairs in my pyjamas like I used to. My sisters and I knew it would make no difference; sometimes it made things worse. Instead, I stayed close to my pillow, whispering the richest lines to myself, whispering and whispering, so that their rhythm swelled against the other stabbing up from downstairs.

We lowered our voices and turned down the volume on Piccadilly Radio when Dad hauled himself out of bed on Sunday afternoons. He would sit at the dining table in his bedraggled dressing gown, rubbing his eyes, while we waited with bated breath to see which side he had got out of. Some Sundays it was smiles all round, even when there was no bacon to go with his egg and beans, before he hunkered down to the *News of the World*.

On days when his face remained stiff, the rest of us froze too. Easter Sunday turned out to be one of those days.

'You have got to be fucking joking.' Dad's mouth crimped at the sight of our lavish roast, a golden-backed chicken burying its head in a bed of roast potatoes. Laurie and I had been up for hours, helping our mother to clean the house and cook up a storm.

'Call this shit gravy?' He sneered at the deliciously thick stuff I had bought from the chippy, thinking he would be thrilled.

'We'd no OXO, love...' Our mother's apology was cut short by a hail of peas, potatoes and gravy showering her chest.

'Fuckin'... fuckin'...' Dad grabbed the electrical carving knife, whacked it into the glistening roast, and whirled the chicken against the window. It splatted on to the net curtains, then thudded to the floor. Clutching the knife like a miniature chainsaw, he looked at us looking at him, all five of us wondering what was coming next.

Then he sat down at the table and rubbed his eyes once more. 'Jesus Fuck Me Christ.'

He was only just waking up.

That day, I was certain my dad was going to do my mother in. More terrified than decisive, I ran to the police station. Two constables took ages fastening shirt cuffs, buttoning jackets, stapling helmets under chins, before they strolled up the road behind me.

Dad opened the door himself. 'Sorry to bother you, like.' He gave them one of the boyish smiles he always had ready for strangers: 'I'm afraid it's a load of hoo-ha over nowt, lads.' The officers took a quick look at our mother, still in one piece, and the furniture in the dining room, which had been shuffled back into order. There was no sign of the chocolate Easter eggs that had been shattered against the wall. Our mother was too crushed to give anything away when they asked her what had been going on. But this time I found the nerve to speak up about the punches and kicks and the way our dad had been throttling our mother when I ran to fetch help.

'Right, Sir.' They turned to Dad. 'Word in your ear?'

The men disappeared into the living-room and shut the door.

'Don't worry, Mum.' I held her to calm her shaking in the wake of the fight and at the prospect of Dad being carted away by the police. 'It's for the best.'

When the living-room door opened, I suffered a pang myself, expecting to see Dad's head bowed over handcuffed wrists. Instead, he looked almost chipper, acting pally with the officers. They smiled at our mother as they reached for the door: 'No more silly stuff?'

'Wait!' I rushed to block the way out. 'Is that it?' Trembling, trying to speak calmly: 'Aren't you going to do anything?'

'Now, now, girls.' The officers were keen to get back to their Sunday shift of tea and cigarettes at the station. Laurie, Sarah and I burst into tears, while our mother stood behind us, unable to open her mouth.

'No need to go getting hysterical.' The older policeman ticked us off. 'That's not going to do anybody any good now, is it?'

'I'll fucking brain you!' Dad's words were slathered in saliva as he lunged to whack the other side of my head. I had lost the knack of keeping my mouth shut when he went for my mother, whose pills made her too sluggish to look out for herself.

'Do it, Dad!' Instead of cowering and straining for peace

and quiet, I felt so fearless it was scary. I thrust out my face to catch his fist: 'Just do it.'

'Swine!' Dad lowered his swing, so that his fist collided with my thigh instead of my head.

The pain felt purple. 'Go on!' It unleashed everything under my tongue: 'Go on, you bullying bastard! Treat yourself! Put me in hospital, why don't you? Anything to get out of this fucking hell-hole.'

For a long time now, I had been harbouring fantasies of waking up in a white bed surrounded by nurses like angels, after stepping in front of a slow-moving bus or falling down the cellar's stone steps.

'Andrea!' My mother gasped, her nails digging into Dad's jumper to hold him back. He looked at me, as hot-faced and wet-mouthed as him. Our eyes locked; his muscles unclenched.

'Leave it, Lorraine.' He eased free of her grasp and went out to drive around in his truck: 'For a think.'

I had to keep reminding myself that it wasn't my fault when Dad finally packed his gear and took off. He had lost a few friends by turning his temper on them, disgusting others by stooping to beat a woman, but he still had plenty of pals from his prison days, and one of them would put him up while he looked for a place of his own.

'We've got to call it a day.' He had broken down in tears with our mother after a long, ugly night that kept us all up beyond dawn. Whereas before there had been funny moments, even whole sweet days and smooth weeks to put us back on track after he and our mother had spun off the rails, for ages now there had been nothing to make up for the bad times. Dad got down on his knees with our mother where their struggle had left them, breathless, at the bottom of the stairs. 'We're killing each other, Rainie,' he whispered.

Half of me was as excited as Laurie and Sarah at the prospect of having our mother safely to ourselves, without the worry that one extra nasty thud might steal her from us for good. The other half wanted to cling to him and kiss him and tell him he would always be our dad, no matter what his wild side had made him do. All the fun we had ever had with him flashed in front of my eyes, watching him strap his guitar into the passenger seat.

'Dad!' I ran out to the truck and pressed an ivory plectrum into his palm. Nearly heart-shaped, I had been saving it for his birthday, to encourage him to break the silence of his Spanish guitar, to tease sweet stuff out of it like he used to, in the old days.

Our mother was standing in the window, a ghost, watching through the nets.

18

'Jammy bugger,' our mother muttered, when the BBC played repeats of *The Fall and Rise of Reginald Perrin*. She sighed over his clothes and shoes on the beach, abandoned at the edge of the sea, which, he left everyone to assume, had swallowed him up.

I kept my eye on her tranquillizers.

'God knows I want to.' Our mother pined, as if suicide was a luxury holiday she had her heart set on. She spent hours discussing 'the end' and 'the way out' with me and sometimes Laurie, hushing up in front of Sarah: 'But I could never do it to you kids.'

The doctor had given her a sick note with her latest batch of tranquillizers.

'The girls at work'll be gossiping me into the ground.' She was terrified of losing her job, but depression had seeped into her bones, making them too heavy to get out to work.

I spent days on end sitting with her by the fire, the gas turned up to full blast so that I sweated while she lay shivering on the settee. I tried not to think about college: it was selfish to worry about all the time I was missing, and dwelling on it only made me sweat more. Clinging to my mother's hands, I massaged the knuckles and rubbed them between my palms.

We sipped coffee to kill time: cup after cup after cup.

Occasionally, my mother would claw in her purse for twenty

or thirty pence and send me to Gateways for a packet of biscuits: 'Summat to cheer us up.' I ached for air not made stale by cigarette smoke and coffee, but I sprinted there and back; I couldn't leave my mother a moment too long. My head pounded as I faced the shelves in a fluster to find the perfect biscuit, the one that might lift her out of her mood. Marshmallow? Chocolate chunks? Coffee icing? All-butter shortbread? I imagined a single crunching bite restoring her will to live.

Sometimes, when I rushed back through the door, she had hauled herself off the settee to make another coffee.

'Bit of oomph!' She half laughed, surprised at her own legs, which could barely drag her to the loo.

I held up the fancy biscuits – lemon creams, fig rolls – but there was no flicker in her eyes. 'Lovely.' She had already forgotten what she had sent me to buy; her treat was just to have me back.

I tried to regard it as medicinal when she spluttered curses off her chest.

'I know, Mum.' I crooned and nodded when she claimed that something massive was against her. Life, the whole malarky, was shitting fucking unjust. 'I know, Mum. I know.'

'No!' My mother practically spat in my face, which seemed to stand for the outside world: 'You bleeding well don't.'

Her eyes blackened over: 'You've no fucking idea, thank Christ.'

'I've not suffered like you, Mum,' I tried soothing. 'But I do have some idea.'

My mother sneered: 'What do you know? You've got your whole life ahead of you. You'll soon be away in the bloody world.'

My English teacher, Mrs Wallis, had put forward my name

as one of the twelve students from Xaverian chosen to sit the Oxford Entrance Examination. Every time I opened a book and flicked pages, my mother heard me flapping my wings.

'You'll never know how it feels to be trapped. Truly, utterly trapped. Not just by pissing circumstances.' Her knuckles knotted, a tiny bomb: 'But buried a-stinking-live. Locked inside yourself.'

My mother's first baby, a boy, had lived for less than twelve hours after he had been born with water on his brain.

'Stephen.' She sometimes murmured his name, wondering what life would have been like if he had survived and grown up into a strapping lad: 'He would've looked after us all.'

'Tony.' She mulled over memories of my father, too.

Grandad had died on her. Gran.

'And that shithead,' she glared at the chair that used to be Dad's throne, 'may as well be dead.' There had been none of the usual crawling back to plead. No late-night phone calls, although she often slept downstairs to be close to the phone as well as the fire.

'Not a whiff,' my mother moaned, sitting bolt upright on the settee when a flash of blue passed outside the window. 'I could have sworn it was his truck.' She settled back under the quilt that went wherever she did, wrapping her head to toe, from bed to settee to the loo.

'He may have had his faults,' my mother turned misty-eyed, wondering where Dad had got to, 'but at least, with him, I knew where I was.'

I was tempted to stick a mirror in front of her face, where sores were still smouldering, to remind her of the fireworks.

'I've lost the knack of being me own person, Andy, without a fella telling me what to do.' Her face collapsed: 'I'm nothing by meself.'

I poured all my spirit into trying to pep my mother up, reminding her that she was only thirty-six – she had the rest of her life ahead.

'Jesus! Perish the thought.' She looked sick at the idea. 'I'll never get anyone now. Who'd want me? I just want it all to be over.'

Clouds sagged against the windows; the afternoon stood still.

It was always on the edge of turning dark outside when we reached the point where there was no use arguing. My mother would give herself up to her gloom, slumping into the very pit of it, while I sat stunned by the massive sense of her deadend.

Getting up from the fire, I switched on the light, making my mother blink like a creature startled by headlights. I put on the kettle while she worked herself back into a rant: 'What's to stop me from topping meself, eh?'

I cleared my throat to remind her: 'Us three love you, Mum.'

'Don't say it.' She recoiled under her quilt: 'That's a dirty word, that is. Love's bloody lethal.'

When Sarah clattered in from school, our mother let her put on old Drifters and Otis Redding records, but drew the line at Earth, Wind and Fire. It was hard to make my eleven-year-old sister understand, since she had spent the day outside the house, that something twisted and ached inside your ears if you listened to jangling, bouncy music when your heart was banging to a slow, heavy beat. She tried hugging and kissing our mother, who had developed a habit of pushing us all away whenever we expressed affection.

'Stop trying to take care of me, will you?' She shoved us back when we came close. '*I'm* supposed to be the mother. *Me.*' Often she let her head sag into her hands, wailing the same awful things: 'Christ, what a mess I've made of it all. You'd be better off without me.'

Sarah learnt to make more friends outside, toughening up her act and her accent, getting in with a gang of girls whose boredom drove them to bullying. Laurie kept herself to herself, mostly diving into the French and German dictionaries that she had won by coming top in tests at school. I let crosses mount up against my name in the college register, missing day after day after day, holding my mother's hand at home, to keep her from doing anything silly.

'I wish you lot'd stop bombarding me with these flamin' things.' Our mother sighed over the Catherine Cookson romances we had chosen for her at the local library, hoping to persuade her to lose herself in one the way she had when Dad slotted something Kung-Fu into the video, then rubbed and chop-chopped her feet. Now she only ever opened books to let off steam at the size of the overdue fine.

'You could do a night class in French.' My sisters and I had gathered leaflets from the library. 'Or pottery. What about Flamenco dancing?'

Our mother puffed on her cigarette, pursed her lips, and let out a smoky snort.

Finally she put aside coffee, cigarettes and curses, steadying her nerves and hands to make a flower out of an empty Tuesday afternoon.

'It's amazing, Mum!' I looked at the lily she had copied from a library book of photographs, using watercolour paints that Sarah had been given for Christmas but declared too wishy-washy. The stem looked slightly twisted, yet the petals appeared ready to flutter off the paper. My mother's face grew shaky, looking at the lily, as if the sight of it made her shy. I stared at the lily too, pink veins painted ever so faintly in, and wondered when she would be strong enough to venture beyond the front door.

Leaving her sedated with tablets, asleep on the settee, I risked one day away at college to sit my mock A-level exams. I had been revising late at night, after seeing Sarah and Laurie to bed and watching my mother take her goodnight pill then curl under her quilt in front of the fire. The gas jets were turned down to blue dwarfs, humming and muttering to guard her until dawn, when worry would yank her awake in spite of exhaustion and pills. I sometimes left my books and crept downstairs to treat myself to the sight of her face, unwrinkled in sleep, in the low blue light.

In the blaze of the hall lights at college, the swotty side of my brain woke up. Equations and formulae unfurled to help me glide through the Chemistry test; light, oxygen and energy still made exquisite sense when it came to Biology; my head spilled purple passages from *Antony and Cleopatra*, analysing poetic and killing passions, weighing up justice against the juicier urges raging in Angelo in *Measure for Measure*. I came out of the exams feeling as if I hadn't missed a day. In spite of my absences, everyone seemed pleased to see me, ribbing me about my time off, egging me to come to this gig or that party as soon as my mother got over her illness. Because I didn't want anyone to know about her depression, I told them she had a hernia; in fact, she *had* pulled muscles in her stomach, stretching them while they were stiffened by stress.

Her fingers hooked my wrist like a handcuff as soon as I got back in.

'I can't breathe, Andy, love!' She sat on the edge of the settee, heaving, thumping her chest to persuade it to let in air. Cradling her ribs with one arm, my other was free to massage her back. Circles, flowers, figures of eight: my fingertips tingled with so much rubbing.

My mother hiccuped, then swayed, drunk on sudden, deep breaths.

'Bless you.' She grabbed my hand to give it a rest, stroking my fingers for once. 'What would I do without you?'

After a long silence, her face buried in cushions on the settee, my mother sometimes hoisted up on to her elbows and swore. It was as if she was stammering to say something, like the men who staggered by our windows after the pub closed, cussing, taking swings at each other's mouths. Fuck pissing cunting bloody buggering flaming fuck.

To insulate myself against my mother's rants, I composed rhymes in the red-black murk of my head which I could copy out on to paper when I was alone in my bedroom after midnight. When my own fragments seemed too flimsy, I would resort to lines of real literature which I memorized at night and nursed through the day. As soon as the afternoon swelled into dark, I was ready to dip into Donne or Coleridge or Keats, lacerating myself with gorgeously morbid lines:

> *Darkling I listen; and, for many a time*
> *I have been half in love with easeful Death,*
> *Call'd him soft names in many a mused rhyme,*
> *To take into the air my quiet breath . . .*

'Soup for brains.' My mother chided me when my face slid into its faraway look. I strove not to look gormless while my mind flitted and soared over sonnets and odes that made miserable things seem sublime.

Now more than ever seems it rich to die,
To cease upon the midnight with no pain,
While thou art pouring forth thy soul abroad
In such an ecstasy!

One rare, sunny afternoon I read my mother a bit from *Paradise Lost* to persuade her to think herself out of her dead end.

'The mind is its own place,' I pronounced with hushed breath, 'and in itself / Can make a Heav'n of Hell, a Hell of Heav'n.'

'All's that means' – she made mincemeat of Milton – 'is mind over bloody matter. Let the fella who wrote that walk a mile in my shoes, then try saying the same again.'

Water pounded to fill the bath. Smacking and swishing to build up bubbles, I made a castle of froth for my mother. She undressed under her quilt, then shed it and stepped in.

'Perfect.' She gasped, relishing the sting of hot water.

I knelt by the bath to soap her back.

'Harder.' She urged me to dig in with the sponge, scrubbing up and down her brittle spine. The flesh seemed paper thin, as though it might rip if I rubbed too hard. My mother liked me to leave the bathroom before her wall of bubbles had burst. She was so thin, it was painful to see. Her ribs jutted so that her body seemed like a cage.

When her teeth weren't chattering with cold, my mother was tormented by hot flushes. She would jerk the quilt aside and peel off her jumper, panting for breath in her underwired bra, which seemed to be all that was holding her together. The next moment she would pale and slide back under her layers, shivering violently, finally snuggling down to sleep. As soon as her eyes closed, I opened my school books, thinking of the Oxford exam less than a fortnight away.

'Eh?' She eventually stirred and rolled over, her face emerging out of the cushions where they had been buried all day. My heart leapt a mile in a moment, before I saw what was wrong: the pattern of the settee had printed itself on her skin, making it appear scarred and red raw, as if it had been burned.

'I said, do you want me to go for the doctor?'

My mother's eyes were muddied by something more disquieting than misery. She had been taking one or two more pills than prescribed. 'Stop shaking,' – she wrestled with the awkward lid – 'help me sleep.'

'Mum?' I nudged her shoulder after her face sank back into the cushions. 'I'm going for the doctor, okay?'

My mother was dead to the world. It was too late to be afraid that she would kill me for bringing outsiders in.

19

If I knew you were coming, I'd have baked a cake – an old fat lady wailing down the corridor of the psychiatric ward. She bent to grab the hem of her nightgown, then pulled it up over her head. *Baked a cake.* Laurie, Sarah and I gawped at masses of flesh, wrinkles heaving and splashing as she ran, naked, from a grim-faced nurse. We heard her warbling – *Baked a cake, Baked a cake* – until a door slammed on the song.

'I shouldn't bloody well be in here!' Our mother began carping as soon as she came to meet us in the waiting area. She looked directly at me: 'I may have godawful nerves, but there's nowt wrong with my flaming head, thank you very much.' I perked up at the sight of my mother's temper, good as new, setting off sparks in her eyes as she led us down the hall to her room: 'Away from the Loony Tunes.'

My sisters and I couldn't resist peeking into each doorway. 'Alfred!' Screeches exploded out of one room as we tiptoed past. 'Al-fred!' Inside, a woman was lashing out at the face of another, the pair of them clawing over a pot of banana yoghurt whose lid ripped and belched yellow gunk. 'She's trying to steal my Alf!'

'Poor thing thinks it's her dead hubby,' our mother explained. 'She's forever looking for him in the fridge.'

*

After little more than a week in the ward, our mother claimed she was ready to be weaned off her medication, the first step towards getting out.

'If I thought I was on the verge of doolally before,' she found it in herself to laugh during our family sessions with the social worker who did the rounds at the hospital, 'a holiday with this lovely lot's put me well straight!'

I squeezed out a giggle to please the social worker, scratching notes on a clipboard, although I wasn't convinced by my mother's brave face.

'You seem much happier,' the woman said to me, when we were alone for a few moments. My eyes were no longer as swollen as they had been when my mother was first taken into hospital. A rash had exploded across the lids, but it had stopped burning when the doctor prescribed hydrocortisone cream and told me to stop worrying so much. I didn't mention the palpitations that quivered in my chest in otherwise calm, quiet moments; I was afraid of pills like the ones my mother had been given.

'I've been crying less . . .' I began. 'I . . .'

The woman scribbled on a form, smiled, 'Good,' and stood up to see me out.

Empty Coke bottles piled up in the pantry. Laurie, Sarah and I sagged home from the hospital, too anxious to bicker between ourselves like we used to, then filled up on fizz, glugging to get through the night. Laurie and I swotted harder than usual, as if it might make things better, before flaking out in front of the telly with Sarah. Extra chocolate was called for on Saturday nights and Sunday lunchtimes, to comfort my sisters while I went to work at The Princess, the new pub where I was being paid a pittance to collect glasses and wash plates, until I was old enough and busty enough to pull pints.

I was fascinated by the way ladies' faces lit up or turned melty when they started drinking, before more glasses made them look craggy and tragic.

'What's a nice girl like you . . . ?' Blokes' leers drowned in their beer.

I tottered past on heels that the landlord ordered barmaids to wear, pint glasses teetering up my arm. I stacked them in breathtaking towers that never smashed, except in my nightmares, where tables slanted and jerked as if the pub were a ship in a storm. I found funny lines to throw back in the face of corny come-ons and slurred innuendoes – all the while memorizing dribs and drabs of poetry as if my life depended on it.

'I don't give a shit,' the landlord had let me know, when I hinted that the Oxford entrance exams were on Monday and I could do with Saturday night or Sunday lunchtime off. 'You do your regular hours, or you don't do no more hours whatsonowt. Savvy?'

> *The trees are in their autumn beauty,*
> *The woodland paths are dry,*
> *Under the October twilight the water*
> *Mirrors a still sky*

On Sunday I collected dirty dishes as fellas finished their fryups. Cigarettes stubbed in yolks, glinting knobs of bacon gristle, ketchup smeared in mindless swoops.

> *Upon the brimming water among the stones*
> *Are nine-and-fifty swans*

I had tucked chunks of Yeats' poems inside my bra to smuggle them into the pub kitchen, where I worked alone. There, I stuck them to the steamed-up tiles above the sink, so that I could read them over and over while I scrubbed.

But now they drift on the still water,
Mysterious, beautiful . . .

My face sweated over the sink. Behind me, smoke hissed off the griddle where one of the kitchen women had slipped and fried her hand last week.

Among what rushes will they build,
By what lake's edge or pool
Delight men's eyes when I awake some day
To find they have flown away?

The scraps of paper dampened and peeled off the tiles to flop into the suds. I finished the dishes and pulled out the plug.

'You're made of bloody good stuff!' My mother was back on her feet at home by the time the news came through. Of the twelve Xaverian students who had sat the exam, I was the one invited to Oxford for an interview.

I was nervous about leaving my mother and sisters alone, since Dad was back on the rampage. Parking his truck far away from our house so that he could creep up without warning, he would emerge from the hedges after midnight, tapping on windows, crouching to post promises or spit threats through the letterbox.

'Open this door, y'bitch! Open it, if you don't want me to open your fuckin' skull!' He knelt at the flap night after night, lurching between acid outbursts and sweet nothings: 'Rainie, love, I can't sleep without you. It's not right. We should be together, Rainie.'

Our mother sat on the stairs like she used to, the eye of her cigarette blinking and flaring in the dark. She craned her head, listening to his hissings, whisperings, croonings, as if they were radio adverts for things she knew she couldn't afford.

On the morning I was due to go to Oxford for my interview, I was alone in the house, ironing my smartest clothes, when his face popped up outside the living-room window. The iron bounced and singed my finger. 'Open the door, Andy, love,' he mouthed through the glass.

'I can't, Dad.' I hadn't seen his face in daylight for a long time. The eyes reminded me why, against all wisdom, we always used to welcome him back in. My finger throbbed under its burn, my throat swelled with the pressure of tears. 'Dad, I can't.'

He beckoned me to the letterbox, where his words rushed through.

'Don't do this to me, Andy, love. Please.' He was weeping. 'Why're you treating me like a dog?'

'I love you, Dad.' I knelt at the flap, eye to eye. 'But you know it's no use.'

He pulled a beer bottle out of his jacket and smashed it against the steps: 'Open it or, so help me God, Andy, I'll top meself!'

He held the broken bottle in front of his stomach: 'Harry Carry!'

I screamed as he jerked the jagged end and keeled over.

My mother fumed when she got in from the shops to find me huddling on the stairs, my blouse burnt on the ironing board, a sultana of a blister on my finger.

'If he's done himself in, he's done a flaming fantastic job of tidying up.' She held my finger under the cold water tap. 'Where's the bloody corpse?'

My mother lanced the blister with a safety pin, stitched to

hide the burn in my blouse, and rode with me on the bus to town, to stash me safe on the coach for Oxford.

Someone had spilt dark blue ink across the sky. Spires were fingers, grasping at stars. Drunk on tequila and cold air, I lay on my back in the quadrangle court of Hertford College, my eye on the moon. It shimmered, a coin I dreamt I could pocket. Crashed out on either side of me, two boys – real Oxford undergraduates – lay in gowns. Exhausted bats, knocked flat by throat-stripping spirits after finishing their preliminary exams and whooping through Radcliffe Square, past a huge wedding cake made of pale stone – a library, where I would read if I got in. The moment my interview was over, my feet had left the ground as they dragged me between them, gowns flapping like wings I might grow myself.

The eve of Christmas Eve. I went hot and cold and turned deaf for a split second when my mother unfolded the letter.
    'You're in!'
    'Wow!' My sisters wreathed me in hugs and kisses.
    They looked at me differently for the rest of the morning. You could practically see the EXIT signs lighting up Laurie's eyes: if I could get out, so could she. Her teachers were predicting that she would pass her O levels with ten straight-A grades. Across Sarah's eyes, though, I saw shutters. She had taken to truanting, picking up a different kind of education, hanging out in cemeteries and deserted warehouses with her dodgy mates. Oxford meant nothing to her, except that I would be gone in a few months' time. She smiled nervously, as if she was already expecting me to go up in a puff of smoke.

*

Snow was straining the edge of the air; light stabbed out of a crystal sky as my mother and I stepped into the street. She couldn't resist holding my hand and parading me around the shops, boasting to everyone we bumped into. Local jaws dropped, old ladies clutched at my wrist, while I swayed, gagged by the grin of an idiot. I wandered around with my mother, on her quest for Liebfraumilch in two-litre bottles, feeling sick with excitement and the sharpness of everything. My eyes smarted at the splatter of blood on butchers' aprons, a pyramid of clementines in the greengrocer's, the warty faces of potatoes.

'Hiya,' 'Hello,' 'Hi,' 'All right?' I greeted everyone as usual, thinking all the while, *Goodbye.*

Christmas Day, and Mum and Dad were reunited. He had rolled up with presents on Christmas Eve. Our mother, made bubbly by Liebfraumilch, giddy at glittering thoughts of the future inspired by my letter from Oxford, opened the door and invited him in. Twinkling red, blue, pink, yellow lights, the Christmas tree made it feel almost safe. After a day or two, waking for breakfast with someone who had been terrorizing us in the middle of the night, my sisters and I got used to our dad again.

But when Auntie Pauline and Auntie Livia found out, they could not get over what they saw as our mother's gobsmacking stupidity: welcoming the mad bugger back with open arms! They summoned a kind of family conference which ended in tears and terrible words: Auntie Pauline accused her sister of being a bad mother. Our mother protested that Dad had really changed this time, she could see it in his eyes. Our aunts had heard it all before: over and over and over again.

'It's the same old broken record, Lorraine.' Auntie Pauline was not swerving from her ultimatum: 'It's him or the kids, and you know it. You've got to get rid of him now, else those poor blighters're going to end up paying for it, big time.'

Our mother was not about to budge: our aunts had got a bee in their bonnets over something they knew sod all about. She appealed to my sisters and me to speak up and vouch for our dad's new, improved mood. Our voices were wobbly, but we backed up her story.

Our aunts looked at each other and decided to wash their hands of the situation.

'Don't come running to us next time it all goes haywire,' Auntie Pauline warned. After sticking by us and bailing us out all these years, she and Auntie Livia had had more than enough of our mother's shenanigans.

'Sheer suicide.' They shook their heads.

It was time to draw the bloody line.

After that, we knew we were on our own. We put on our best behaviour and prepared to tiptoe about in a world of eggshells, praying that things wouldn't crack. Our hearts stopped if one of us spilt tea or said something thoughtless at home, waiting for the creases to freeze around his blue eyes. But his smile showed no signs of slipping. The monster who had howled and banged to break down the front door seemed like some other man.

Dad took great, swaggering pleasure in the fact that I had earned a place at Oxford, beating all them other posh gits to it. 'One in the eye,' he called it. He was flabbergasted and chuffed when Laurie outstripped kids who had visited Europe, to win a national competition for young modern linguists. But Sarah was his real pride and joy: he spent hours urging her to take a slug at his jaw, oiling her swing so that she would do better next time she faced Sharon Corkhill and her gang after school.

'I wish you wouldn't be encouraging her to fight,' our mother moaned while she fried kidney and onions for tea. 'She's only eleven.'

'She's got to learn how to stand up for herself.' Dad offered his chest as a punchbag to Sarah: 'Gwan, sock it ter me!'

Thwud! He thrilled when Sarah's left hook hit home.

The rest of us marvelled that he never raised his own hands to land a smack or a punch nowadays.

Being on the dole no longer seemed to torment our dad. He took carpentry and bricklaying work where he could. When hard times left him stuck in the house, he spent hours striking match after match after match, blowing each one out as soon as its pink head had spluttered and sighed to a bald, charred tip.

'Unbelievable,' our mother whispered, peering over his shoulders while he stuck them together. Following no pattern but the one in his head, he squinted, bit his tongue, and caressed his matchsticks with glue to make them grow, one by one, into a gypsy caravan.

I was still terrified that Dad might blow his lid when we were least expecting it, but I was no longer ashamed of his swearing and ranting from behind the *Sun*; the smoke that hung about his head in his own private cloud; or the strange, thin taste of tea in our house, made with recycled teabags and powdered milk. I lost my old dread that people would turn up their noses if they knew where and what I came from. My place at Oxford was not just about books; it made me suspect I might be as good a person as anyone else.

After hearing a talk at college about charities and fundraising, I sent off for sponsorship forms from the National Society for the Prevention of Cruelty to Children. Within a fortnight

I had raised seventy pounds. Now I had to go through with the aerobatic flight I had been sponsored to do. Mum and Dad were as excited as I was: they drove me all the way to Blackpool, where a tiny, two-seater plane was waiting to take off. I climbed in and sat next to the pilot, my knees trembling at the sight of the glamorous man at the controls and the prospect of shooting up in the air.

A clatter, an awesome roar, and we were shaving the clouds.

'Guts in your mouth?' the pilot's voice crackled through the headset over my ears. 'You've gone green!'

Then a nose-dive and a barrel roll, a loop-the-loop, and another barrel roll. I thought of us up there, drawing shapes in the sky. *This is my life*, my insides were shouting.

'One more loop-the-loop?' the headset fizzed.

I nodded and gripped my knees. Inspired by the next swoop, a glob of vomit shot out of my mouth and landed between my feet, where it stayed even when we arced upside-down.

'Don't worry,' the voice came through the roar. 'Defies gravity every time.

'The sickness goes if you focus on the horizon,' he shouted. 'Here, take the stick!'

I prised my right hand off my knee and clamped it around the knob of the steering rod.

Whish! We lurched down towards Blackpool beach, which bloomed suddenly: hundreds of faces looking up. You could see the ice-creams cradled in kids' fists.

'Blimey!' The pilot put out his hand to steer us up and away from the sea. 'Trying to take us for a swim?'

He chuckled and guided us back to the airfield. I scanned the ground until my eyes brushed across Mum and Dad: two pale specks, next to a dab of blue, the truck. A rush of guilt thwacked my gullet as we glided down.

Small. They looked so small, and far away. *Another world.*

A strange shyness came over me as I climbed out of the plane, my whole body shaking, while Mum and Dad rushed towards me, shining with pride.

'How did it feel?' they were dying to know. 'Could you see us from up there?'

'Clear as day.' I took my mother's hand to steady myself, while Dad ruffled my hair.

I wanted to forget how small they had seemed from the sky.

Now that I was no longer tied down, worrying about Mum and Dad, I was free to lose myself in the whirl of drinking and dancing that everyone else at college had been in for ages. Venturing inside Deville's nightclub, I tried not to stare into shadowy corners at two-headed monsters, hands all over the place: slithering up and down backs, loitering around hips, disappearing inside clothes. I knocked back the vodkas lads urged me to try, and found that they acted like keys: unlocking something inside, they let me slide into a paradise of sweat, saliva and pelvises, slinking and grinding to head-swerving sounds.

Mind, heart, muscles, lips, nerves, fingertips, toes, soul: everything came together when I finally fell in love.

Because his house was not far from mine, Jamie had been the one to walk me home when we reeled out of parties and found the streets fabulously still. No cars, no buses, no people. It was as if we were the last pair of souls on earth. My mind rocked full of echoes after hours of ear-bashing bass. Over time, this came to be drowned under a more tormenting throb. Desire. I found it deafening, strolling home from party upon party, my head pounding with the din of so many things not said. It was a victory to walk in a straight line, dizzied not just by drink but by thrumming suspense – aching for something to come out at last, before we reached my front door and I had to endure one more chaste and fidgety goodnight.

Long before the first kiss, I knew that he was the one. A hot, blanket-twisting dream, vivid with vodka, spat me out of sleep in the night. I swayed downstairs to the bathroom and found the mirror lit up by a swipe of moonlight: even after a splash of cold water, there was his face, mingled with mine.

Throughout that spring, as I looked forward to Oxford and became more and more tangled in love, my family actually felt normal. Happy, even, most of the time. Except for the chicken in our cellar. Having hatched eggs in her science class, Sarah begged Dad to let her bring home a ball of fluff. It lived with cuddly toys in front of the fire until its first feathers began to come through and it was no longer so cute. Then Dad made us spread newspaper across the floor of the cellar, where he kept it in the murky cold, glaring at it to lay eggs for him to fry. My sisters and I would go downstairs and make clucking noises to cheer it up. We shovelled up the foul mess it continually made, then hustled back upstairs, where we tried not to think of the thing pining away under our house. No sign of an egg.

Meanwhile, Dad conjured rose bushes to crawl up the front wall and spread pink petals outside our freshly painted green door. My sisters and I kept shtum about the skinny chicken hobbling about in our cellar, but were quick to show off the glorious explosion of roses to friends, now that our parents allowed us to bring them round. The doorway was just beyond full bloom – some of the fatter flowers turning blowsy, smaller buds clinging, tight-lipped, to the last of their lustre – when we got home one afternoon and our mother came out blushing furiously, asking us to send our friends away, not to bring them inside the house.

That night, we watched her sniffling tears into toilet tissue, while Dad fumbled with shattered fragments of criss-crossed matchsticks, like parts of a jigsaw puzzle, trying to glue his precious caravan back into one piece. Nothing was said about how it broke, but it never looked the same again.

On May Day, Mum and Dad lined up my sisters and me in front of the telly.

'Guess what?' They couldn't stop grinning. 'We're going to tie the knot!'

'When?' Sarah was dying to know. The news made up for the misery they had begun to ooze across the house again lately. My sisters and I were elated to think that they would be married at last; we imagined it could seal things with an air of for ever, changing our lives for good.

I was touched when they chose my birthday, the 16th of May, to be their big day too. It felt like a special gift to me and my sisters, the promise they were going to make on paper to love and to cherish and everything. The day I turned eighteen, I put on a short, short summer dress, all lemony and see-through, under the battered brown leather pilot's jacket my dad had given me for my birthday – the one he used to huddle in for hours when he went fishing, crouching in silence behind his rod on the edge of the water at Sale Park. Laurie wore black clothes and dark sunglasses that made her look slinky and cool as a cat. Sarah loaded her earlobes with earrings that didn't match, cramming as many as possible into the extra holes she had pierced herself.

We clambered into the back of the truck and took off to the town hall: Mum in a peach satin dress; the pinstripes of

Dad's old suit jazzed up by a carnation whose petals were the exact same peach. We tried not to stare at the other people outside the Registrar's office, all waiting like us in their shiniest clothes. An old lady, with rotten teeth, even had a too-big tiara: she kept chuckling, revealing brown stumps and gums, and shoving the tiara back into place when it refused to stay put. Some of the brides-to-be grimaced and looked the other way, as if they were trying to avoid their own reflections. Others glared around the waiting room, looking everyone else up and down: their wedding was the real McCoy, you could see they were thinking, not like the rest of these quickie affairs.

Once our parents' papers had been signed and stamped and they had paid for an instamatic photo of the just-married kiss, snapped by a doddery old geezer, we went to climb back into the truck.

'Spot of pub grub, eh?' Dad was ready to hang the expense. 'It's only once in a lifetime!'

He coughed into his carnation: he had in fact been married once before; there were even two children with his eyes and nose floating around somewhere. At the same time, our mother stroked the peach satin of her dress as if to smooth the creases out of her own history. She adjusted the ring on her finger (which she wouldn't really consider hers until they had completed the payments for it), and laughed a little laugh: 'Third time lucky!'

We shot out for a frolic in the country, the way we used to, back when Dad had only just moved into our lives. After baked potatoes in a pub, we went for a long walk. Dad splashed out on proper Mister Softee ice-creams: 99ers, complete with a chocolate chimney of Flake and great swirly squirts of raspberry syrup, which we licked frantically to keep it from bleeding on to our fingers and clothes.

Mmm. The five of us wandered along the bank of the canal

near New Mills, trying to eke out our ice-creams and what was left of the day.

The sun blazed like an egg yolk, slithering down the sky. It wasn't dying, our mother murmured, only heading to light up somewhere else, far away. But we couldn't help feeling deserted when the horizon of livid pinks faded to a purple haze and the dark made us turn to go home.

20

A few weeks after the wedding, our bedraggled chicken slumped in the cellar, choked by a lump in its craw. Our mother carried the chicken upstairs and laid it in a cardboard box by the fire to warm it up. When it failed to stir, she crushed aspirin in water and tried to stop the squawking that way.

'It's breaking my heart.' She was near to tears as the gasps continued.

Dad put the hopeless bird in its box with a pile of newspapers and a hammer, then headed back down to the cellar, looking yellow: 'A man's gotta do what a man's gotta do.'

Spring warmed up into summer. Our mum and dad went through a phase of concocting fantastic plans for the future. They pored together through *Exchange and Mart*, eyes peeled for things to buy and sell.

But as Dad's ideas grew more and more extravagant, Mum grew less and less keen. He decided we should go and start a farm on one of the Maldive islands.

'We're not the Swiss-Family-flamin'-Robinson!' she chided: 'We couldn't even keep one buggerin' chicken alive, remember?'

We knew they had ditched their dreams when we got up one morning to find a row of headless stalks under the front window sill outside the house, daffodil faces lolling in the soil. They had gone wild with knives the night before, our mother explained wearily, hacking the flowers they had planted so carefully, out of protest at their sodding suffocating life together.

Soon they were back shrieking at each other until they were hoarse and blue in the face. Between bouts of shouting, they settled down to wage a sly kind of indoor war: our mother hunched over the tape recorder upstairs, playing her Leonard Cohen cassette over and over at full blast; Dad in the living-room, spinning his ancient Rod Stewart album, a gravelly racket. Laurie, Sarah and I took turns with the kettle, brewing pots of tea in an effort to keep the peace.

Occasionally, they would snap out of it to join forces and turn their anger on us kids. Every day, before and after school, they would bark at us to brush, scrub, polish to keep the house in spanking order.

'You know the rules,' Dad glowered, when we sighed to lift stray shoes, clothes and books out of the dirt at the bottom of the cellar stairs. Anything left lying around in the living-room, he hurled down into the dark.

Along the settee – its Dralon nap combed, according to our mother's screeched orders, in a different direction each day – we had to space the cushions as if with a ruler. Every leaf of every plant had to shine.

It was worse when the last chore had been done and redone, giving everything an eerie gleam. Mum and Dad would sit, empty-faced, saying nothing, at opposite ends of the settee. Two bluish snakes of smoke writhed up from their estranged cigarettes, while the rest of the house stood horribly still.

*

When they did break into talk, it was in low murmurs, listing the various ways – crude, quick, luxurious, artistic – in which they planned to do one another in.

'What you waiting for?' Dad ripped open his shirt – pinging buttons across the room – to thrust out his bare chest, the night our mother helped herself to one of his screwdrivers. Though I stayed stony-faced to reassure my sisters, I was on the verge of wetting my pants at the sight of the screwdriver and bare flesh: in my mind, I saw them coming together. But I was even more shaken by the regret I felt when my mother grunted and swung up her arm and plunged the screwdriver harmlessly into the wall.

I smiled as brightly as ever at college, even through the exams.

'Nerves of steel,' friends marvelled when I stayed calm in the face of each paper. Only Jamie knew why: he could see how my fear of our house made everything else a breeze.

As soon as the exams were over and I stopped going to college, an awesome headache settled on me: sometimes a helmet of metal, biting; when I was lucky, it pulsed and slopped around my skull.

After tea one night, I went upstairs to my bedroom with a can of Coke and a bottle of paracetemol tablets, determined to put an end to the headache. Mum and Dad were at it downstairs. Sitting cross-legged on the floor, I poured the tablets on to the carpet and contemplated the powdery pile. I imagined taking so many that they would have to bring their fighting to a full stop, to call an ambulance and take care of me.

One. Two. Three. Four. Five.

I forced down the bitter, fat tablets until my throat seized up against swallowing more.

It wouldn't bring them to their senses. It would just be letting everyone down and making things worse, if I were to crumple.

Andrea was the steady one.

I had stiffened myself so much on the outside, my insides were clogged up: it was too exhausting even to cry, to rinse things out that way. And crying was dangerous – it made Mum and Dad even more angry, if any of us burst into tears.

I fed the rest of the tablets back into the bottle and lay down on my bed with the poems of Hopkins, which I'd been told to read in preparation for my first term at Oxford. *I caught this morning morning's minion, kingdom of daylight's dauphin* – my eyelids drooped – *dapple-dawn-drawn Falcon* – afraid of falling asleep with the tablets inside me – *My heart in hiding / Stirred for a bird* – I gave in to my pillow – *Fall, gall themselves, and gash gold-vermilion.*

I had submitted fifty lines of verse to a literary society in London, at the suggestion of my English teacher; one morning a certificate for creative writing arrived through the post. It made me feel invincible, for a moment. I could put poetry into clouds and puddles and gutters and all kinds of filth. I could turn nasty things at home into stories. I could cut myself off.

Instead of clustering in front of the telly like we used to, keeping an eye on Mum and Dad, my sisters and I went out more and more often to do our own things. We never left them alone when a fight was in the offing; we waited for the air to clear, then we crept out.

I might take the bus to visit Tamsyn or to go out with Helena and Sasha and other girlfriends from college, to the pub or the pictures, sometimes even the theatre. But usually my head was too fuzzy for that, and I went straight round to Jamie's instead, even though I had already spent most of the day with him. Now that college was over, we had summer jobs at Manchester Unemployment Benefit Office. At first, the pair of us had rejoiced at being assigned to the same workfloor. Then we were shoved into the front line, on the counters shielded by bullet-proof glass, where we parried insults from people sick of the shitting arsing System that was trying to screw them over. Still, we were able to sail through the day, glimpsing each other across the office, revelling in gooey feelings and looking forward to the hours we would steal, smooching in his bedroom all evening, until his mother pounded up the stairs to announce that the party was over.

I would come away from him in a gorgeous fluster, my fingertips burning after playing up and down his back, hot beneath his T-shirt. He was good-looking and clever and funny, but what really touched me was his gentleness. I was obsessed by the softness of his skin, and its smell.

At home I suffered a constant buffeting against my ribs, from the storms inside me; but a secret sun shone under my skin when I was with Jamie. As things grew darker in my house, I could look at him and see the future, fabulously bright. He was going to study in London while I was in Oxford, so we could be together every weekend. Being close to him gave me a blissful ache. Clothes came loose under his covers, though I always clung to some shred, no matter how fast our breathing grew. Desire spingled along my nerves, delirious. But something told me to wait, to save the precious thing in my hands until I was far away from home, where nothing could spoil it.

One night, after I had torn myself away from Jamie, I got back to my house around midnight. I slid my key into the front door quietly, hoping no one would be awake, so I could go straight to bed with my thoughts.

A strange sort of music was seeping out of the living-room. Mum and Dad. Their voices were sputtering and purring and sputtering. Behind them, I could hear Laurie and Sarah sobbing. I pushed open the living-room door.

They were circling each other, slowly. My mother was clutching the big kitchen knife, jerking it in front of her face to ward off Dad, who had the huge marble ashtray raised in his fist, ready to smash it against her skull as soon as he could get close enough.

'Andy!' Laurie and Sarah were cowering against the wall, watching the stuff in front of them which they were helpless to stop.

'I – want – you – out – of – here – you – *bastard*.' My mother gritted her teeth and ground out her words slowly, as if she were spelling.

Dad's voice was wet with bloody determination: 'Over my dead body!'

He lunged towards her, dropping the ashtray, reaching out to grab the knife from her hand. She yanked it back, out of the way of his fingers. Then she shrieked; he turned deadly quiet. The blade had caught Dad's thumb and sheared a slice of flesh off the tip. A line of blood jetted up the wall, spattering a fantastic pattern over the white paint.

'Shit!' Dad gave a strange laugh, as if the whole thing was happening to someone else.

My mother nudged him out of his stupor and led him by the wrist to the kitchen, where she ran a bowl of cold water and plunged in his hand. Laurie, Sarah and I stood by, watching the sink turn pink. Then she pulled out his thumb and wrapped the gash under acres of toilet paper, which I tried to bind with Sellotape.

Dad had to sit with his hand above his head, pressing his

finger over the cut to slow the flow of blood, still pumping through his home-made bandage.

'Ta, love.' He gave me a shaky smile when I put a mug of tea, loaded with sugar, into his other hand. 'Ta.'

My sisters and I went to bed, leaving him stunned on the settee, contemplating the red across the wall, while our mother bent over a bucket of soapy water, wringing a rag and rubbing to wash it away.

But the paper would not let go of its stain: a great patch of rouge stayed on the wall.

'Dad, we've got something to ask you.' Laurie's voice trembled. She and Sarah and I were lined up in front of the settee, where he was sprawled out on his back. 'We've been thinking, and we don't know what else to do.' Laurie nudged me.

'We're afraid that if you don't move out, Dad,' I stammered, 'something's going to happen.'

He hoisted himself up until he was sitting, feet flat on the floor, his face hung down so we couldn't see it.

Sarah dared to reach out and hold his hand. 'It doesn't mean we don't love you.'

'I know, ducky.' Dad squeezed her hand and looked up, smiling sadly, 'I know.'

'So you'll go?' I asked softly.

'Will I buggery!' He pulled his hand away, his face hardening: 'I'm not moving out. The rent book's got my name on it, don't forget.'

Our mother had, in a gesture of trust, transferred the tenancy to him on their wedding day.

'So it's technically my bloody house, see?' Anger clouded his eyes. 'Mine!'

'But you're going to kill each other, Dad,' I pleaded.

'So be it,' he shrugged. 'If you want me to shift' – he sat squarely in the middle of the settee – 'you'll have to put a bomb under me.'

My mother took my sisters and me on the bus to pay a secret visit to Auntie Livia, who was too worried, when she saw the state we were in, to waste time on 'I told you so's'. Uncle Max picked up the phone, muttered a bit under his moustache, then clicked it back down with a grim smile. It would cost no more than fifty quid, a pal of his had come up with the best price: 'for a kneecap'.

'We can lend it.' Uncle Max assured our mother that she could pay him back over as many months as she liked. 'Just say the word.'

She looked sick, chewing over the idea, twizzling her wedding ring.

It was only a few seconds, though it felt to us like a lifetime, before she shook her head. With nowhere else to go, no aunties with the patience to put us up, no car to take us anywhere, we got back on the bus and sloped home to our dad.

It was hard to look at him without thinking of the kneecap plot. When he launched into a rage, my head was blasted clear of any thoughts, reduced to a hot, tight redness – panic, in case this time it would be the end of everything. But when he was in one of his mercifully mild, trancelike moods, my mind was stalked by men in balaclavas. I saw them homing in on him down a dark alley, taking crowbars and bricks to his bones.

Nights in white satin, never reaching the end – he let his Moody Blues album crackle quietly when exhaustion had robbed him of his anger – *Letters I've written, never meaning to send.*

He didn't hum or jiggle his toes like he used to. He just sat there, slumped in the song. I cringed when the chorus broke into its wail of *I love you*s. But my eyes welled when they met my dad's, and I found myself kissing the cheeks with his tears on them.

It was always a worry to leave the house, not knowing what Mum and Dad would do while they were by themselves. One day, when Dad had gone out to cash his dole cheque, our mother had grabbed his stonking great electric drill and changed the locks behind his back. Instead of hurling his body against the door and howling (the way he used to when Mum locked him out), he had spent hours sweet-talking his way over the threshold, back into the house. Then, our mother told us later, he let his nice front-door face drop off, and got stuck in. He smashed her head against the wall and knocked her to the floor, where she lay in a daze while he let loose with his boot.

Alarmed because she couldn't open her eyes properly, Dad had grabbed the kettle and chucked hot water into our mother's face to wake her up. She had blinked and seen him rush off in his truck, terrified, before she passed out.

When our mother came round, she had to call the ambulance herself, with a handful of broken fingers. The police were brought to her bedside at the hospital, where she was hooked to a machine that would let her sleep off the shock without sliding into a coma. Laurie, Sarah and I stared at it, willing the bleeps to stay nice and steady. The police put on gentle, spongy voices as if to protect her face and neck from any more damage.

'We'll have to press charges, love.' A sergeant explained that, because the doctors had called them in the light of her injuries, there would have to be a prosecution whether she liked it or not.

'It'll only rile him,' my mother mumbled, groggy with painkillers. It would be better to leave things as they were, she struggled to make clear, or this would not be the end of the story.

The police arrested him. Laurie and I had to go with our mother when the case finally came up at Manchester Crown Court; a solicitor told us that we might be called upon to testify, if our mother's word was not deemed enough. If the law hadn't dragged its feet, our mother pointed out, her face would not have had time to mend and the crime could have spoken for itself.

'If only someone had had the nous to take a photo.' She shook her head.

She went in to be questioned first, while my sister and I waited in the hall outside the courtroom. Then Dad turned up, dressed in the pinstriped suit he had worn to get married. Laurie and I squirmed, tortured by shyness rather than fear. He sat on the bench opposite, holding his head in his hands, lifting it now and then to smile meekly at us. When it was his turn to go in, we went to peek through the pair of glass portholes on the double doors of the courtroom. We couldn't hear what he was saying, but we watched our dad acting like the docile, put-upon husband, defending himself with sparkly eyes and honest hands (no sign of his knuckle-duster gold ring). Laurie and I bristled outside the doors, our breath steaming up the glass of the portholes, dying to be called in to tell the truth. But when Dad had finished his performance, the judge just leaned back and looked down at his own hands. Then he sat up straight again and adjusted his wig to make a pronouncement, before pushing his papers to one side and stealing a look at his watch. We saw something crash inside our mother's face, as if she had been walloped again.

Although they had let him off with a fine of one hundred and fifty pounds, Dad went berserk. He came pounding on our front door, screaming that my mother owed him a hundred and fifty quid and he would kill her, no messing around this time, if she didn't come up with the dosh. By the time the police had come at our call, he had disappeared. For days, he prowled around the streets, chasing our mother if ever she dared to step out through the door. Once he caught her and pinned her against the glass wall of a bus shelter to spoil her healed face by giving her a split lip. Our mother cried out for help, but men and women just passed by, looking the other way.

'I should have had the bastard kneecapped when I had the chance.' She lurched between steaming up, furious, and breaking down to weep, finding herself trapped in her own home, as miserable and frightened as ever.

He had caught her and Sarah out shopping one afternoon, revved up his truck and tried to ram them both against a lamp-post.

After that, none of us went out after dark, for fear of being spotted and followed by Dad. Sometimes Jamie would come round, or Laurie would bring her boyfriend Christopher home. Although we felt safer when they were there, we could see that our mother was uncomfortable about it. The air inside the house would become clogged with embarrassment as well as the usual nerves and dread, waiting for Dad to turn up. It was easier not to see anyone at all, to stay in with our mother in the evenings, ready for his banging on the door and windows, the swearing in a voice that didn't sound human.

The hedges looked different, knowing he could be creeping up behind them or crouching inside them at night: watching, listening, hissing about a petrol bomb; shovelling dogshit through the letterbox; trapping the telephone line so that we couldn't dial 999 when he took a crowbar to the back door. Some nights we felt as if we'd been caught in a horror film: Dad smashing glass, bloody fingers scrabbling inside the kitchen window to lift the latch; our mother whacking the knuckles with a plate, sweating to keep him at bay without crippling him, while I dashed for a hammer and nails from the cellar, to board up the weak spot in the window.

Sleep wasn't always to be had in our beds: we got something more like rest when we lay side by side on the living-room floor, ignoring the hard boards under our bones, hugging tennis racquets, the rolling pin, a baseball bat. Our mother rummaged around in the cellar, came up with a poker, a great knob of metal for a head, and chose to sleep with that.

When Dad surprised us in the doorway – he had shimmied up the drainpipe to the attic and let himself in through a bed-room window – none of us reached for a thing. My legs gave way: I couldn't stand up. Laurie and Sarah took their cue from me, and stayed rooted to the settee. Our mother floated in front of us, looking like death in her nightie. Her body seemed drained of blood, filled with air, bones showing through her skin. She sort of smiled. Dad was wearing his pinstriped suit, which showed no trace of his scramble to reach the roof. He seemed to have dressed up to see her. As if it was the last time.

Our mother shifted towards the phone, shivering, to dial the police.

'Terry . . .' she began, when he slid the receiver out of her hand.

I prayed for the lead in my legs to melt and let me move.

'Mum . . .' It was as if we had already lost her.

Our dad looked around the room, his eyes sweeping up tennis racquets, the baseball bat, the rolling pin and poker, before throwing them back in our faces with a laugh: 'Red alert, eh?'

He placed the receiver coolly back on the cradle of the phone.

'You needn't worry,' he murmured into our mother's face, 'if I wanted to get you, I could do it like that' – he clicked his fingers.

Then he unhooked the chain on the front door, sliding the bolts across – one, two, three, slowly – and saw himself out.

21

Her wails sliced the air, so that we all felt it when she cried.

'The loneliness...' Even her whimpering got into our bones: '*It's killing me.*'

My sisters and I tried huddling close to our mother, but she would burst out shrieking: 'I wish the lot of you would just fuck off!' She shoved us from her, snarling: '*Don't touch me!*'

Then she would cave in, subsiding into hushed, shallow sobs that grated her chest.

'Forgive me, forgive me,' she snuffled, while Laurie, Sarah and I clustered around her in one of the clammy hugs that kept us together.

On good days, instead of screaming so that her face looked like it was about to rip, our mother would tuck her knees under her chin and rock back and forth, crooning about pushing up daisies. Her eyes would take on a horrible brightness as she reached to grasp one of us by the hand – 'You know I want to be cremated, don't you, when it comes to the crunch?'

Then she would sit, as still as stone, on the settee, staring at the walls.

Dad's truck growled past our windows – once, twice, sometimes several times a day. Our mother would snap out of her trance as soon as she heard the buzz of his engine and caught sight of the blue cruising by.

My sisters and I watched her face, scrutinizing it for signs of what was running through her mind.

Her temper flared when she saw us fretting. 'I've no intention of letting that devil back into our lives!' Her voice cracked: 'Don't you think I've learnt my lesson?'

Laurie wasn't convinced. After appealing for help from her teachers, she moved into a council hostel for girls whose families were a threat to their mental or physical health.

My mother went white. She wept into my chest while I held her: what was the point of carrying on? She was so worthless, her own child couldn't bear to be near her.

'It's not you, Mum.' I rocked her in my arms, half singing, repeating it like a nursery rhyme: 'It's not you.'

But I knew how Laurie felt: the same desire to escape careered through me – making me feel drunk, almost ill, with anticipation – whenever I flicked the pages of my Oxford prospectus, sneaking a peek at those spires.

My mother was still struggling to get over Laurie, when a social worker knocked on the door. Sarah had heard about Childline on TV, and had rung up to speak to someone – anyone. She was truanting from school and getting into scrapes with the police over rough lads and booze. Worse than that, my little sister was damaging herself in secret: she took safety pins, razors and burning cigarettes to her arms. I winced at the sight of the patterns, all those ugly, hidden things, etched into her skin. For so long she had been going around smiling and pretending nothing was up. Now official plans were being filed to remove her from our mother's custody and place her in a foster home. Sarah rolled her sleeves back down to her wrists, while our mother ranted and raved: 'Why do you want to hurt yourself in that foul way?'

'It hurts less,' Sarah murmured.

'Less than what?' our mother fumed, more angry than frightened, it seemed. Her eyes, crowded with pain, were dry: they no longer took in anything they couldn't bear to see.

I would have to leave in a matter of days.

'Don't be ridiculous,' my mother said stiffly, after I suggested that I could telephone Hertford College: perhaps they would let me postpone entry for a year, so that I wouldn't be leaving her and Sarah alone. The two of them were always having terrible fights, laying into each other with foul words, yanking and slapping in their rage. I thought about what would happen when I was no longer there to pull them apart and stick them back together. The glue of the family, my mother called me.

'You've got your own life to be getting on with.' Her gaze burrowed to hide in the carpet. 'You have to go.'

She stayed up smoking to get through my last night at home. I woke to find her in the murky living-room, her face floating above the round marble ashtray, a dirty moon, crammed with pale flakes and cigarette stubs. Scattered by her feet was a jumble of photos, some black-and-white, turning tea-coloured at the edges, colour ones hacked here and there where her emotions had sent her to the scissors.

'I didn't want to let you go without a picture to remember us all by.' Her voice shook. 'But I can't find the right one.'

'Oh, Mum.' I tried laughing. 'I'll only be gone for eight weeks.'

I drew back the curtains and banged to open the window, hoping to shift the morbid cloud around her with a blast of fresh air. Sunshine spilled across her face: grooved with non-stop smoking, its lines said everything her lips were too dry to get out.

I held my own face still to hide the guilty thrill that swirled through me as I gazed around the living-room.

It was like looking at someone else's life.

The settee, the telly, the curtains, the stereo with its wonky turntable, the sparse-looking ornament stand, the rubber plant battling on in the corner, the muzzy pink patch on the wall. Leaning against the window sill, as if it were waiting for Dad to stroll back in, was the battered Spanish guitar: three of the strings had snapped, the neck had been broken and was trying to hold up under a sorry-looking splint.

That and the huge marble ashtray brought me back to my mother.

She made me a cup of coffee and I cradled it between my hands, taking loving glugs that made my throat ache because it was so tight with excitement. I murmured silly nothings to take the edge off her silence. Then I kissed her and went upstairs to squash the last things into my suitcase.

'Aren't you going to leave your toothbrush?' Sarah lingered around my case.

I rummaged for the brush and jangled it back into the toothmug to join hers and Mum's. Pulling Sarah close for a hug, I breathed in cigarette smoke and hairspray and lipstick, mingling with that yeasty scent of her skin that still made me think of her as my baby sister. I took care, when my feelings welled, not to squeeze her arms where they were raw under her uniform. She left for school just before a black cab turned up, honking.

*

'Your carriage awaits you.' My mother attempted a smile. She stood in the doorway, clutching the collar of her housecoat. 'Here, love.' Pressing a five-pound note into my hand, she ignored my attempts to refuse: it would be my first ride in a black cab, and she had her heart set on paying for it. 'Let me,' she said.

The cab rumbled and purred while I hovered at the top of the steps.

'Go on.' She nudged me, trying to sound jolly: 'You don't want to miss that coach!'

My skin felt as hot as my mother's when I pressed my cheek against hers.

'It's not for ever.' My words came out wet.

She clutched my hair and branded my forehead with a vicious, burning kiss.

Then she warbled, finally overtaken by weeping: 'You're my hope.'

I lugged my suitcase down the steps, feeling dizzy, blinking at the glare of the morning sun off the wet road. It had rained during the night, leaving the sky glassy and full of reflections. Climbing into the back of the cab, I turned and strained to blow kisses through the rear window as it pulled away from our house.

My mother blurred into the hedges and was gone.

ACKNOWLEDGEMENTS

This is a work of non-fiction. Some names have been changed to protect the privacy of those involved.

I would like to thank some special people who have helped me to bring this book into being.

Michelle Kass is a fairy godmother of an agent: she has believed in me from the first line, and has guided me through blank pages and murky places, offering me the courage of her convictions when my own went awry. She knows how to make things happen, and she has both my admiration and my deep gratitude.

The wonderful team at Picador have made publishing feel like serious fun; their enthusiasm has been infectious and is precious to me. Above all, I have enjoyed the generous ministrations of Ursula Doyle, who has helped me to shape this story out of chaos. As well as being a delight to know as a friend, she is that rare thing, a real and marvellous editor. It has been my privilege and saving grace to be able to trust utterly in Ursula's judgment.

To Julia Briggs I would like to express my profound and enduring thanks; she has helped me to save myself, to create myself over and over, and to celebrate that ongoing regeneration.

I will always be grateful to Barbara Wallis, who was my superb English Literature teacher at Xaverian College, and through whom I became enchanted with the memorable bits of literature that buoyed me when circumstances were sinking. Before that, at Oakwood High school, it was my great fortune to be taught and inspired by Jude Cooper: she radiated a crucial sense of possibility and cast a benign, probably life-saving, spell on me.

David Bowker has my enormous, special thanks for sharing his extraordinary wizardry with words. I would also like to let Tishna Molla know how much I appreciate her great skill and good humour in dealing with the nitty-gritty side of things.

There are others who lie closer to the heart of this book than they might realize. Hayley Boyle was my best friend and a precious beacon while I was growing up. Manuel Puro gave me hope and made me happier than I can say. These days, Gerald Lang is the funniest, most thoughtful and admirable friend I could wish for.

Finally, I would like to extend loving thanks to my family and to Mick. Brilliant and judicious, Mick Imlah has sustained me and propelled me to the end. I am forever grateful to him for his influence on this book and on the person who wrote it. My sisters, Lindsey Nefesh Clarke and Sarah Tompkins, have comforted me and truly encouraged me by their brave and beautiful ways of living. I thank my mother for her blessing and for the example of her awesome spirit. A last kiss goes to my shiny niece, Hannah – the future.